Sport Speed and Agility Training

John M. Cissik, MS, CSCS*D
and
Michael Barnes, MEd., CSCS*D

COACHES
≡ CHOICE™

ISBN: 1-58518-875-1
Library of Congress Control Number: 2003115156
Cover design: Jeanne Hamilton
Text design: Jeanne Hamilton
Diagrams: Kerry Hartjen
Text photos: John Cissik
Front cover photos: Rick Stewart/Allsport (football); Allsport (track);
    Matthew Stockman/Allsport (men's basketball); Doug Benc/Getty Images (soccer);
    Al Bello/Getty Images (baseball)

Coaches Choice
P.O. Box 1828
Monterey, CA 93942
www.coacheschoice.com

Acknowledgments

We would like to acknowledge the following individuals for their contribution to Chapter 5 and their commitment to agility theory and practice:

- Jerry Attaway, Physical Development Coordinator of the San Francisco 49ers
- Steve Plisk, MS, CSCS, Sports Performance Director, Velocity Sports Performance
- Tom Billups, CSCS, Head Coach, USA Eagles Rugby
- Greg Halberg, MS, CSCS

Contents

Preface

Speed and agility are two of the most misunderstood components of sport. How to train for speed and agility is even more misunderstood. This book breaks down speed and agility into manageable components and analyzes those components to give coaches and athletes a strategic and methodical approach to training.

Many coaches consider speed and agility to be characteristics that athletes must be "born with." It is true that everyone is limited by his own genetic potential, and it is in fact very difficult to develop speed and agility. However, once you break down speed and agility into their respective components, the situation becomes very manageable. With proper training, a slow athlete can become faster, a fast athlete can become even faster, and a good athlete can become great.

Examples of athletic performance include the ability to change direction easily, make an over-the-shoulder catch at full speed, create separation between you and your opponent, react to a changing environment, and start, stop, and reaccelerate. Many coaches do not have an integrated approach to training for athletic performance. Traditional methods consist of weight training for several weeks, followed by the incorporation of linear running. What is often missing from traditional training methods is agility and speed development. The traditional approach is a huge mistake, especially in the off-season, because it does not address specific neuromuscular responses, such as co-contractions of muscles (hamstrings and gluteus) with the displacement of body mass, possibly with a reactionary component (ball or opponent).

Athletes do need to train to become more effective at specific components of their game. For instance, training a football lineman would include weight training and cardiovascular training. It is also desirable for athletes to have strength and an efficient metabolic system. But according to the SAID principle (Specific Adaptations to Imposed Demands), if an athlete is concentrating on strength and metabolic training, he will improve only in those areas.

The best way to train for any sport is to practice the sport itself. If done properly, speed and agility training addresses sport-specific skills and the neuromuscular system in a manner that most closely resembles the sport itself—often called "functional training." The less the method of training resembles the sport, the less functional it is.

Speed and agility development also requires a different timeline than traditional training. The nervous system, motor abilities, and sport-specific movements will have little time to develop if they are not addressed outside of the pre-season. It takes weeks and sometimes months of training to see any significant results in speed and agility. It takes professional athletes years to refine sport-specific technique. Even then, fundamental errors occur with the most proficient athletes in game situations. Gone are the days of getting into shape during training camp. Today's professional athlete will take only two weeks off immediately following the season before beginning training for the next season.

This book has two basic parts. Part I covers the information that a coach or athlete needs to have to design and implement successful speed and agility programs. It presents scientific foundations that support speed and agility training. It also discusses, in detail, safety considerations, the warm-up, a dynamic flexibility program, speed training drills, and a theory of agility training.

Part II offers specific examples of speed and agility training programs for several sports (baseball, basketball, football, hockey, rugby, and soccer) that rely heavily on speed and agility for success. The authors developed these programs using what they believe to be the most methodical and practical approach to speed and agility development. The programs may or may not be appropriate for a particular program (collegiate, high school, club, or otherwise) because so many variables (including the competency of the instruction) need to be identified before implementing a speed and agility program. Therefore, the programs are based on a methodical and progressive model that can be adapted for use by any coach or athlete at any level.

Part I:
Principles and Fundamentals

The first part of this book covers the information that a coach or athlete needs to have to design and implement successful speed and agility programs. The first chapter details safety considerations for speed and agility programs and discusses injury prevention. The next few chapters describe the various components in a speed and agility training program. Chapter 2 covers warming up—why it is important and how to do it most effectively for speed and agility training. Chapter 3 describes speed training—what factors affect speed, the components of speed, technique, and how to train each component. Chapter 4 outlines selected speed drills. Chapter 5 covers agility training—the science behind it (physiology, biomechanics, and motor learning), its constituents, training variables, and program design information. Chapter 6 describes the importance of the cool-down and how it can be implemented. Chapter 7 puts everything together and covers program design, including information on principles of exercise, analyzing the needs of the sport and the athlete, and how the sport's competition season affects program design.

1

Safety Considerations for Speed and Agility Training

Several broad-based issues directly pertain to safety for speed and agility training:

- pre-exercise health screening
- nutritional status
- footwear
- how to choose a strength and conditioning coach
- industry standards and guidelines
- training surfaces
- environmental conditions

An entire book could be devoted to a discussion of these issues. This chapter will provide only an overview, along with references to assist you in furthering your knowledge of these important safety considerations.

Pre-Exercise Health Screening

A medical doctor should clear everyone who is participating in a structured speed and agility program. The trainer that is designing and implementing the program should have formal communication with the doctor. For details pertaining to pre-exercise health screening, refer to the Industry Standards and Guidelines provided by the National Strength and Conditioning Association (*www.nsca-lift.org*).

Nutritional Status

Serious athletes take their nutrition as seriously as they do their training. For athletes to perform at peak levels, their bodies must be properly fueled with a balanced diet that addresses hydration status. Athletes should not engage in fad diets that are outside of the guidelines of professional associations or state and federal nutrition policy. Contact the American Dietetic Association (*www.eatright.org*) for more information and a list of qualified nutrition professionals.

Footwear

Proper footwear is essential for speed and agility training. Footwear should be evaluated on function and fit. Choose footwear that is specifically designed for the activity and playing surface. For example, molded and screw-in-type cleats are designed for use on natural grass surfaces. Different lengths of screw-in cleats can be used, depending on the size of the athlete, the requirements of the activity, and the training and competition surfaces. All of the sports discussed in this text have specialty footwear.

The fit of the footwear is critical for comfort and performance. An athlete should select the footwear that is best for his foot. Disregard companies, superstar endorsements, style, and price. When it comes to footwear, choose function over form.

How to Choose a Strength and Conditioning Coach

Before choosing a professional strength and conditioning coach, athletes should ask the following questions:

- What education do they have?

They should have at least a four-year degree in exercise science or a related field.

- Do they hold a relevant certification?

The CSCS® (Certified Strength and Conditioning Specialist) offered by the National Strength and Conditioning Association is the most relevant certification for speed and agility instruction.

- What experience have they had with speed and agility training?

They should have relevant experience working with athletes with speed and agility goals.

- Do they have references?

They should be able to provide references from individuals they have worked with on speed and agility training.

These questions offer only a start to choosing a trainer. The National Strength and Conditioning Association offers assistance in selecting a qualified trainer on-line at *www.nsca-lift.org*.

Industry Standards and Guidelines

The National Strength and Conditioning Association recently released their professional standards and guidelines (www.nsca-lift.org). These standards and guidelines are areas of liability for the practicing strength and conditioning coach and will also ensure that athletes are training in a safe and effective environment.

The NSCA has identified the following nine areas of liability:

- preparticipation screening and clearance

- personnel qualifications

- program supervision and instruction

- facility and equipment set-up, inspection, maintenance, repair, and signage

- emergency planning and response

- records and record keeping

- equal opportunity and access

- participation in strength and conditioning activities by children

- supplements, ergogenic aids, and drugs

Training Surfaces

Ideally, athletes should train on the same surface on which they compete. However, some circumstances warrant a difference, for example, weather that presents a safety issue (soft, wet, and/or slippery). The preferred surface for conditioning and performing agility-training drills is natural grass. The ground under natural grass most often has shock-absorbing properties that are conducive to training. Again, because of safety issues, natural grass may not be optimal in some circumstances, such as when it is too soft, wet, and/or slippery. Surfaces should be smooth and the area should be clear of any obstacles that could obstruct moving in all directions. Stay clear from things like trees, drainage, playground equipment, blocking sleds, sidewalks, and training equipment that isn't being used.

Environmental Conditions

A combination of heat and humidity can pose a threat to an athlete's health status. Many athletes die every year as a result of heat illness (including dehydration, heat syncope, heat exhaustion, and heat stroke) suffered during competition or training. Strength and conditioning professionals should be able to identify contributing factors and take precautionary measures to prevent heat illness. Contact the National Athletic Trainers Association (*www.nata.org*) for more information on this topic.

2

The Warm-Up

Before beginning a workout of any type, it is important to warm up. Done properly, the warm-up serves two important functions: it prevents injuries and it helps to maximize performance. Warming up is a vital component of training, yet it is often one of the most overlooked. Coaches and athletes may feel pressed for time, they may find it boring, and they may elect to shorten or even skip the warm-up. But a complete, proper warm-up is essential because warming up prepares the body for work. This chapter will discuss the benefits of warming up, types of warm-up exercises, and how to design a warm-up for speed and agility training.

Benefits of Warming Up

Warming up has two broad benefits: it improves performance and it helps to prevent injuries. The warm-up accomplishes this in a number of ways. First, a warm muscle will contract more forcefully and relax more quickly than one that is not warm, thereby potentially increasing speed, strength, and power. Second, warming up will increase both the sensitivity of nerve receptors and their transmission speed, thereby increasing an athlete's speed and reaction time—sometimes referred to as "cueing the nervous system." Third, warming up will increase the temperature of the blood, leading to more oxygen being released from hemoglobin and myoglobin, and allowing more oxygen to be available to the exercising tissues. Fourth, warming up will enhance vasodilation, which will allow for more substrates to enter exercising tissues and for enhanced removal of waste products. Fifth, muscle elasticity and joint range of motion will be enhanced with increased blood saturation and temperature. In other words, a warm-up can help to prevent injuries by increasing the deformability of muscles and the range of motion around joints.

Many of the benefits of the warm-up result from an increase in body temperature. The increase in temperature is an outcome of the metabolism of fuels during the warm-up—the friction of actin and myosin during a muscular contraction (theoretically), and vasodilation leading to increased blood saturation of the exercising tissues. These actions are responsible for assisting to further increase the temperature in the working muscles and joints.

Another benefit of warming up that should not be overlooked is the fact that warming up allows an athlete to practice the event. By performing parts of a movement at lower intensities, the athlete can work on technique and gradually become more psychologically focused.

Effective warm-ups should be centered around increasing body temperature and allowing for practice or rehearsal of the upcoming event, whether it is competition, skills training, or the first exercise to be performed. The warm-up should be a gradual process that increases in terms of complexity and speed of motion. To accomplish this goal, the warm-up is typically divided into two phases: general and specific.

The primary purpose of the general warm-up is to elevate body temperature. A general warm-up usually consists of five to ten minutes of some type of aerobic exercise, calisthenics, and static stretching.

The general warm-up is followed by the specific warm-up. The purpose of the specific warm-up is to perform exercises that simulate those to be performed either in practice, training, or competition, but at a lower intensity. The specific warm-up activates the muscle groups in a fashion that is similar to practice or competition.

Types of Warm-Up Exercises

Jogging, static stretching, and dynamic flexibility exercises are commonly used in a warm-up for a speed and agility workout.

Jogging

Jogging is a favorite method that many athletes use to help warm up for a speed and agility workout. It elevates the heart rate, increases respiration, moves blood into the muscles of the lower extremity, and increases core temperature. Athletes need to be careful when using jogging during the warm-up, however. Jogging does not do a good job of reinforcing correct sprinting mechanics. Relying too much on jogging can lead to the development of bad habits during sprinting. Another drawback is that jogging for long distances will develop the wrong energy systems for sprinting. The best approach is for athletes to jog for a few minutes (less than five) and then move on to another warm-up mode.

Static Stretching

Another common component of warming up is static stretching, which involves holding a stretch for a period of time (generally 10 to 30 seconds). Stretching is generally performed to help decrease injuries by, in theory, directly decreasing muscle stiffness via viscoelastic changes in the muscle or indirectly increasing muscle stiffness due to reflex inhibition and decreased myosin/actin cross-bridging.

Unfortunately, not much evidence exists to support the hypothesis that the flexibility gained from stretching reduces injury or improves performance. In fact, stretching may impair performance and may increase the risks of injury because it is a passive activity that does not result in a significant temperature increase to the exercising tissues. Static stretching does not increase temperature for many reasons: it causes only minimal friction of actin and myosin; it provides little increase in the rate of fuels being metabolized; and it does not require intramuscular blood vessels to dilate.

In addition to having only minimal effects upon temperature, flexibility training may also inhibit force production by decreasing the sensitivity of the muscle spindles—a factor that has implications for strength and power events. For example, Church, et al. (2001) found that performing PNF stretches prior to an activity resulted in a significant decrease in one-step counter-movement jump performance compared to only performing calisthenics prior to the activity.

Stretching may contribute to decreases in force production in other ways. Muscles that are lengthened through stretching may be unable to produce forceful contractions compared with those that have not been lengthened, because muscles that are lengthened too much will have myosin and actin filaments that do not overlap, resulting in fewer cross-bridges being formed and less force being generated.

In summary, stretching is not an ideal warm-up exercise for several reasons. First, stretching does not increase temperature. Second, very little evidence exists to indicate that static or PNF stretching before activity will decrease risks of injury. Third, static or PNF stretching performed before an activity may decrease performance due to reflex inhibition or a reduction in cross-bridges. As a result, dynamic flexibility exercises may be a better form of exercise to include in the warm-up than traditional stretching.

Dynamic Flexibility Exercises

Dynamic flexibility exercises closely duplicate the movement requirements seen in training or in competition. They are functional-based activities that increase balance, flexibility, coordination, and speed. They also help to teach sport-specific movements.

Dynamic flexibility is the ability to flex and extend the joint quickly, with little resistance to the movement, regardless of the ability to achieve an extreme range of motion. It may be more applicable to athletics than other forms of flexibility training because the ability to move a joint quickly through its range of motion resembles real-life situations. In addition to providing the benefits of balance, flexibility, and sports-skill crossover, dynamic flexibility exercises are excellent for warming up. Dynamic flexibility exercises involve flexing and extending the muscles about a joint, thereby causing friction from sliding actin and myosin filaments, vasodilation and increased blood flow, and breakdown of substrates for energy. In other words, dynamic flexibility exercises will continue the warming up process and apply it specifically to the muscles and joints that will be used in competition or training.

Fredrick and Szymanski (2001) identified several categories of dynamic flexibility exercises: joint mobility, general movement preparation, general linear preparation, and general multidirectional preparation.

Joint Mobility Exercises

Joint mobility exercises are almost traditional calisthenic exercises (i.e., toe touches, jumping jacks, squat thrusts, etc.) that are meant to increase the active ROM of a joint. They include exercises like neck rotations, arm circles, leg swings, etc.

General Movement Preparation Exercises

These exercises are primarily designed to warm up the muscles and joints of the lower body through forward, backward, or lateral movements. Exercises usually focus on specific muscle groups. For example, heel/toe raises may focus on muscles that move the ankle, straight-leg marches may focus on the hamstrings, butt kicks may focus on the quadriceps, etc.

General Linear Preparation Exercises

These exercises help prepare the athlete for straight-ahead movements like sprinting. They may include sprinting lead-up exercises such as high knees or A-skips (some of which are described in Chapter 4).

General Multidirectional Preparation Exercises

These exercises help prepare the athlete for agility work. Exercises may include lateral marches or skips, crossover exercises, or running backwards.

Refer to Table 2-1 for examples of dynamic flexibility exercises by category. The remainder of this section will describe how to perform some of the more unusual dynamic flexibility exercises.

Classification	Sample Exercises
Joint Mobility	Ankle Circles
	Knee Circles
	Forward/Backward Leg Swings
	Lateral Leg Swings
	Kick the Fence
	Hip Circles
	Eagles
	Stomach Eagles
	Windmills
	Wheelbarrows
General Movement Preparation	Walk on Toes
	Walk on Toes/Arm Circles
	Toe Taps
	Walk Forward, Bend and Touch Toes
	March
	March and Touch Toes
	Inch Worm
	Knee-Down Butt Kicks
	Forward Lunges
	Posterior Lunges
	Angle Lunges
	Side Lunges
	Lunges with Upper Body Rotation
	Walk Forward, Abduct Hip
General Linear Preparation	Ankling
	Butt Kicks
	High Knee
	High Knee Pulls
	High Knee Pulls/Lunge
General Multidirectional Preparation	Side Shuffle
	Step Backs
	Backpedal
	Carioca

Table 2-1. Dynamic flexibility exercises

Joint Mobility Exercises

These exercises are meant to increase the active ROM of a joint. In general, they will target a specific joint or group of joints. These exercises are normally performed for 10 to 20 repetitions.

Figure 2-1. Forward/backward leg swings

Forward/Backward Leg Swings

Purpose: To loosen up the hip joint and the muscles that act upon it.

Start: Stand tall, shoulders back, next to a fence or a partner. The left side of the body should be next to the fence or partner, with the left hand holding the fence or partner for support.

Action: Staying tall, swing the right leg from the hip forward and backward. Keep the knee straight and try to swing the leg as high as possible. While performing this exercise, keep the ankle dorsiflexed and lift up the big toe. After performing the desired number of repetitions, switch sides and repeat.

Finish: This drill is completed after the desired number of repetitions has been performed on each side.

Figure 2-2. Lateral leg swings

Lateral Leg Swings

Purpose: To loosen up the hip joint and the muscles that act upon it.

Start: Stand facing a support, such as a fence or a partner. The right foot should be a step or two in front of the left and should not touch the ground.

Action: Lean forward from the waist slightly and place the right hand on the support. Keeping the right leg straight, swing the leg from side to side from the hip. Try to move the leg as high as possible in both directions. At the same time, swing the left arm, counteracting the movements of the right leg. When the right leg crosses the body's midline, so should the left arm. After performing the desired number of repetitions, switch sides and repeat.

Finish: This drill is completed after the desired number of repetitions has been performed on each side.

Kick the Fence

Purpose: To teach the high-knee action and to loosen up the hip flexors and knee extensors.

Start: Stand tall, shoulders back. Face a fence or wall (something that provides a target that will not move).

Action: Lift the right knee as high as possible. As the right foot leaves the ground, the foot should be dorsiflexed with the big toe lifted up. As the right knee reaches its highest point, extend the knee and drive the right foot into the fence or wall. Immediately retract the foot and repeat with the left leg. The advanced version of this drill involves kicking over a hurdle or other obstacle.

Finish: This drill is completed after the desired number of repetitions has been performed.

Figure 2-3. Hip circles

Hip Circles

Purpose: To loosen up the hip and the muscles that act upon it.

Start: Stand upright, with arms at the sides of the body and feet hip-width apart.

Action: Start by raising the right leg until the top of the thigh is parallel to the ground. As the leg rises to a parallel position, externally rotate the leg and hip. Return the leg back to the ground behind the body, moving backwards. Immediately switch legs and repeat. The upper body will work opposite of the lower body, assisting in rotation of the hips.

Finish: Perform a "speed turn" after completing the hip circles and sprint for 10 to 20 yards.

Figure 2-4. Eagles

Eagles

Purpose: To loosen up the hip and the muscles which act upon it.

Start: Lie on your back with your legs extended. Your arms should be extended straight out to the sides, making a "T" with the body.

Action: Keeping the knees extended and moving from the hip, move the right leg across the body, attempting to touch the right foot to the left hand. Do not move the hands. Try to keep the shoulders on the ground. Switch sides.

Finish: This drill is completed after the desired number of repetitions has been performed.

Figure 2-5. Stomach eagles

Stomach Eagles

Purpose: To loosen up the hip and abdominal muscles.

Start: Lie on your stomach with your legs extended. Your arms should be extended straight out to the sides, making a "T" with the body.

Action: Bending the left knee, attempt to touch the right hand with the left foot. Repeat with the right side (right foot touches left hand).

Finish: This drill is completed after the desired number of repetitions has been performed.

Windmills

Purpose: To loosen up the shoulder and the muscles which act upon it.

Start: Stand up tall. Hold the arms out to the sides so that they are parallel to the ground.

Action: Moving from the shoulders, move the arms in a circular motion.

Finish: This drill is completed after the desired number of repetitions has been performed.

Wheelbarrows

Purpose: To strengthen the muscles of the upper body.

Start: This exercise requires a partner. Assume the push-up position, with the arms extended. Spread the feet so the partner may step in between them. The partner will squat down and grab one ankle in each hand. The partner will then stand up, holding one ankle in each hand.

Action: Keeping the trunk straight, walk forward on the hands while the partner walks behind, holding the ankles. This drill is typically performed for 10 to 30 yards.

Finish: After performing the drill for the prescribed distance, the exercise is complete.

General Movement Preparation Exercises

These are exercises that are primarily designed to warm up the muscles and joints of the lower body, using forward, backward, or lateral movements. Exercises usually focus on specific muscle groups and wherever possible good sprinting technique should be emphasized (i.e. dorsiflexion, high knees, tall posture, etc.). Generally these drills are performed for 10 to 30 yards.

Walk on Toes

Purpose: To loosen up the ankles and develop balance.

Start: Stand upright, arms relaxed and held at the side of the body, feet hip-width apart.

Action: Plantarflex both feet. Walk forward on the balls of the feet, without letting the heels touch the ground.

Finish: After performing the drill for the prescribed distance, the exercise is complete.

Walk on Toes/Arm Circles

Purpose: To loosen up the ankles and shoulders while developing balance.

Start: Stand upright, arms relaxed and held at the side of the body, feet hip-width apart.

Action: Plantarflex both feet. Walk forward on the balls of the feet without letting the heels touch the ground. While walking forward, rotate the arms to the sides so that they make large circles.

Finish: After performing the drill for the prescribed distance, the exercise is complete.

Figure 2-6. Walk forward, bend and touch toes

Walk Forward, Bend and Touch Toes

Purpose: To loosen up the hamstrings.

Start: Stand upright, arms relaxed and held at the side of the body, feet hip-width apart.

Action: Take a step forward with the left foot. Keeping the left leg straight, bend forward and touch the left foot with the right hand. Straighten up as you step forward with the right foot. Bend forward and touch the right foot with the left hand. Continue alternating for 10 to 30 yards.

Finish: After performing the drill for the prescribed distance, the exercise is complete.

March

Purpose: To loosen the hamstrings and improve hip flexion.

Start: Stand upright, arms relaxed and held at the side of the body, feet hip-width apart.

Action: Step forward from the hip, keeping the knee straight. As you step forward, dorsiflex the foot and pull the big toe up. When marching, try to lift each leg as high as possible.

Finish: After marching for the prescribed distance, the exercise is complete.

Figure 2-7. March and touch toes

March and Touch Toes

Purpose: To loosen the hamstrings and improve hip flexion.

Start: Stand upright, arms relaxed and held at the side of the body, feet hip-width apart.

Action: Step forward with the left foot. Step from the hip, keeping the knee straight. As you step forward, dorsiflex the foot and pull the big toe up. When marching, try to lift each leg as high as possible. As you lift the left leg, try to touch the left foot with the right hand. As the left foot contacts the ground, repeat with the right leg (left hand touches right foot).

Finish: After performing the drill for the prescribed distance, the exercise is complete.

Inch Worm

Purpose: To loosen up the hamstrings.

Start: Lay facedown on the ground in a push-up position, with chest touching the ground.

Action: Extend the arms at the elbow, performing a push-up. Hold the top position in the push-up. While holding the push-up position, walk the feet to the hands (or as close to the hands as possible), while keeping the hands in contact with the ground. Once the feet are as close as possible to the hands, walk the hands away from the feet, returning to the top of the push-up position. Repeat this sequence until the drill is complete.

Finish: The drill is complete after performing the prescribed distance.

Figure 2-8. Knee-down butt kicks

Knee-Down Butt Kicks

Purpose: To loosen the quadriceps.

Start: Stand upright, arms relaxed and held at the side of the body, feet hip-width apart. Lean forward slightly, putting your weight on the balls of the feet.

Action: Pointing the right knee down, bring the right foot up towards the hips (try to contact the right heel to the hips). Place the right foot down in front of the body and pull yourself forward. As this is being done, point the left knee down and bring the left heel up towards the hips.

Finish: After performing the knee-down butt kicks for the prescribed distance, the exercise is complete.

Figure 2-9. Forward lunges

Forward Lunges

Purpose: To warm up the muscles of the lower body, especially the quadriceps, while developing balance and flexibility.

Start: Stand upright, arms relaxed and held at the side of the body, feet hip-width apart.

Action: Take a large step forward so that the heel strikes the ground first (heel to toe). As the heel strikes the ground, flex the front hip and knee so that the front thigh is parallel to the floor. The back knee should be flexed, though it should not be touching the ground. Extend the front knee and hip and pull yourself forward. Switch sides and repeat.

Finish: After performing the forward lunges for the prescribed distance, the exercise is complete.

Posterior Lunges

Purpose: To warm up the muscles of the lower body, especially the hamstrings, while developing balance and flexibility.

Start: Stand upright, arms relaxed and held at the side of the body, feet hip-width apart.

Action: Take a large step backwards. The front knee and hip should flex until the front thigh is parallel to the floor. The back knee should be flexed, though it should not be touching the floor. Extend the front knee and hip and pull yourself backwards. Switch sides and repeat.

Finish: After performing the posterior lunges for the prescribed distance, the exercise is complete.

Figure 2-10. Angle lunges

Angle Lunges

Purpose: To warm up the muscles of the lower body, while developing balance and flexibility.

Start: Stand upright, arms at sides, feet hip-width apart.

Action: Begin by taking a step forward at a 45-degree angle. (Note: The step should be longer than normal walking stride.) Once the foot makes contact with the ground, flex the knee of the walking leg until the top of the thigh is parallel to the ground. The trail leg will also have a slight flexion at the knee. Arms may be used in a walking fashion or they can be used for balance. Repeat by switching legs with each step.

Finish: After performing the lunges for the prescribed distance, the exercise is complete.

Figure 2-11. Side lunges

Side Lunges

Purpose: To warm up the muscles of the lower body, especially the hamstrings, while developing balance and flexibility.

Start: Stand sideways, arms relaxed and held at the side of the body, feet hip-width apart.

Action: Begin by stepping out to the side with the lead leg. Once the foot makes contact with the ground, flex the knee of the lead leg until the top of the thigh is parallel to the ground, and do not allow the knee of the lead leg to pass the toes. The trail leg should be extended. This position will require flexion at the hip with a flat back and the head in a neutral position. The arms are either flexed at the elbow and held alongside of the body or extended in front of the body for balance. Extend the knee and hip of the lead leg and pull yourself sideways. The lunge is generally performed for a distance of 10 to 30 yards on each leg.

Finish: After performing the lunges to each side, the exercise is complete.

Figure 2-12. Lunges with upper body rotation

Lunges with Upper Body Rotation

Purpose: To warm up the muscles of the lower body, while developing balance and flexibility.

Start: Stand upright, arms relaxed and held at the side of the body, feet hip-width apart.

Action: Place hands on the head with the elbows pointing out. Begin by taking a step forward that is longer than a normal walking stride. Once the foot makes contact with the ground, flex the knee of the walking leg until the thigh is parallel to the ground. Once in this position, rotate the upper body to both sides. The trail leg will also have a slight flexion at the knee. Do not allow the knee of the lead leg to pass the toes and do not allow the knee of the trail leg to rest on the ground. Repeat the movement, switching legs with each step.

Finish: After performing the lunges for the prescribed distance, the exercise is complete.

Walk Forward, Abduct Hip

Purpose: To warm up the hip while enhancing hip flexion and balance.

Start: Stand upright, arms relaxed and held at the side of the body, feet hip-width apart.

Action: Lift the right knee high, with the foot dorsiflexed and big toe pulled up. From this position, abduct the hip so that the knee moves away from the midline of the body. Without lowering the foot, adduct the hip so that the knee moves back towards the midline. Step forward and repeat with the left leg. Repeat until the drill has covered 10 to 30 yards.

Figure 2-13. Walk forward, abduct hip

Finish: After performing the drill for the prescribed distance, the exercise is complete.

General Linear Preparation Exercises

These exercises help prepare the athlete for straight-ahead movements like sprinting. They help to reinforce technique on specific parts of the sprinting motion. These exercises are typically performed over 10 to 30 yards.

High Knee

Purpose: To teach lifting the knees during the sprinting motion.

Start: Stand upright, feet hip-width apart. Place your hands behind your head so that you cannot use them.

Action: Lift the right knee as high as possible, and dorsiflex the right foot as it leaves the ground. Step forward. Repeat on the left side. Visualize stepping over a tall object.

Finish: After performing the drill for the prescribed distance, the exercise is complete.

Figure 2-14. High knee pulls

High Knee Pulls

Purpose: To reinforce lifting the knees while working on flexibility and balance.

Start: Stand upright, arms relaxed and held at the side of the body, feet hip-width apart.

Action: Lift the right knee as high as possible, and dorsiflex the right foot as it leaves the ground. Grab the right leg just below the knee and pull up, stretching the leg. Step forward. Repeat on the left side.

Finish: After performing the drill for the prescribed distance, the exercise is complete.

High Knee Pulls/Lunge

Purpose: To reinforce lifting the knees while working on flexibility and balance.

Start: Stand upright, arms relaxed and held at the side of the body, feet hip-width apart.

Action: Begin by raising one leg until the top of the thigh is parallel to the ground, keeping the knee flexed. Grab the leg with both hands (just below the knee), and carefully pull the knee to the chest, keeping a flat back with chest up. As the leg is returning to the ground, extend the leg and perform a forward lunge. Repeat this exercise by switching legs.

Finish: After performing the drill for the prescribed distance, the exercise is complete.

General Multidirectional Preparation Exercises

These exercises prepare the athlete for agility work. They teach fundamental movement patterns while warming up the muscles and joints. They are performed at higher speeds than the other exercises described in this chapter and are generally performed over 5 to 20 yards.

Side Shuffle

Purpose: To warm up the hip and lower body muscles, and to teach lateral movement patterns.

Start: Stand sideways in the "ready" position: feet shoulder-width apart, knees and hips flexed, back flat, arms flexed.

Action: Step sideways with the lead leg, and lightly drag the trail leg on the ground toward the lead leg. Keep the legs shoulder-width apart. While pushing with the trail leg and stepping out with the lead leg, keep the body in the "ready" position. Repeat for 5 to 20 yards.

Finish: After performing side shuffles for the prescribed distance, sprint for 10 to 15 yards.

Step Backs

Purpose: To warm up the hip and improve backward movement.

Start: Stand upright, arms relaxed and held at the sides of the body, feet hip-width apart.

Action: Raise the left leg until the top of the thigh is parallel to the ground. As the leg rises to a parallel position, externally rotate the leg and hip. Return the leg to the ground (moving backwards), then immediately switch legs and repeat. Perform this action slowly and methodically. The upper body will work opposite of the lower body, assisting in the rotation of the hips. Performed over 10 to 30 yards.

Finish: After performing the step backs for the prescribed distance, the exercise is complete.

Backpedal

Purpose: To teach movement patterns.

Start: Begin in a crouched position, back flat, feet staggered. Arms should be flexed at the elbows.

Action: Push with the front foot while stepping backwards with the rear foot. Maintain the crouched position and use the arms in the normal running motion. Perform for 5 to 20 yards.

Finish: Perform a "speed turn" at the end of the backpedal and finish with a 10- to 20-yard sprint.

Carioca

Purpose: To warm up the hips and muscles of the lower body, and to teach lateral movement patterns.

Start: Stand sideways in the ready position: feet shoulder-width apart, knees and hips flexed, back flat, arms flexed.

Action: Move laterally, alternately crossing each leg in front of the other. Stay in the ready position. The legs should move as quickly as possible as they cross in front of one another. Perform over 5 to 20 yards.

Finish: After performing the carioca for the prescribed distance, complete the drill with a 10- to 15-yard sprint.

Organizing the Warm-Up

The duration and intensity of the warm-up will depend upon the level of the athlete, the nature of the workout to follow, and other factors, such as the ambient temperature in which the workout is going to be performed. Workouts performed by advanced athletes, intense workouts, or workouts performed in cold environments all require more thorough warm-ups.

As mentioned previously, warm-ups consist of a general warm-up followed by a specific warm-up. Jogging and dynamic flexibility exercises make a great general warm-up for speed and agility workouts. Two to three minutes of light jogging followed by one to two exercises from each category of dynamic flexibility exercises should make up the general warm-up. The specific warm-up should consist of the sprint and agility technique exercises.

Each exercise in the general warm-up should be performed for one to three sets of 10 to 30 yards (or repetitions). The number of sets and yards (or repetitions) per set will depend upon the level of the athlete and the nature of the workout. More advanced athletes or preparation for more difficult workouts will require a greater volume of warm-up exercises. The specific warm-up exercises should be performed for three sets of 10 to 30 yards. Table 2-2 outlines an example of a basic warm-up. For advanced athletes, on cold days, or prior to strenuous workouts, add jogging to some of the dynamic flexibility exercises to increase the level of difficulty. (See Table 2-3.)

Warming up is an important component of a speed and agility workout. Done properly, it can prevent injuries and improve performance. Warm-ups should be constructed in a way that allows the athlete to prepare for the workout that lies ahead. With regards to speed and agility workouts, the best way to prepare is through dynamic flexibility exercises, perhaps combined with limited jogging. In addition to warming up the tissues, dynamic flexibility exercises warm up the muscles and joints in a manner similar to how they will be used in the workout. Dynamic flexibility exercises also provide a way to make the warm-up interesting and challenging. Failing to warm up, or doing so improperly, could lead to injury and will limit the effectiveness of the athlete's training experience.

General Warm-Up	Specific Warm-Up
Jog, 400 meters	Ankling, 3 x 20 yards
Walk on toes, 2 x 20 yards	Butt kicks, 3 x 20 yards
March, 2 x 20 yards	High knee, 3 x 20 yards
Eagles, 2 x 10	Backpedal, 3 x 10 yards + 10-yard sprint
Stomach eagles, 2 x 10	Side shuffle, 3 x 10 yards + 10-yard sprint
Lateral leg swings, 2 x 10	sprint
Forward lunges, 3 x 30 yards	Carioca, 3 x 10 yards + 10-yard sprint
Side lunges, 3 x 30 yards	
Posterior lunges, 2 x 20 yards	
Step backs, 2 x 20 yards	

Table 2-2. Sample basic warm-up

General Warm-Up	Specific Warm-Up
Walk on toes, 2 x 20 yards; jog back	Ankling, 3 x 20 yards
March, 2 x 20 yards; jog back	Butt kicks, 3 x 20 yards
Eagles, 2 x 10; jog 20 yards in between sets	High knee, 3 x 20 yards
Stomach eagles, 2 x 10; jog 20 yards in between sets	Backpedal, 3 x 10 yards + 10-yard sprint
Lateral leg swings, 2 x 10; jog 20 yards in between sets	Side shuffle, 3 x 10 yards + 10-yard sprint
Forward lunges, 3 x 30 yards	Carioca, 3 x 10 yards + 10-yard sprint
Side lunges, 3 x 30 yards	
Posterior lunges, 2 x 20 yards	
Step backs, 2 x 20 yards	

Table 2-3. Sample advanced warm-up

Training for Speed

Running speed is important for success in sports. Even though the exact requirements may differ for each sport, almost all sports consider speed an important quality. Speed influences an athlete's ability to get to the ball, get to the base, get to the goal, outrun a defender, catch an opponent with the ball, block a scoring attempt, etc. Speed is such an important quality that it is frequently used to help determine who makes the team and who starts.

This chapter begins with a discussion of the factors that influence speed and how they may be affected through training. It then describes the proper technique behind running at maximal speed, and how to train for it. The chapter concludes by describing technique and training for acceleration and speed endurance.

Factors That Determine Speed

Muscle Structure

Distribution of Muscle Fiber Types

The distribution of muscle fiber types (i.e., fast twitch vs. slow twitch) could affect how fast an athlete can be. In theory, a greater percentage of fast-twitch muscle fibers, which generate a large amount of force over a short period of time, would enable an athlete to run faster. Costill, et al (1976) found that sprinters have a greater percentage of fast-twitch muscle fibers than middle-distance and distance runners (71.8 to 79% for sprinters versus 26.2 to 59.5% for distance runners). Whether this difference is a result of training or whether it is inherited is not clear, but it does indicate that those athletes with a higher percentage of fast-twitch muscle fibers may have a greater potential to be faster.

Length of the Muscle Fibers

The length of the muscle fibers could affect speed. Muscles with longer muscle fibers (i.e., more sarcomeres in series) have a lower reduction in force at higher velocities. Length is also important because longer muscle fibers will have a greater shortening velocity. In other words, muscles with longer muscle fibers will be able to generate more force against the ground at higher speeds and will be able to contract more quickly.

Shape of the Muscles

The cross-sectional area (CSA) of a muscle is important for performance. Muscles with a larger CSA will be able to produce more force. However, CSA alone may not be as important as the shape of the muscle. According to Kumagai, et al (2000), faster sprinters have greater muscle thickness in the upper portion of their thighs (anterior and posterior). Abe, et al (1999) compared black and white football players and found that black offensive and defensive backs had faster times in the 40-yard dash than white players did (mean of 4.63 seconds vs. 4.90 seconds) and that those black players had larger muscle thickness at the upper portions of the quadriceps and hamstrings. It is unclear if this difference is a result of training or if it is inherited. However, this information may demonstrate that not only is the cross-sectional area of a muscle important, but the location within a given muscle of the hypertrophied tissue may affect speed.

Ability to Use Fuel

Speed is a short-duration, maximal intensity activity. Therefore, it will be affected by how much ATP and CP are present in the body. If not enough ATP is available, it will limit an athlete's ability to contract his muscles. Without enough CP, the athlete's ability to resynthesize ATP after contractions will be limited. Long-term speed training may increase the activities of the enzymes involved in ATP breakdown and ATP resynthesis, which could speed the breakdown of ATP and its resynthesis during activity, thereby allowing an athlete to exercise faster and for longer periods of time.

In some instances, speed must be maintained over a period of time (i.e., speed endurance). Speed endurance is limited by the presence of glycogen stores and by the ability of the tissues to resist the effects of lactic acid. Training has been found to increase the activity of the enzymes involved in the breakdown of glycogen and the production of lactic acid.

Fatigue

Fatigue interferes with speed. Performing speed work under fatigued conditions will teach the athlete the wrong things. Allowing an athlete to run slowly or with bad technique will reinforce those poor motor patterns. Speed work should be performed when the athlete is fresh so that he may learn good technique and be fast. When fatigue sets in and performance of the exercises begins to suffer, the speed workout should be terminated for that day.

Flexibility

Flexibility, as it relates to speed training, is the ability to move a joint through an unrestricted range of motion (not the ability to stretch a muscle and hold that extended position for a period of time). The greater an athlete's flexibility, the less impedance he will experience during fast movements. Chapter 2 details dynamic flexibility exercises that can assist with this ability.

Stride Length and Stride Frequency

Stride length and stride frequency determine speed. To improve speed, an athlete must improve one or both of these parameters. Stride length refers to the distance that the hips travel with each stride. The ability to take longer strides will potentially allow an athlete to get where he's going faster. Stride frequency refers to the number of foot contacts with the ground per unit of time. Taking more frequent strides also potentially means that an athlete can arrive at his destination faster. Both qualities are trainable. However, keep in mind that more is not necessarily better. For example, after a certain point, too much stride length will slow an athlete down because it will cause him to brake while running. Elite sprinters, who have already optimized their stride length, focus on increasing stride frequency to improve their speed. For most athletes that are not elite sprinters, the trick is to find the optimal relationship between the two.

Technique

In sprinting, a number of complicated movements are taking place in a short period of time. The ability of the athlete's nervous system to link together the action of the muscles will determine that athlete's ability to run fast. In other words, the limiting factor in speed development is technique. Not only is technique important for performance, it is also important for the prevention of injuries. Poor sprinting technique can place too much strain on the hamstrings, groin, and shins, leading to injuries in those areas. Therefore, a significant part of an athlete's training should be spent on developing sound technique, using drills that are specifically designed to develop an "ideal" sprinting technique.

Maximum Velocity Running

Technique

Maximum velocity running is often divided into two phases: support and recovery.

Support Phase

The support phase starts when the leading foot makes contact with the ground and ends when it breaks contact with the ground. The leading foot should land on the ground slightly ahead of the athlete's center of gravity. The foot should be driven down by the hip extensors (i.e., the hamstrings and glutes should be performing the majority of the work during the hip extension). The quadriceps play an important role at touchdown in keeping the athlete's knee from flexing excessively and dissipating elastic energy. As the foot lands on the ground, it should be dorsiflexed, with the big toe pulled up to help maximize elastic force production. The outside of the forefoot should contact the ground.

The athlete should think about pulling himself over the foot. He should continue exerting force until his center of gravity passes over and in front of the foot. When the toes leave the ground, the support phase has ended.

Recovery Phase

The recovery phase starts when the leading foot breaks contact with the ground and lasts until it again makes contact with the ground. As the athlete enters the recovery phase (i.e., as the foot leaves the ground), the ankle should immediately be dorsiflexed, with the big toe pulled up. As the foot leaves the ground, the athlete should flex the knee and bring the heel up to the hips as quickly as possible. This movement allows the athlete to swing his recovery leg faster by shortening the lever and bringing the mass of the leg closer to the hip's axis of rotation.

As the heel reaches the hip, the leg should be swung forward. The athlete should aim to step over the opposite knee with the ankle, to keep the lever shorter for a longer period of time. The athlete should begin unfolding the swing leg as the ankle steps over the opposite knee. The hip and knee extension is due to a transfer of momentum, not an active quadriceps contraction. As the leg unfolds, the athlete aims to drive it down via hip extension, thus going back into the support phase.

Other Technique Considerations

The head should be kept in natural alignment with the trunk. The shoulders and trunk should be kept steady to avoid twisting. The exact angle of the body will depend upon acceleration, but at maximum speed it should be 80 to 85 degrees. The muscles of the face, neck, shoulders, arms, and hands should be relaxed because tension in those muscles will slow down limb speed and range of motion.

Arm action during maximum velocity running is very important. The swinging of the arms balances the forces created by the legs and initiates the actions of the legs. According to Bodyen (1978), the total power output during sprinting can be no more than the latitude allowed by the weakest link. In other words, a weak and ineffective arm swing will limit running speed. Therefore, the action of the arms during running is very important to achieving and improving maximum velocity.

Contrary to popular belief, the elbow angle should vary from 60 degrees (when the arm is in the front of the body) to 140 degrees (when the arm is in the back). When running, the emphasis should be on driving the arm backward (not on driving it forward). If the arm is driven backward with enough force, it will be pushed forward due to the stretch reflex at the shoulder (i.e., the athlete should not have to think about pushing the arm forward). The following pointers will help athletes achieve proper arm action:

- The hand should travel from the height of the face or shoulder to the hip.

- If the arm is driven backwards properly, then the elbow will open to 140 degrees on its own (it should not be a "forced" movement).

- The arms should not cross the midline of the body because that movement will cause the athlete to begin twisting, which will interfere with speed.

Evaluating Speed

Flying sprints or middle distance sprints will be best for evaluating speed. To evaluate maximal running velocity, a test needs to last five to seven seconds. Tests that are too long (for example, 100-yard dash) primarily evaluate speed endurance. Tests that are too short (for example, 40-yard dash) primarily evaluate acceleration. Tests that could be used to evaluate speed include a "flying" 40 (20-yard acceleration zone followed by 40-yard all-out sprint, but only the 40 gets timed) and a 60-yard sprint (tests acceleration plus maximal speed).

Principles of Training

Maximum velocity training should not take place in two consecutive training sessions. In general, it requires one to three days of recovery between sessions. Maximum velocity training is conducted over distances of 20 to 80 yards, with three to five minutes rest between repetitions, and six to eight minutes rest between sets. Because the aim of maximum velocity training is to become as fast as possible with good technique, athletes must be allowed to fully recover between efforts. In addition, athletes should be encouraged to run as fast as possible because learning to run slowly is undesirable. The intensity of maximum velocity exercises should be close to 100%. Table 3-2 at the end of this chapter provides a breakdown of repetitions, intensity, rest, and recovery for training for different speed qualities.

Whether the athlete should focus more on developing stride length or stride frequency will depend upon the individual's ability, his level of development, and his training age. Table 3-1 details some areas of emphasis according to an athlete's level.

Athlete's Level	Qualities to Develop
Youth	Strength Power Mobility Technique
High School	Strength Power Mobility Technique Stride Length Stride Frequency
College	Strength Power Mobility Technique Stride Length Stride Frequency
Professional	Strength Power Mobility Stride Frequency

Table 3-1. Speed-related qualities to focus on according to an athlete's level of development

Youth and high school athletes are still growing, so stride length will be an issue for them, because they have not yet achieved the full length of their limbs. In addition, technique will be very important to develop during those phases.

Collegiate athletes will need further emphasis on technique and refinement of their stride length, especially if they have not had much specialized instruction in speed training at previous levels. College is the time to begin heavily emphasizing stride frequency training because the athlete's other physical qualities (strength, power, and mobility) are peaking.

With professional athletes, it will probably be impractical to attempt to teach them technique. They are not developmental athletes and placing too much emphasis on technique may alter their movement patterns and adversely affect their performance. The focus with professional athletes should be on the other physical qualities (i.e., strength, power, and mobility), as well as increasing their stride frequency.

Modes of Exercise

A number of modes of exercise are used to improve speed. These include:

- Drills—used to develop technique or to enhance a part of the sprinting motion

- Varied pace running—helps the athlete to break through the speed barrier

- Resisted running—requires an athlete to increase the amount of force required to run at maximum speed

- Assisted running—helps the athlete run faster than he is normally able to

Drills

Drills facilitate the development of an "ideal" sprinting technique, with resulting benefits to maximum speed. Drills allow the techniques of sprinting to be broken down into components and perfected at slower speeds so that they may be transferred to maximum velocity runs. Note that while drills are important for good technique, they are not a substitute for actual sprinting. Chapter 4 provides detailed descriptions and illustrations of several maximum velocity running drills.

According to West & Robson (2000), coaches should use the following guidelines when employing drills for speed training:

- Understand the drill.

If the coach does not understand the techniques behind the drill, he cannot expect the athletes to learn it.

- Understand the drill's purpose.

Each of the drills listed in this book serves a role, but each drill also has limited application outside of that purpose. For example, while high knee drills do a good job of reinforcing frontside mechanics during sprinting, they do not teach backside mechanics. Relying solely on high knee drills will limit the athlete's development.

- Pay attention to speed drills during every training session.

Devote time and attention to speed drills. Do not perform them as an afterthought or only as a warm-up. The drills will not be beneficial without the proper time and attention.

- Introduce drills with a proper sequential progression.

Introducing an advanced drill before an athlete has mastered the basics will not help the athlete. Just like any other type of conditioning, speed training has a logical series of progressions that athletes should master before moving to more advanced drills.

- Athletes must possess the physical qualities necessary for the drills.

Athletes must have a degree of dynamic flexibility, strength, and maturity to master many of the drills outlined in Chapter 4. An athlete who is lacking in those qualities will not derive the full benefit from the drills.

Varied Pace Running

Once an athlete has developed sound technique through drills, varied pace running is probably the best method to improve the athlete's speed. The most effective training takes place under "normal" conditions that do not disrupt technique. Therefore resisted and assisted running, which disrupt an athlete's technique, are less effective than varied pace running, which does not. (Resisted and assisted running are discussed in detail later in this chapter.). Varied pace runs allow for several changes of speed to take place during the exercise. As a result, the athlete gets the feel of running at different speeds, learns to run relaxed, and avoids making costly mistakes during the run (for example, overstriding as speed increases). The varied pace also gives the nervous system a chance to recharge between high speed segments.

A common method of varied pace training is called "ins and outs." An "in" refers to a period of 100% intensity, when the athlete should be running with maximum velocity. During the "in" phase, emphasize good technique, especially an active foot strike/pawing motion. An "out" refers to a maintenance phase, where speed is maintained. During the "out" period, emphasize relaxed running and good technique.

"Ins" generally cover 10 to 20 yards, while "outs" cover 5 to 20 yards. Use the first 15 yards as an acceleration zone, then alternate "ins" and "outs." The drill should always end in an "in." Figure 3-1 shows an example of "ins and outs."

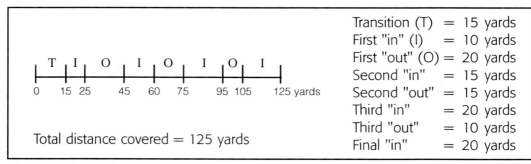

Transition (T)	= 15 yards
First "in" (I)	= 10 yards
First "out" (O)	= 20 yards
Second "in"	= 15 yards
Second "out"	= 15 yards
Third "in"	= 20 yards
Third "out"	= 10 yards
Final "in"	= 20 yards

Total distance covered = 125 yards

Figure 3-1. Ins and outs

Varied pace running can be manipulated to provide more sport-specific speed work. For example, in soccer, most sprints will cover 5 to 30 yards with a 1:3 work:rest ratio. Therefore, when training for soccer, the "ins" should cover 5 to 20 yards and the "outs" should cover 15 to 60 yards. (See Chapter 13 for more on soccer training.)

Another approach to varied pace running is called a "flying" sprint. This exercise involves the athlete jogging for 10 to 15 yards and then running at maximal velocity for a specified distance. For example, with a flying 40, an athlete would jog for 10 to 15 yards and then run at maximal velocity for 40 yards. This approach is very applicable to sports, because athletes are often called upon to change speeds in the middle of a play.

Resisted Running

Resisted running involves the athlete pulling something. The idea behind this technique is that by making the sprinting motion more difficult, the athlete will have to learn to recruit more muscle fibers and achieve greater neural activation, which will then carry over and allow the athlete to run faster when unencumbered. Resisted running includes the use of chutes, towing, weighted vests, uphill running, sand/water running, etc.

Figure 3-2. Resisted running

While it is a useful tool, resisted running does have limitations. Letzelter, et al. (2000) studied the effects of towing 2.5kg, 5kg, and 10kg sleds on female sprinters whose mean 100 meter time was 12.50 seconds. They found that as little as 10kg of resistance will decrease stride length by 13.5% and stride frequency by 6.2%. Athletes spend more time on the ground as a result of resistance (up to 21% more support time), thereby altering muscular contraction patterns and force application. Athletes who are towing may increase their upper body lean to compensate for the added weight, in some cases by more than 20%. This forward lean will also result in an incomplete hip extension during the sprinting motion, which will limit force production and speed. Obviously, such dramatic changes to sprinting technique are undesirable, as they will teach the athlete bad habits. For this reason, Jakalski (2000) recommends that resisted training methods should not reduce the athlete's speed by more than 10%.

Assisted Running

Assisted running (also known as overspeed training) usually involves the athlete being pulled by something. This technique allows the athlete to achieve a greater stride frequency than is normally possible. The purpose of assisted running is to teach the athlete to run faster through numerous repetitions, so he will be able to run faster under normal circumstances. In assisted running, the athlete may be towed (by a vehicle, by another athlete, or by an elastic cord) or he may use other approaches such as running on a high-speed treadmill or running downhill. The benefits of assisted training include an increase in stride frequency, increased muscle stiffness, and increased stores of elastic energy—all of which improve speed.

Like resisted running, assisted running also has limitations. Assisted running that involves speed above 106% of maximum leads to an increased stride length, which increases the braking phase of each foot contact, and, in turn, slows stride frequency. Therefore, assisted running should not employ speed greater than 106% of the athlete's maximum speed because it will disrupt technique and teach the athlete bad habits. Downhill sprinting and high-speed treadmills also have limitations. Downhill sprinting that involves a greater than 3% decline results in increased stride length (i.e., braking), which is undesirable. Faccioni (1995) points out that running on a high-speed treadmill could be disruptive because the athlete is running on a surface that moves horizontally backwards, as opposed to the athlete having to propel himself forward, which could interfere with normal sprint kinetics on unmoving ground.

Summary

When training for maximum velocity running, keep in mind the following:

*   Technique is the limiting factor for speed. This quality must be progressively developed and refined. Without good technique, other training tools are useless and could be dangerous.

- Physical qualities such as strength and mobility are extremely important to enable an athlete to master drills and be fast.

- Drills should be learned progressively. Advanced drills should only be attempted after the beginning drills have been mastered.

- Varied pace running will be one of the most effective methods for increasing maximum velocity because it does not interfere with mechanics.

- When using resisted running, an athlete's speed should not decrease by more than 10%, or mechanics will suffer.

- Assisted running, while effective, does have limitations in terms of the speed or the decline that should be observed to keep the athlete from developing inefficient mechanics.

- Exercises should be employed in a progressive manner and will be most effective if used in a periodized program.

Acceleration

Technically, acceleration refers to the process of increasing speed until you reach maximum velocity. Elite sprinters may accelerate for as long as six to seven seconds before reaching maximum velocity. Because most athletic events involve running shorter distances than sprinting does, in this book acceleration will refer to the first 10 to 20 yards of the athlete increasing his velocity. Running mechanics will be different over the first 10 to 20 yards than they are during the maximal velocity running described previously.

Acceleration is an important skill to develop because it is a huge component of most athletic plays. Rarely do athletes get to run all-out in a straight line for the 50 to 70 yards that would be required to reach maximum velocity. Since most plays will take place over shorter distances, this skill needs to be developed.

Technique

Acceleration differs from speed in two key areas. First, stride length increases during acceleration, so the strides will initially be shorter than they are at full speed. As a result, the shin angle will be less during acceleration than during maximum velocity running. Second, due to the reduced stride length, the emphasis during acceleration is on frontside mechanics, with little or no emphasis on backside mechanics. Therefore, during acceleration, the athlete should focus on toe up, high knee, vigorous arm action, active "pawing" action at footstrike, and maintaining a tight back and stomach.

Evaluating Acceleration

Acceleration is best evaluated through short distance sprints from a standing or crouching start. The exact distance and starting position should be determined by the needs of the sport. Sprints of 20 to 40 yards are good tests of acceleration. Longer sprints from a standing or crouching start can also help to evaluate acceleration while combining it with other qualities (for example, the 60-yard dash mentioned previously in the maximum velocity section).

Principles of Training

Like speed training, acceleration training should not take place in two consecutive training sessions and requires one to three days of recovery between sessions. Acceleration training is conducted over distances of up to 80 yards, with one to two minutes rest between repetitions and five to seven minutes rest between sets. Acceleration training may be combined with maximum velocity training. However, due to the importance of acceleration in athletics, some training sessions should be set aside just for acceleration. Table 3-2 at the end of the chapter provides more detailed information about volume, intensity, etc. when training for acceleration.

Acceleration Drills

Starts are the primary method for developing acceleration. Starts involve the athlete beginning the drill in a stationary position. After receiving the start command, the athlete leaves the position and attempts to increase his velocity while covering the specified distance. Start drills are effective because beginning from a stationary start requires the athlete to accelerate and reacting to the start command enhances his reaction time. "Unusual" starting situations (for example, a push-up) can be used to enhance the athlete's ability to react quickly and to accelerate. Long drills (i.e., 30 yards or more) will enhance maximum velocity running in addition to acceleration. Start drills may also be combined with other exercises (for example, performing a long jump to a sprint) to increase the difficulty level.

As with the maximum velocity drills, acceleration drills should be used in a progressive manner. They should only be made more complex and more difficult as the athlete's technique and fitness allow. Chapter 4 will cover acceleration drills in detail.

Speed Endurance

According to Winckler (1995), speed endurance refers to the ability of the athlete to maintain high levels of speed for long periods of time. Speed endurance (also referred to as conditioning) is an important ability for an athlete whose sport (e.g., soccer) or position (e.g., football receiver) requires repetitive sprinting.

Evaluating Speed Endurance

Speed endurance can be evaluated by several methods, including long-distance sprints (e.g., 100 yards and greater) that have the ability to evaluate multiple qualities (acceleration + maximum velocity + endurance). Another method involves running numerous short-distance sprints with little or no recovery between each sprint. The 300-yard shuttle run is an example of one such test. For this test, place cones 25 yards apart. The athlete should sprint back and forth between the cones for a total of six round trips (i.e., 12 x 25 yards = 300 yards). Record the time it takes the athlete to complete six round trips. Allow the athlete to rest for five minutes and then have him repeat the test. Take the average of the two times and record it.

Principles of Training

In general, speed endurance involves training over distances of 30 to 600 yards at 75 to 100% intensity. Depending upon the distances involved, rest may range from 30 seconds to 15 minutes between each repetition, and anywhere from two minutes to full recovery between each set. As with acceleration and maximum velocity, speed endurance should not be trained during successive workouts.

The large possible range of distance, intensity, and recovery variables available for speed endurance training can make program design confusing. To make it easier, Plisk and Gambetta (1997) suggest the following process for structuring speed endurance training and making it sport-specific. First, analyze what is occurring during competition: time spent working, time spent in recovery, nature of the work and recovery, average number of plays per unit of time, length of plays, etc. Then, based on this information, structure training to meet the needs of competition: similar work:rest intervals, work and rest resembling what is seen in competition, etc. Finally, modify the training based upon the needs of different positions.

As an example, during an average quarter an offense makes 15 plays. Each play (on average) lasts 4 seconds, with 30 seconds of rest. Play consists of short sprints, rest generally consists of walking. A speed endurance workout would consist of sets of five 40-yard sprints, with approximately 30 to 45 seconds recovery between each sprint. This approach to training design will be described and applied in greater detail in the event-specific workout chapters. Table 3-2 provides general volume, intensity, and rest guidelines for programming components of speed endurance.

Conclusion

Speed is an important quality for success in athletics. Speed is made up of different components, depending upon the distance to be covered. These components include maximum velocity running, acceleration, and speed endurance. Each one requires slightly different techniques, methods for evaluation, and approaches to training. Understanding these differences is important because not every sport will require the same emphasis on the same components.

Table 3-2 provides general programming guidelines in terms of volume, distance, intensity, and rest for training various speed-related qualities. Note that the volume per session is for collegiate-level 100-meter sprinters, so this number will have to be adjusted downward for younger athletes.

Component	Length of Reps	% of Best Speed	Rest Intervals Between Reps/Sets	Volume per Session (College)
Acceleration	20-80 yards	90-100%	1-2'/5-7'	300-500 yards
Maximum Speed	20-80 yards	90-100%	3-5'/6-8'	300-800 yards
Anaerobic Capacity	80+ yards	80-89%	30"-5'/3-10'	800-1800 yards
Speed Endurance	80-150 yards	90-100%	5-10'	300-900 yards
Long Speed Endurance	150-300 yards	90-100%	10-15'	600-900 yards

Table 3-2. Programming recommendations for collegiate sprinters. Adapted from USA Track and Field Coaching Education Program (2001). Level II Course: Sprints, Hurdles, Relays. USA Track and Field.

4

Speed Training Drills

This chapter describes drills that can be used to enhance maximum velocity running and acceleration. Some drills reinforce aspects of technique, some enhance stride frequency or stride length, and others work on explosiveness.

Maximum Velocity Running Drills

The drills that will be covered in this section are designed to break the sprinting motion down into parts to make mastery easier. These drills should be done in the following order:

- Arm swing drills

- Ankling drill

- High knee drills

- Butt kicks drill

- A drills

- B drills

- Fast leg drills

- Stride length drills

❑ Arm Swing Drills

Arm swing drills are designed to teach the correct arm action during maximum velocity running. As was discussed in the last chapter; arm action balances the forces created by the legs, initiates the actions of the legs, and potentially limits running speed. As a result, it is important to develop correct arm swing mechanics during maximum velocity running. The arm swing drills described in this chapter start with the simple and move to the complex. Athletes should not progress to each more advanced drill until they have mastered the basic drills that precede it.

Figure 4-1. Arm swing drill, seated

Arm Swing Drill, Seated

Purpose: To teach correct arm swing mechanics.

Start: Sit down and extend the legs in front of the body. The torso should be tall, with the shoulders back. Flex both elbows and make loose fists with both hands. The right elbow should begin at approximately 60 degrees, with the hand located between the shoulder and the eyes. The left arm should be placed behind the body so that the left hand is next to the left hip.

Action: While seated, drive the right arm backwards aggressively so that the right hand ends up next to the right hip. At the same time, drive the left arm forward so that the left hand ends up between the left shoulder and eye. As the right arm moves forward as a result of the stretch reflex, drive the left arm backwards. Repeat until the desired time has elapsed.

Finish: The drill is completed when the desired time has elapsed.

Arm Swing Drill, Standing

Purpose: To teach correct arm mechanics while standing.

Start: Stand tall, shoulders back. Flex both elbows and make loose fists with both hands. The right elbow should begin at approximately 60 degrees, with the hand located between the shoulder and the eyes. The left arm should be placed behind the body so that the left hand is next to the left hip.

Action: Focus on swinging the arms in the manner described in the seated arm swing drill.

Finish: The drill is completed when the desired time has elapsed.

Arm Swing Drill, Walking

Purpose: To teach correct arm swing mechanics while moving.

Start: Use the same starting position described in the standing arm swing drill.

Action: While walking forward for 10 to 20 yards, focus on swinging the arms in the manner described in the standing arm swing drill. Try to swing the arms faster than the feet move.

Finish: The drill is completed when the desired distance has been covered.

Arm Swing Drill, Jogging

Purpose: To teach correct arm swing mechanics while moving.

Start: Use the same starting position described in the standing arm swing drill.

Action: While jogging forward for 10 to 20 yards, focus on swinging the arms in the manner described in the standing arm swing drill. Try to swing the arms faster than the feet move.

Finish: The drill is completed when the desired distance has been covered.

❑ Ankling

Ankling teaches the athlete how to lift his feet off the ground during maximum velocity running.

Figure 4-2a: Ankling drill—plantarflexion

Figure 4-2b: Ankling drill—"cocking" of the ankle

Ankling Drill

Purpose: To teach "cocking" of the ankle.

Start: Stand tall, shoulders back.

Action: Keeping the legs straight, step forward with the right foot. As the right foot lands on the ground, the left foot should enter plantarflexion and begin to lift off the ground.

As the left foot is lifted (the leg remains straight), the ankle should be "cocked." (i.e., dorsiflexion with the big toe pointed up). The ankle should remain cocked as the foot swings forward. Attempt to land on the outside edge of the foot. Repeat this movement pattern with both sides until the desired distance has been covered, usually 10 to 20 yards. Note that this drill is not done for speed, but rather for technique.

Finish: The drill is completed when the desired distance has been covered.

❑ High Knee Drills

High knee drills teach the athlete to lift the knees during maximum velocity running. This technique is important to master because it results in a more powerful leg drive by allowing the athlete to use his gluteus maximus to help power the motion. High knee drills start with a walking motion, focusing on one side at a time. Eventually, both sides are alternated, then skipping is added to make the movements more complicated. At first, these drills are performed without any emphasis on the arm motion. As the athlete becomes more proficient, the arm motion can be added. High knee drills are performed for 10 to 20 yards. As with most technique drills, the emphasis should be on quality of movement as opposed to speed.

High Knee Drill, Walking, One-Side

Purpose: To teach the high knee motion while focusing on one side of the body at a time.

Start: Stand tall, shoulders back.

Action: Maintaining a tall posture, lift the right knee as high as possible. As the right knee is lifted, the right foot should be cocked. Maintaining the cocked position, lower the right foot so that it lands on the outside edge of the foot. Take a normal step forward with the left leg. Repeat the drill with the right side for the desired distance, then switch sides.

Finish: The drill is completed when the desired distance has been covered with both sides of the body.

High Knee Drill, Walking, Alternate Sides

Purpose: To teach the high knee motion while alternating both sides of the body.

Start: Stand tall, shoulders back.

Action: Perform the high knee walking motion with the right leg. As the right foot lands on the ground, perform the high knee walking motion with the left leg. Continue alternating for the desired distance.

Finish: The drill is completed when the desired distance has been covered.

High Knee Drill, Skipping, One-Side

Purpose: To teach the high knee motion in an explosive manner while focusing on one side of the body.

Start: Stand tall, shoulders back.

Action: Maintaining a tall posture, perform a forward skip with the right leg. As the right leg is skipped, the right knee should be lifted high with the right foot cocked. Maintaining the cocked position, lower the right foot so that it lands on the outside edge of the foot. Take a normal step forward with the left leg and repeat the skip with the right side. Repeat the skips for the desired distance and then switch sides. Focus on getting off the ground with the skipping foot as quickly as possible. Note that stride length will not be very great during this drill, so the distance will not be covered quickly.

Finish: The drill is completed when the desired distance has been covered with both sides of the body.

High Knee Drill, Skipping, Alternate Sides

Purpose: To teach the high knee motion in an explosive manner while alternating both sides of the body.

Start: Stand tall, shoulders back.

Action: Perform the high knee skipping motion with the right leg. As the right foot lands on the ground, perform the high knee skipping motion with the left leg. Repeat the skips for the desired distance. Focus on getting off the ground with the skipping foot as quickly as possible. Once again, stride length will not be very great during this drill, so the distance will not be covered quickly.

Finish: The drill is completed when the desired distance has been covered.

❑ Butt Kicks

Butt kicks teach backside mechanics. Note that when used for maximum velocity running they are somewhat different than traditional butt kicks.

Butt Kicks Drill

Purpose: To reinforce cocking the foot and to teach bringing the foot to the hip after push-off.

Start: Stand tall.

Action: Lift the right foot off the ground, cocking it as it leaves the ground. Immediately bring the foot to the right hip, flexing the right hip somewhat so the knee does not

point straight to the ground. As the right foot lands on the ground, repeat this drill with the left side. Continue alternating until 10 to 20 yards have been covered. Note that this is a technique drill, not a speed drill.

Finish: The drill is completed when the desired distance has been covered.

Figure 4-3. Butt kicks

❏ A Drills

A drills are designed to bring together ankling, high knee drills, butt kicks, and, eventually, arm swing drills. They are designed to be performed faster and more explosively than these basic drills and are meant to reinforce a tall posture, ankling, heel to hip, high knees, ankle dorsiflexion, and driving the foot towards the ground. Like the high knee drills, A drills start with a walking motion, focusing on one side at a time. Eventually, both sides are alternated, then skipping is added to make the movements more complicated. At first, these drills are performed without any emphasis on the arm motion. As the athlete becomes more proficient, the arm motion can be added. A drills are performed for 10 to 20 yards. As with most technique drills, the emphasis should be on quality of movement as opposed to speed.

A Drill, Walking, One Side

Purpose: To begin teaching the sprinting motion by focusing on one side of the body at a time.

Start: Stand tall.

Action: Bring the right heel to the right hip and cock the foot. When the heel reaches the hip, lift the right knee. As the knee is lifted, the foot will separate from the hip. The knee should be lifted high enough so that the right foot "steps over" the left knee. The foot must remain cocked as this occurs. Using the hip, drive the leg into the ground just in front of the body's center of gravity, with the outside edge of the foot landing on the ground. Use a pawing motion to pull the body's center of gravity over the foot. Take a normal step forward with the left leg. Repeat until the desired distance is covered. Switch sides.

Finish: The drill is completed when the desired distance has been covered with both sides of the body.

A Drill, Walking, Alternating Sides

Purpose: To begin teaching the sprinting motion by focusing on alternating both sides of the body.

Start: Stand tall.

Action: Perform the walking A drill with the right side. As the body is pulled over the foot, lift the left heel to the left hip and perform the walking A drill with the left leg. Continue alternating until the desired distance has been covered.

Finish: The drill is completed when the desired distance has been covered.

A Drill, Skipping, One Side

Purpose: To teach the sprinting motion in an explosive manner while focusing on one side of the body.

Start: Stand tall.

Action: Maintaining a tall posture, perform a skip with the right leg. As the skip is performed, the right foot should be cocked and the heel should be brought to the hip. The knee should then be raised and the foot should be aggressively driven into the ground in a pawing motion. Walk forward with the left leg. Repeat until the desired distance has been covered. Switch sides.

Finish: The drill is completed when the desired distance has been covered with both sides of the body.

A Drill, Skipping, Alternate Sides

Purpose: To teach the sprinting motion in an explosive manner while focusing on alternating both sides of the body.

Start: Stand tall.

Action: Maintaining a tall posture, perform a skip with the right leg, focusing on the mechanics described in the previous drill. As the right foot makes contact with the ground, immediately perform a skip with the left leg, once again focusing on correct mechanics. Strive to get off the ground as quickly as possible. Repeat until the desired distance has been covered.

Finish: The drill is completed when the desired distance has been covered.

Figure 4-4a: A drill—heel to hip

Figure 4-4b: A drill—lifting the knee

❏ B Drills

B drills build on the skills taught by A drills and help the athlete to focus on an active landing with the foot during the sprinting motion. The landing is important because a poor foot strike can result in braking, which can slow the athlete down. Like the high knee and A drills, B drills are performed slowly with one side at first and gradually progress to a skip using both sides of the body. Initially, the arm swing motion should not be included, but it should be added as the athlete progresses in proficiency. These drills are typically performed for 10 to 20 yards.

B Drill, Walking, One Side

Purpose: To teach the active landing during the sprinting motion while focusing on one side of the body at a time.

Start: Stand tall.

Action: Bring the right heel to the right hip and cock the foot. When the heel reaches the hip, lift the right knee. As the knee is lifted, the foot will separate from the hip. The knee should be lifted high enough so that the right foot "steps over" the left knee. Allow the right knee to extend so that the foot travels out in front of the body. Let this movement occur naturally, as a result of the hip flexion. Do not force or exaggerate it. The foot must remain cocked as it moves in front of the body. Using the hip, drive the straight leg into the ground just in front of the body's center of gravity, with the outside edge of the foot landing on the ground. Use a pawing motion to pull the body's center of gravity over the foot. Take a normal step forward with the left leg. Repeat until the desired distance is covered. Switch sides.

Finish: The drill is completed when the desired distance has been covered with both sides of the body.

B Drill, Walking, Alternate Sides

Purpose: To teach the active landing during the sprinting motion while focusing on alternating both sides of the body.

Start: Stand tall.

Action: Perform a walking B drill with the right leg. As the right foot makes contact with the ground, perform a walking B drill with the left leg. Repeat until the desired distance has been covered.

Finish: The drill is completed when the desired distance has been covered.

B Drill, Skipping, One Side

Purpose: To teach the active landing in an explosive manner, focusing on one side of the body.

Start: Stand tall.

Action: Maintaining a tall posture, perform a skip with the right leg. As the skip is performed, the right foot should be cocked and the heel should be brought to the hip. Raise the knee and then allow it to extend as the foot travels out and away from the body. Remember to keep the foot cocked throughout. The knee extension should happen as a result of the hip flexion. It should not be forced or exaggerated. From the hip, aggressively drive the straight leg into the ground just in front of the body's center of gravity, with the outside edge of the foot landing on the ground. Use a pawing motion to pull the body's center of gravity over the foot. Take a normal step forward with the left leg. Repeat until the desired distance is covered. Switch sides.

Finish: The drill is completed when the desired distance has been covered with both sides of the body.

B Drill, Skipping, Alternate Sides

Purpose: To teach the active landing in an explosive manner, focusing on alternating both sides of the body.

Start: Stand tall.

Action: Maintaining a tall posture, perform a skipping B drill with the right leg. As the right leg makes contact with the ground, immediately perform a skipping B drill with the left leg. Continue alternating for the desired distance.

Finish: The drill is completed when the desired distance has been covered.

❏ Fast Leg Drills

Fast leg drills are advanced drills that combine the qualities of a number of the drills described previously. Fast leg drills should only be performed after athletes have mastered the more basic drills.

Fast Leg Drill

Purpose: To help improve stride frequency.

Start: Stand tall.

Action: Shuffle on straight legs, cocking each foot as it leaves the ground (i.e., a fast ankling motion). On every third step, perform a "fast leg" motion: bring the heel to the hip, cycle the leg forward (stepping over the opposite leg), and lift the knee, allowing the foot to separate from the hip. Using the hip, drive the foot down towards the ground in a pawing motion so that the outside edge of the foot makes contact with the ground. The foot should remain dorsiflexed throughout. This fast leg motion should take place as quickly as possible. Perform the drill for 10 to 20 yards. A variation of this drill is to take every left (or right) stride as a fast leg.

Finish: The drill is completed when the desired distance has been covered.

❏ Stride Length Drills

Stride length drills are designed to help improve an athlete's stride length. When implementing these drills, keep several points in mind:

- Too much stride length (i.e. overstriding) is just as bad as not enough stride length.

- An athlete's ideal stride length generally should be 2.3 to 2.5 times leg length for women and 2.5 to 2.7 times for men.

- Improving stride length requires several factors, including sound sprinting technique, strength, and dynamic flexibility.

With a stride length drill, the coach should give the athlete 10 to 15 yards to accelerate. After that point, the coach should put some type of marker on the ground at a percentage of the athlete's ideal stride length (generally 80%). The coach can place 10 to 15 markers the same distance apart. To execute this drill, the athlete will accelerate and then attempt to have a foot strike after each marker.

For example, if a male athlete has a 36" leg, then his ideal stride length is 90 inches (2.5 x 36). After a 10- to 15-yard acceleration zone, a marker should be placed every 72 inches (80% of 90). The athlete will be expected to have a foot strike after each marker.

Another approach is a scaling foot strike drill, where the distance between markers is gradually increased. The athlete should still have a 10- to 15-yard acceleration zone. After that, the first marker should be placed at a distance of 60% of the athlete's ideal stride length. The next marker should be at 65%, then 70%, and so on, with each marker increasing by 5%, all the way up to 105% of the athlete's ideal stride length. Using the same athlete as the previous example, the markers would be placed 54, 58.5, 63, 67.5, 72, 76.5, 81, 85.5, 90, and 94.5 inches apart.

During stride length drills, sound technique must be emphasized. Athletes will attempt to overstride or run on their toes during these drills, but these actions should be discouraged because they develop bad habits.

Acceleration Drills

Accelerating includes starting the motion (from a stationary or moving start) and increasing velocity. Acceleration drills can go from simple to sport-specific. The acceleration drills in this chapter use the following progression:

- Standing

- Crouching

- Lying

- Changing directions

- Sport-specific

Standing Start

Purpose: To teach the arm action that accompanies the start and to develop acceleration.

Start: The non-power foot begins two foot-lengths behind the start line. The power foot begins three foot-lengths behind the start line. Feet are placed less than shoulder-width apart. Squat down, keeping the head and trunk in alignment. Keep the weight on the balls of the feet.

Action: Begin acceleration by "falling" forward and then stepping with the power foot to break the fall. As the power foot steps forward, drive back the arm on the same side. Run the prescribed distance.

Finish: The drill is completed when the desired distance has been covered.

Figure 4-5a. Standing
start

Figure 4-5b. Standing
start—first step

Crouch Start

Purpose: To develop acceleration from the crouched position.

Start: Assume either a three-point or four-point stance.

Action: On command, sprint forward and cover the desired distance. As the power foot steps forward, drive the arm on the same side backward.

Finish: The drill is completed when the desired distance has been covered.

Figure 4-6a. Crouching
start

Figure 4-6b. Crouching
start—first step

Push-Up Start

Purpose: To make the starting motion more difficult by requiring the athlete to stand up before accelerating.

Start: Lie down behind the start line and assume the starting position for push-ups.

Figure 4-7. Push-up start

Action: On command, stand up and sprint forward, covering the desired distance.

Finish: The drill is completed when the desired distance has been covered.

Prone Start

Purpose: To make the starting motion more difficult by requiring the athlete to get off the ground before accelerating.

Start: Lie down on the stomach.

Action: On command, stand up and sprint forward, covering the desired distance.

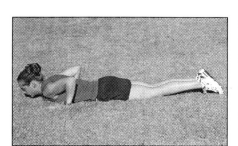

Figure 4-8. Prone start

Finish: The drill is completed when the desired distance has been covered.

Standing, Back-to-Course Start

Purpose: To make the starting motion more difficult by requiring the athlete to change direction before accelerating.

Start: Stand with the back to the course.

Action: On command, turn around and sprint forward, covering the desired distance.

Finish: The drill is completed when the desired distance has been covered.

Broad Jump + Start

Purpose: To make the starting motion more complex and more sport-specific by combining motions.

Start: Stand tall.

Action: Execute a standing broad jump. Upon landing, immediately sprint forward and cover the desired distance.

Finish: The drill is completed when the desired distance has been covered.

Vertical Jump + Start

Purpose: To make the starting motion more complex and more sport-specific by combining motions.

Start: Stand tall.

Action: Execute a vertical jump. Upon landing, immediately sprint forward and cover the desired distance.

Finish: The drill is completed when the desired distance has been covered.

Medicine Ball Toss + Start

Purpose: To make the starting motion more complex and more sport-specific by combining motions.

Start: Stand tall.

Action: Execute a forward or backward medicine-ball toss. Upon releasing the ball, sprint forward the desired distance.

Finish: The drill is completed when the desired distance has been covered.

5

Agility

Agility is the ability to effectively and efficiently change direction. In an athletic context, agility can take on a much greater meaning, for instance, the ability to coordinate sport-specific tasks (like eluding a defender, carrying a ball, and evaluating the defensive scheme), the ability to coordinate several skills simultaneously, and even the ability to effectively decipher a novel situation. Studies show that, outside of sport-specific skills, agility is the primary determining factor for success in a sport.

Like any physical component of a successful athlete (e.g., strength, power, balance, coordination, etc.), agility (or athleticism) is largely determined by genetics. Many coaches and athletes think that agility cannot be influenced or improved to any significant degree. Agility is difficult to influence and improve, but agility training is still important, just like strength training, flexibility, and metabolic conditioning. Agility is a neural ability that is developed over time with many repetitions. Depending on the physical requirements of the sport, agility training may be the most important aspect of training out of season.

Traditionally, off-season programs have focused solely on strength and conditioning, without sport-specific application. The problem with this approach is that when the season starts, the athlete is in top physical shape that does not necessarily apply to the sport's specific needs. Agility training bridges the gap between strength and conditioning and competition, and helps athletes apply their hard-earned strength and conditioning gains to the playing field. Agility training should be incorporated into all off-season strength and conditioning programs for sports that require the athlete to compete in open space, change direction, or compete in an unpredictable environment.

This chapter will cover the science behind agility training, constituents of agility, training principles of agility training, and program design information relating to agility training.

Science and Agility Training

It is important to understand some of the mechanisms associated with acquiring agility skills. Many coaches quickly incorporate drills into team practice, with little understanding of the whys behind the drills. As a result, athletes of varying degrees of experience and skill may be grouped together, and many of the athletes may receive inappropriate coaching. Before implementing agility training, a coach needs to understand the science behind agility to avoid some common coaching pitfalls. Agility training draws from a number of important sport science disciplines: physiology, biomechanics, and motor learning.

Physiology and Agility Training

Metabolic conditioning and agility training should be considered inseparable. Appropriate agility training drills can duplicate movement skills that tax the metabolic system in a specific manner. Although the intensity of competition can never be exactly duplicated in practice, the intensity, duration, and rest periods of drills can be adjusted to simulate game situations and elicit the desired metabolic effect. The drills should be modified according to the nature of the sport (work/rest or work/active rest).

Many coaches line up their players single file to participate in a drill. For instance, the soccer coach instructs one player to possess the ball while another player acts as the defender. The ball handler tries to run by the defender, while the rest of the team stands in line and watches. In essence, two players are active, while 10 or more are metabolically at rest. Clearly, this situation rarely happens in a game. As an alternative, divide the players into groups of three. In each group of three, two can compete or be active and one can rest. Even if the coach cannot instruct all the players, they are active and they are learning on their own. This simple strategy can increase the metabolic intensity of practice and keep the players interested in the drill.

Biomechanics and Agility Training

The basis of all human movement is muscles applying torque to bones rotating around joints. The human body is a very complex series of systems that are coordinated to make even basic movements happen. While training for agility, or in athletic competition, the biomechanics of the movements become very important and can have a pronounced effect on the outcome. If a batter were to adjust his swing even a quarter of an inch on a pitch, it could mean the difference between a routine pop-up and a home run. The same thing can be said for foot placement on the basketball court. If two players are scrambling for a loose ball and one can apply more properly placed foot contacts, then he is in a better position to win the ball.

When it comes to biomechanics and agility training, a coach should take into account the following four interrelated considerations:

• the location of the center of gravity

• the importance of acceleration and deceleration

• efficiency of movement

• the importance of body positioning

Location of the Center of Gravity

The center of gravity or center of mass is the point at which all of the mass of the body would be condensed into considering all body segments and their positions. The higher the center of gravity, the more unstable the athlete. A high center of gravity can sometimes be advantageous, for example, when a basketball player would desire to remain elevated for a longer period of time. Advanced players will raise their center of gravity while in the air to give the visual illusion that they are somehow suspended. The athlete's center of gravity will have an ideal location depending on the situation.

Most often, a higher center of gravity will not be to the athlete's advantage. Consider the following situation: two opposing players are positioning for a loose soccer ball. As they both race toward the ball, one drops his center of gravity by bending at the hips, while the other also lowers his center of gravity, but not as much. During incidental contact as they move toward the ball, with all other variables held equal, the lower player can better position himself by pushing off the opponent.

Lowering the center of gravity by bending at the knees and hips often results in a better position to push the athlete in the desired direction when accelerating. As a simple example, take a shoulder-width stance, bend at the knees slightly, and then take a forceful lateral step. Next, take the same shoulder-width stance, but this time bend further at the knees and hips, lowering your center of gravity, and take the lateral step. You will quickly notice that you can take a bigger and more forceful step in the lower position.

The universal "athletic stance" is a position where the knees and hips are bent, the torso leans forward slightly, the back is flat, and the head and eyes are up. This stance is observed in many different sports, such as football, basketball, and tennis. This stance is the best position to apply force in all directions. The linebacker can either take on a blocker by quickly moving forward or react to cover a tight end. The tennis player can move in multiple directions to return a serve with a backhand or forehand. And the basketball player is best positioned to defend an opponent that is trying to run by with the ball. The center of gravity is low and the body is positioned to move in many different directions.

Importance of Acceleration and Deceleration

Acceleration can be defined as a change in velocity, usually in the positive direction. Deceleration, or stopping ability, is simply moving from a high to low velocity or to a stop. Many situations in sport require the athlete to be able to accelerate and decelerate. The more proficient the athlete becomes at these skills, the better his performance potential. The ability to accelerate and decelerate is important because it creates space between opposing players. Its importance is especially evident in football between defensive backs and the receiver position.

Great receivers can accelerate and decelerate more rapidly than defensive backs. For example, take a simple out pattern of the receiver into account. The receiver will accelerate off the line of scrimmage rapidly and, depending on the situation, the defensive back will start moving backward quickly. Great receivers can disguise their routes using acceleration off the line to keep the defensive back positioned not to give up the deep pass. The receiver route requires them to quickly decelerate and make a 90-degree turn. The defensive back should then change direction and accelerate toward the receiver. Once again, the receiver will want to disguise which direction he is going to turn, leaving the defensive back with little information to react to. If the receiver decelerates quickly enough, he will create space between himself and the defensive back. However, a good defensive back will be in position to defend the receiver. As the pattern continues and the receiver changes direction, he will have another opportunity to accelerate more rapidly than the defensive back. The great receivers can accelerate, decelerate, and re-accelerate better than their opponents. On the other hand, a great defensive back can do the same.

Efficiency of Movement

Efficiency of movement is critical for effective agility to occur. Athletes should be trained enough and familiar enough with the required skills of the sport to move efficiently in various situations. In open skills, the athlete may be able to decipher the offensive and defensive schemes, which can be a very effective way to conserve energy. However, when isolating specific agility skills, efficiency of movement is paramount. Foot placement, location of the center of gravity, torso positioning, arm action, head positioning, and the focus of the eyes are all very important. The athlete should strive to expend all of his efforts moving in the most efficient manner toward his objective, which may involve an array of different movement patterns like backpedaling, side shuffling, using the crossover step, or turning and running. An experienced coach will be able to identify unnecessary movements of the body, usually of the feet and arms. The coach should give information to the athlete before, during, and after the drill. This strategy has been proven to be most effective for athletes to learn and acquire skills. The bottom line is that the athlete should strive to bring about some end result with maximum certainty and minimum outlay of energy, or of time and energy.

Importance of Body Positioning

The importance of body positioning cannot be overstated. In team sports, using correct body position enables the athlete to best apply force. The resistance that needs to be overcome is the athlete's own body weight, an opponent's resistance, an implement/object, or a combination of these factors. The athlete should maintain a neutral spine and have the ability to keep the correct body position. The term "core stability" is sometimes used to define the ability to maintain this position.

The "core" of the body refers to the musculature that supports the spine of the body. If the spine is viewed as a lever and it is *not* rigid, the limbs cannot generate maximal force. On the other hand, if the spine is neutral, and the body is in position, then the athlete can significantly increase the amount of force that can be applied. This force can be used to accelerate, decelerate, change direction, win a loose ball, return a serve, drive block a defender, etc.

Motor Learning

Motor learning is a set of internal processes associated with practice or experience leading to a relatively permanent gain in performance capability. The following section pertains to motor learning and skill classification. It is important to understand skill classification and its implications. The information that follows will help the practitioner to discern between each skill taught and give a strategic approach to coaching. Coaches should be familiar with the types of skills that their sport requires and with basic concepts underlying motor learning. Skill classification and practical application for the coach and athlete will be discussed.

Discrete, Continuous, and Serial

• Discrete: A skill where the action is usually brief and with a recognizable beginning and end. The serve in tennis is an example of a discrete skill. Elite players recognize the importance of the serve and practice it for hours on end.

• Continuous: A skill where the action unfolds continuously, without a recognizable beginning and end. Playing the game of rugby incorporates many actions without a recognizable beginning and end. Therefore, rugby would be classified as a continuous skill.

• Serial: A skill composed of several discrete actions strung together, often with the order of actions being critical for success. Some drills used in agility training are serial in nature, for instance, using a sequence of changes in direction, reacting to a stimulus (defender), and catching a ball.

Open and Closed

Open skills are skills that take place in an unpredictable and changing environment. With open skills, it is recommended that the athlete focus on the environment. Most team sport competitions (i.e. basketball, rugby, football) are open skilled.

Closed skills are movements that take place in stable environments. The athlete should be focusing on the preprogrammed motor programs. Many skills in gymnastics are closed skills. The environments (i.e., balance beam, uneven bars, floor, etc.) are clearly stable and unchanging.

Motor and Cognitive

Highly weighted cognitive skills rely on a thinking process and arousal is detrimental to performance. Springboard and diving are an excellent example of highly weighted cognitive skill.

Motor skills rely on movement control and response production. Powerlifting is a wonderful example of a motor skill. Although the lifts themselves are somewhat technical, they rely on motor skills heavily.

Simple and Complex Skills

The concept of *simple* and *complex* skill classification gives room for interpretation. If the skill to be learned is novel and requires a great deal of cognitive awareness, then the skill would be classified as complex. However, if the athlete is advanced and the learning of new skills comes easily, it may be termed simple. Keep in mind the arousal level of the athlete. If the skill appears to require less concentration and arousal levels are advantageous, then the skill would be simple. Olympic lifting is very technical and requires a certain level of arousal, but not so much as to compromise the successful execution. Weightlifting is classified as complex.

Concepts of Motor Learning

The following concepts of motor learning are important for agility training:

- Perceptual emphasis

- Sequential dependencies

- Automatization

- The importance of errors

- Motor stage of mastery

- Arousal levels

• Perceptual Emphasis

Perceptual emphasis is a key area to training for agility. To perform in an unstable environment, the athlete must be aware of sensory information. For instance, many situations in the game of soccer, like time on the clock, surface conditions, team tactics, and the opponent's strengths, weaknesses, and tendencies all require a perceptual emphasis—in contrast to discrete skills like gymnastics, where the focus is mainly on movement control.

• Sequential Dependencies

Sequential dependencies are skills or tasks that interrelate or depend on each other strongly. The bicycle kick in soccer has a strong sequential dependency. If a skill has a strong sequential dependency, then it is best to practice all the skill's movements together, not independently. Many times, skills can be broken down, but it is important to always train the skill in its entirety.

• Automatization

If the skill, or part of the skill, can be automated, then the athlete can free attention for higher order aspects of the skill. As an example, the offensive lineman's footwork of the pass set in football can be automated. Automatization of the footwork can free attention to process other coordinative abilities and the opponent's strategies and tact.

• Importance of Errors

It is important to determine how costly errors are to the performance. In many team sports, errors can be extremely costly, therefore practicing for automatization is less important than being able to decipher sensory information. Sensory information is critical to transferring agility training to the field of competition. Therefore, supplying a significant level of sensory information when appropriate is important. The *transfer* of agility training to competition is what is most important.

• Motor Stage of Mastery

Motor stage of mastery is the level of acceptance where the skill can be repeated successfully without error. This level is important to reach in many skills because it frees up the athlete's attention and that could lead to their success. It is critical for the coach to define the basic skills of the sport. Once the skills have been defined, reinforce those defined skills with practice.

• Arousal Levels

Arousal, or mental excitement, levels will vary from sport to sport and position to position. If the position on a team requires a great degree of skilled ability, then the arousal level is relatively low. As an example, a defensive back may have to process more information than the defensive tackle on the same team during the same play. The defensive back will have to recognize the offensive scheme, align himself against his opponent, determine what the opposition's tendencies and weaknesses are, react to the opponent's body positioning, and react to the ball in open space—all, most likely, in a highly skilled manner. The defensive tackle will have to make some of the same decisions, but he has less information to process and less space to make moves in, and many of the skills required are gross motor movements.

Constituents of Agility

An effective agility-training program will address several components that are the constituents of agility. They are dynamic flexibility, coordination, power, dynamic balance, acceleration, stopping ability, and strength. A moderate to high degree of transfer exists among each sub-component. These components are interrelated, and drills will often emphasize one of the components but do not, and should not, isolate one particular component. The coach should practice subcomponents of agility to improve overall agility.

Dynamic flexibility: Dynamic flexibility exercises closely duplicate the movement requirements seen in training or in competition. They are functional-based activities that increase balance, flexibility, proprioception, coordination, and speed. They also help to teach sports-specific movements. Dynamic flexibility was covered in Chapter 2.

Coordination: Coordination is an athlete's ability to properly manage or process muscle movements to produce certain skills. Highly coordinated athletes will properly coordinate their muscle movements to elicit productive outcomes.

Power: Mechanically, power is work divided by time. If an athlete moves from point A to point B in less time, he has executed the movement more powerfully. Power is one of the many desirable characteristics that make up an agile athlete.

Dynamic balance: Dynamic balance is the ability to maintain control over the body while in motion. While in motion, the body can use various feedback (i.e., sight, kinesthetic awareness, perturbations) to adjust its center of gravity. Adjustments are made by the nervous system.

Acceleration: This element should be considered as the ability to accelerate from a starting position to a greater velocity, and also the ability to change from one speed to another, often referred to as "changing gears." Acceleration was covered in Chapter 3.

Stopping ability: Stopping ability is the ability to come to a complete stop or to decelerate from various speeds. Stopping ability can take on various forms, such as shuffling, backpedaling, using a crossover step, using single or multiple footsteps to stop, etc. Stopping ability and acceleration are two key elements for success on the playing field.

Strength: Strength, in its most basic form, is the ability to overcome a resistance. In many situations surrounding agility, the mass of the body supplies the resistance. When an athlete is engaged with an opponent, the addition of the opponent's resistance *plus* the athlete's own body mass is the resistance.

To maximize performance, strength training should supplement all athletic training. Research has indicated that a significant correlation exists between lower body strength and agility. As a general rule, the more emphasis the sport has on strength and power, the greater the need to strength train. Strength training has numerous beneficial effects for the athlete, including:

- Improve body composition

- Reduce the risk of injury

- Increase muscular strength and endurance

- Improve athletic performance

The ground-based Olympic lifts (snatch, clean and jerk, and their variations) in particular are extremely important to maximizing performance of team and change-of-direction sports. The intermuscular motor coordination of the Olympic lifts is most similar to various athletic competitions. In addition, the rate of force development while using the Olympic lifts is most similar to that of agility movements on the field or court.

Regarding explosive lifts and training, it is the position of the National Strength and Conditioning Association that:

- Resistance exercises characterized by maximal or near maximal rates of force development or by high accelerations, usually referred to as "explosive exercises," are effective for enhancing physical performance.

- Explosive exercises may be necessary for optimal physical conditioning in some sports, particularly those involving high accelerations.

- In keeping with the principle of specificity of training, explosive exercises can be used to simulate movement patterns and velocity and acceleration patterns of many sports movements.

- Explosive exercises should be taught by experienced and knowledgeable instructors.

- When properly taught and supervised, explosive exercises do not involve excessive risk of injury.

These interrelated constituents of agility are underlying components that should be addressed when training agility.

Training Principles and Agility Training

The following agility principles are highly correlated with training for agility and will serve to better define a theoretical agility paradigm:

- Overload principle

- Transfer of abilities

- SAID

- Lead-up skills

The overload principle is simply stressing the body beyond its current state. The stress is exercise. The body makes an adaptation based upon the stress and current fatigue status. This definition is a very simplified version of the overload principle, with no consideration to the appropriate level of stress/exercise that will elicit the optimal adaptation.

Practicing agility movements should reflect circumstances observed in competition. There will be a positive transfer of abilities if appropriate drills are selected. The amount of transfer will depend on the similarity of practice and competition. The greater the amount of similarity between practice and competition, the greater the amount of appropriate transferring.

The specific adaptations to imposed demands (SAID) principle states that the adaptations of the body are specific to the type of activity that caused them. As an example, a distance runner would tax the aerobic system and muscular endurance qualities of the body. The expected adaptations would be an improved aerobic system and increased muscular endurance. In the case of training for agility, the coach will want to make the drills as specific as possible to the demands of the sport. If lateral shuffling is a predominant motor ability of a tennis player, then that specific skill should be emphasized in the agility training program. It is wise to incorporate other factors that are specific to tennis as well, such as having the athlete hold a racquet, use the court to perform the training, and/or react to a tennis ball in an appropriate manner.

The parts of a skill that lead up to more complex skills are called *lead-up skills*. Athletes should learn novel skills first, then the coach can add more complexity to the skill. In gymnastics, for example, it is logical to teach the forward roll before introducing a drive roll.

Program Design Variables and Agility Training

Before beginning an agility-training program, the coach should define the following program design variables:

Exercise interval refers to how long (in time or distance) the drill should last.

Exercise order should be determined by which drills are the most technical or important, either to an individual athlete or to the demands of the sport/position.

Exercise relief is the amount of exercises performed per set, for example, two sets of four reps.

Frequency is the number of training sessions performed in a given time period. Frequency is usually expressed as training sessions per week when referring to agility training.

Intensity is expressed as how quickly (in time) the drill is performed. If the drill is timed, then intensity is the distance covered.

Relief or recovery interval is determined by the objective of the training session. If learning a new complex technique is the objective, then rest should be maximal, allowing the body a complete recovery before the next repetition. However, if sport-specific metabolic training is the objective, then the rest interval should be reflective of the rest interval of competition or demands of the game.

Repetition is the execution of one complete movement skill.

Set is a group of repetition and relief intervals.

Volume is the amount of total repetitions performed.

Drill selection is based on four factors: movement patterns of the sport, work intervals (considering distance and time), rest intervals (which will vary according to training objectives), and complexity. Once motor pattern/ movement is mastered, then adding decision sensory information like balls, implements, and defenders can increase the complexity of the drill. Technique suggestions on how to increase the complexity of the drill will be included in the drill descriptions in this book.

All other program design variables, such as sets, volume, repetitions, frequency, order, and exercise relief, need to take into consideration unforeseeable training factors, including the age of the athlete, experience with training, the maturity of the athlete, training experience, level of play, present fitness levels, history of injury, medications, resistance to training, and other training methods that may be incorporated into training, like plyometrics, strength training, and practice. To specifically recommend definitive programs without the aforementioned information would be inappropriate.

Keep in mind the following factors when planning an agility training program:

- Train quality of movement first.

- Use a progression (simple to complex).

- Train specific motor/movement patterns.

- Incorporate reactive stimulus when appropriate.

- After mastery of movement, and when appropriate, incorporate metabolic conditioning by controlling the rest interval and intensity.

- Train the skill in its entirety.

- After mastery of movement, execute movements at 100 percent intensity.

- Make sure athletes give their undivided attention to the drill.

6

The Cooldown

Towards the end of the workout, it is important to engage in some type of cooldown activity. The cooldown is designed to slowly reduce the intensity of the exercise and serve as a bridge between exercise and rest, which is important because an abrupt stop in exercise may lead to blood pooling in the extremities, dizziness, fainting, and elevated catecholamine levels.

Remember that towards the end of a speed or agility workout, a number of things will be occurring in the athlete's body. First, due to the activity, the athlete's heart rate and respirations will be elevated. Second, the athlete will have an increased blood flow to the exercising muscles (predominately lower extremity). Third, the athlete will have increased levels of lactic acid circulating through his muscles. Fourth, the athlete will be psychologically aroused. A properly performed cooldown is designed to reduce all of these factors gradually, rather than suddenly.

In addition to being a gradual transition from exercise to rest, the cooldown may also be used to address areas that really cannot be addressed well during the warm-up or during the workout itself. The major area that can be addressed during the cooldown is the prevention of shin splints.

Shin splints are an unfortunate reality of speed and agility training. They typically take the form of pain along medial aspect of the tibia. In the beginning stages, this pain occurs at the beginning of a workout but disappears as the workout progresses. In later stages, the pain becomes more severe and more persistent.

Shin splints may result from any one of a number of factors. Athletes may be wearing inappropriate footwear, which will contribute to shin splints. They may be training on a surface without much "give" to it (for example, a concrete parking lot). They may not have enough strength in the muscles on the anterior portion of their lower leg or their feet. They may also be unable to adjust to higher training volumes. Any of these factors, or any changes in these factors, could cause or exacerbate shin splints.

Some of the contributing factors to shin splints are interrelated. Most athletes today are accustomed to training with cushioned shoes. As a result, their feet and shin muscles do not get stronger through training. Unfortunately, common strength training exercises address these areas (feet and shins) inadequately. One way to address this deficiency is by having an athlete perform drills in bare feet during the cooldown. Performing drills in bare feet will help the athlete to strengthen the muscles that support the feet. This chapter describes drills that an athlete can perform with bare feet during the cooldown. The drills are presented in the progression that they should be mastered.

Walk on Toes

Start: Face the course and stand tall. Plantarflex the ankles so that the heels are not touching the ground.

Action: Without letting the heels touch the ground, walk the prescribed distance. This drill is typically performed over 20 yards.

Finish: The drill is completed when the desired distance has been covered.

Walk on Heels

Start: Face the course and stand tall. Dorsiflex the ankles so that the toes are not touching the ground.

Action: Without letting the toes touch the ground, walk the prescribed distance. This drill is typically performed over 20 yards.

Finish: The drill is completed when the desired distance has been covered.

Walk Toes In

Start: Face the course and stand tall. Exaggerate the angle of the feet so that the toes are pointing towards each other.

Action: Maintain the exaggerated foot angle and walk the prescribed distance. This drill is typically performed over 20 yards.

Finish: The drill is completed when the desired distance has been covered.

Walk Toes Out

Start: Face the course and stand tall. Exaggerate the angle of the feet so that the toes are pointing away from each other.

Action: Maintain the exaggerated foot angle and walk the prescribed distance. This drill is typically performed over 20 yards.

Finish: The drill is completed when the desired distance has been covered.

Walk Pronated

Start: Face the course and stand tall. Stand with the feet pronated so that the soles of the feet are facing out.

Action: Maintaining this posture, walk the prescribed distance. This drill is typically performed over 20 yards.

Finish: The drill is completed when the desired distance has been covered.

Walk Supinated

Start: Face the course and stand tall. Stand with the feet supinated so that the soles of the feet are facing each other.

Action: Maintaining this posture, walk the prescribed distance. This drill is typically performed over 20 yards.

Finish: The drill is completed when the desired distance has been covered.

Stand on One Foot

Start: Balance on one foot.

Action: Maintain the position for a prescribed period of time.

Finish: The drill is completed when the desired time has elapsed.

Stand on One Foot and Toss Medicine Ball

Start: This drill requires a partner. The athlete should first balance on one foot.

Action: Once balance has been attained, perform chest passes with the medicine ball.

Finish: The drill is completed when the desired number of chest passes has been completed.

Stand on Balance Board with Both Feet

Start and Action: Step on the balance board and attempt to keep it level. Do not let any part of the balance board touch the ground. This drill is typically performed for time.

Finish: The drill is completed when the desired time has elapsed.

Stand on Balance Board with One Foot

Start: Step on the balance board with one foot.

Action: Attempt to keep the board level, not letting any part of the balance board touch the ground. This drill is typically performed for time.

Finish: The drill is completed when the desired time has elapsed.

Stand on Balance Board and Toss Medicine Ball

Start: Perform with one foot or both feet on the board. Step on the balance board and get the board level.

Action: Once the board is level, toss the medicine ball with a partner. Focus on catching the ball and on keeping the board level.

Finish: The drill is completed when the desired number of tosses has been performed.

Sprinting Technique Drills

Advanced athletes may perform many of the sprinting technique drills (e.g., ankling, butt kicks, high knees, A walks/skips, and B walks/skips) in bare feet during the cooldown. These drills are described in Chapter 4.

Multi-Directional Drills

Advanced athletes may perform many of the multi-directional drills (e.g., side shuffles, cariocas, step backs, and backpedals) discussed in Chapter 2 for 20 yards in bare feet during the cooldown.

The cooldown should begin immediately following the last speed or agility exercise. It should consist of three to five minutes of light exercise designed to gradually bring the athlete to a resting state. The barefoot drills provide an excellent way to transition the body from exercise to rest. Since they are not performed for speed (i.e., the goal is to walk 20 yards in the manner specified), they are a low intensity type of exercise. As a result, even though a training effect is still occurring, heart rate will decrease and blood flow to the exercising tissues will gradually return to normal.

Barefoot drills should be performed for 10 to 20 yards. Generally, they are performed for one set on each exercise and can be performed in a manner of minutes, so they do not require much time. Beginners should focus on the walking drills. As those drills are mastered, the balancing exercises may be integrated into the program for variety. Once athletes are able to perform the balance exercises with the medicine ball and balance board, they are ready for some of the sprinting and multi-directional drills. Athletes should first perform ankling, butt kicks, and high knees with bare feet before progressing to A drills, B drills, and multi-directional exercises.

The cooldown should provide a way to gradually return the body to a resting state. It provides an excellent time to address injury prevention exercises, which are typically performed at a much lower intensity than the actual workout. If the time is used properly, the cooldown can help prevent injuries such as shin splints and could possibly help keep the athlete from being as sore the day or two after training.

7

Program Design

Previous chapters have explored all the components that are required for safe and effective speed and agility training. This chapter is going to focus on putting everything together. To design effective speed and agility programs, one must consider the following:

- principles of exercise

- needs of the sport and the athlete

- the sport's competition season

Principles of Exercise

The following principles should be used as guidelines to maximize the effectiveness of strength and conditioning programs:

- specificity
- overload
- progression

- reversibility
- individualization
- exercise order

The principle of specificity states that an athlete adapts to exercise according to how he exercises. Following this principle allows an athlete to focus conditioning programs to ensure that the desired gains are achieved. Failing to follow this principle means that things will happen by chance as a result of the conditioning program, which may not work out to the benefit of the athlete. When considering the principle of specificity, consider the biomechanical and metabolic demands of the sport and then design the program to address those demands.

The principle of overload states that the body adapts to exercise, and for the exercise to continue producing a positive training effect, it must be made more difficult over time. If this principle is not observed, then exercise will stop producing a positive training effect and development will level off and could actually regress. The overload applied to a speed and agility workout could take the form of more complex exercises and drills, greater volume, greater intensity, modified rest periods, or some combination of these elements.

The principle of progression states that an athlete must gradually increase the complexity and difficulty of training across his training lifetime to ensure that he masters fundamental skills and exercises and develops a fitness base. This approach prevents injuries and ensures better mastery and performance of skills.

The principle of reversibility states that the gains made from exercise can be reversed. If an athlete does not maintain his conditioning levels, then he will regress. Muscles may atrophy, strength levels may decrease, speed and agility may decrease, flexibility may decrease, and body fat levels may increase as a result of injury, inactivity, and reduced training over a long period of time. Loss of conditioning occurs very rapidly after the cessation of exercise.

The principle of individualization states that while certain fundamental principles and concepts should be observed during exercise, everyone will respond to a given stimulus differently. This principle is especially important when it comes to manipulating volume, intensity, rest, and recovery. Some athletes are able to tolerate larger, more frequent increases in volume and intensity, while others will be crushed by the same training demands. Coaches will need to alter their programs based upon how individual athletes respond. This principle explains why it is not recommended for coaches to copy the workout programs of highly successful, advanced athletes.

Exercise order is not a fundamental principle behind program design, but it is an important consideration. Speed and agility training takes place very quickly. It requires proper technique and the athlete's psychological focus or it can be dangerous. As a result, speed and agility training should be performed while the athlete is fresh. It should not be performed as an afterthought following a grueling practice or strength workout. Where possible, new skills should be introduced towards the beginning of the workout, followed by those activities requiring the most speed. In other words, the fastest or most difficult exercises should be performed towards the beginning of the workout. Failure to observe this principle can result in injury and will certainly result in a reduction in the training's effectiveness.

Keeping the principles of exercise in mind, it's important to begin tying everything together to determine what is needed from a conditioning program. To determine the program needs, take a look at the sport or even the position and determine what qualities are necessary for success.

Determining the Needs of the Sport and the Athlete

Before designing a conditioning program, it is important to assess an event or sport to determine exactly what qualities are important for success. Failing to do so could waste an athlete's time and may not provide benefits from the training. The process of assessing an event or sport is called the needs analysis. When performing a *needs analysis*, one should consider the following:

- The biomechanical demands of the sport

- The metabolic demands of the sport

- The injury characteristics of the sport

Biomechanical Demands

The biomechanical demands of the sport refer to the quantity and quality of movements performed in the sport. Consider the following:

- What are the major muscles and motions used in the sport and position?

- What are the speed requirements?

- Do different positions within the sport have different needs?

The first thing to address is how the athlete is using his body to perform the event or sport. Understanding which muscles are involved and how those muscles are used can greatly aid in the design of a conditioning program. For example, is the activity performed standing up? If so, then exercises must be included that are performed standing up to help with the transfer of training gains. Strength training exercises such as squats, cleans, snatches, etc. that involve exerting force against the ground should be included to help with specificity.

Does the sport involve running or quick changes of direction? If so, then running or agility training should be included in the conditioning program. While this statement seems self-evident given the topic of this book, it is not true of every sport. For example, you could argue that volleyball does not involve a great deal of running, and therefore, a volleyball player's conditioning should focus more on weights and jumping than on running.

Obviously, most sports are going to require speed and agility. Understanding the nature of that speed requirement will help in the designing of conditioning programs. Consider the following:

- Does the sport require acceleration? Remember that acceleration refers to changing velocity. Moving from a slow speed (or no speed) and increasing speed is acceleration. Since it takes four to seven seconds to reach maximum velocity, anything under that time is going to be acceleration.

- Does the sport require maximum velocity running? It takes four to seven seconds to reach maximum velocity and it can only be maintained for one to two seconds. Many sports require acceleration, but few will require maximum velocity running.

- Does the sport require speed endurance? The ability to maintain speed is speed endurance. After reaching maximum velocity, the goal is to slow down as little as possible. After five to ten seconds of acceleration and maximum velocity running, speed endurance becomes important. Keep in mind that (except for track events) athletes will rarely have the opportunity to run flat-out for 10 to 20 seconds in sports.

- What type of agility does the sport require? Are athletes required to shuffle to the sides? Are they required to backpedal? Are sudden starts and stops common? Are quick changes of direction combined with sprints frequent?

These considerations should be evaluated and incorporated into a conditioning program. For example, baseball requires an athlete to sprint from home plate to first base, or from a position in the outfield to a fly ball. In other words, baseball requires the ability to accelerate. Baseball does not require an athlete to be able to maintain speed for periods of time (i.e., baseball does not require speed endurance). As another example, soccer has periods of acceleration and maximum velocity running, interspersed with periods of walking and jogging. In this sport, fatigue could be a factor in the outcome of the game. In addition, soccer requires backpedaling, sudden starts and stops, and rapid changes of direction accompanied by sprinting. As a result, soccer would require acceleration, maximum velocity running, speed endurance, and extensive agility training.

Many sports have positions that will have different roles during the game, which may affect that position's conditioning needs. You may understand how long an average play lasts and how long the athlete rests between plays, but if you do not understand how each athlete functions during the plays, you may miss the mark in the conditioning program. For example, in football, the wide receiver and the offensive line are going to have different roles during the game and, therefore, different conditioning requirements.

Once the quantity and qualities of motion used in the performance of a sport are understood, it is time to examine the metabolic demands of the sport, which will help you evaluate potential limitations to an athlete's performance.

Metabolic Demands

The metabolic demands of a sport refer to energy and fatigue. Different sports may rely upon different energy pathways for fuel. Therefore different sports will have different conditioning needs. Understanding which energy system(s) contribute to the sport will help you understand what potentially limits performance and help you design conditioning programs accordingly. To determine which energy system(s) contribute to the sport, consider:

- How long does the event last?

- How much of that time is actually spent moving?

- What are the rest/recovery periods?

- What is the predominate energy system? If the sport uses more than one, how significantly is each involved?

Table 7-1 provides an overview of energy systems by duration of each event. The table includes information on intensity, the primary energy system(s) used, and the major limiting factors for exercise in that energy system. Note that the times listed in the table are only a guideline, and may vary from athlete to athlete due to conditioning levels and genetic ability.

Duration of event	Intensity	Primary energy system(s) used	Limiting factors for exercise
0-6 seconds	Maximal	ATP-PC	• Amount of ATP present • Ability to resynthesize ATP
6-30 seconds	Very high	ATP-PC and glycolytic	• Ability to resynthesize ATP • Ability to tolerate lactic acid
30-120 seconds	High	Glycolytic	• Ability to tolerate lactic acid
120-180 seconds	Moderate	Glycolytic and aerobic	• Ability to tolerate lactic acid • Ability to get oxygen to exercising tissues
180+ seconds	Light	Aerobic	• Ability to get oxygen to exercising tissues

Table 7-1. Overview of energy systems (Adapted from Conley)

The length of the event is going to determine which energy system(s) is providing the bulk of the fuel. For example, the 100-meter sprint may last 10 to 12 seconds. Therefore, results are going to be determined by the ability to resynthesize ATP to continue working at maximal intensity and partially by an ability to tolerate lactic acid to maintain speed towards the finish. By understanding these facts, you know that the majority of the sprinter's training needs to focus on the ATP-PC system, but the training also needs to include some longer-duration (i.e., speed endurance) runs to get him acclimated to large levels of lactic acid.

The length of the event can be deceptive. For example, football is played over four 15-minute quarters. Table 7-1 would indicate that this sport would be fueled by the aerobic system. However, analyzing the game reveals that football plays only last four to six seconds, with perhaps 30 to 45 seconds of recovery. Therefore, instead of aerobic training, the football player needs to focus on training the ATP-PC and glycolytic energy systems. This example serves to reinforce the point that while the length of the event is important, you also need to examine how much of that time is actually spent moving.

Understanding how long the event lasts, how much of that time is actually spent moving, and how much recovery time exists between plays will give you a great deal of important information for the designing of conditioning programs. What is actually occurring during the rest interval is also important. For example, do athletes get to sit down between plays or do they walk around between plays? This factor should be reflected in the conditioning program.

For example, knowing that a typical football play lasts five seconds, with 30 seconds of active recovery (i.e., walking, jogging) in between, you can design running conditioning programs around these values. For conditioning, you may have football players perform 40-yard sprints every 30 seconds and have them walk around between sprints.

Like with biomechanical demands, it should be kept in mind that different positions in a sport may have different metabolic requirements. For example, in baseball, the pitcher and the center fielder are doing very different things. One is active during the pitch and the other is in more of a waiting mode. The pitcher is throwing the ball, catching the ball, then preparing to throw it again. The center fielder, on the other hand, needs to go from essentially no activity to a very intense sprint or jump to react to a play.

In addition to the biomechanical and metabolic demands of a sport, the injury characteristics of a sport or position need to be considered so you can design your program to prevent those injuries.

Injury Characteristics

It's important to have an understanding of what injuries are common in a sport and why those injuries occur. When considering the injury characteristics of a sport, ask the following questions:

- Are certain muscles or joints more frequently injured in a sport or position? Are some athletes prone to certain types of injuries?

- Why?

Do certain injuries occur with great frequency to athletes of a certain sport or position? For example, baseball pitchers are more prone to shoulder and elbow injuries due to a number of factors, including overuse, lack of conditioning, and the deceleration of the arm during the pitching motion. Knowing this tendency, you can design a pitcher's conditioning program around helping to address those factors that contribute to shoulder and elbow injuries.

You may also have specific athletes that are prone to certain types of injuries. For example, you may have a running back that is prone to hamstring and groin injuries. Examining that athlete's conditioning program and running technique may reveal some deficiencies that can be addressed, for example:

- hamstring strength and flexibility

- groin flexibility

- running technique

- agility drill technique

- a need for greater emphasis on agility training in the athlete's conditioning program

In addition to biomechanical, metabolic, and injury characteristics of a sport or position, other considerations should be included when assessing the conditioning needs of a sport or position. For example:

- Does a model exist for the event or sport?

- What kind of testing is appropriate for the sport?

After examining the muscles and motions involved in the sport, its metabolic demands, and its speed of movement requirements, and distinguishing between the needs of different positions, you should determine if a model exists for the event or sport. A model can provide anthropometric data, physical preparation data, and data on ideal performance of the event. In other words, a model tends to be an ideal. It can be a valuable tool in the selection and training of athletes for an activity. Remember, though, a model is meant to be a tool to aid in the conditioning process, not a standard to be achieved.

Table 7-2 provides a sample anthropometric model for Olympic-style weightlifting. It is somewhat dated because it is based upon older weight classes that are no longer used in competition. The height/weight data reveals something important about weightlifters—heavier weightlifters are taller ones, and vice versa. This knowledge can aid a weightlifting coach in the training and selection of weightlifters. Given an athlete's height, you can have some idea of what weight class you should be attempting to get them ready for. For example, if you have an 80kg lifter who is 180cm tall, you know that that lifter should ideally be in the 100kg or 110kg weight class. If the lifter is a junior, then you can design the training program to help put on enough muscle mass to place that lifter in the proper weight class.

Weight Class (kg)	Average Height (cm)
52	149 (+/- 3)
56	153 (+/- 3)
60	159 (+/- 3)
67.5	164 (+/- 3)
75	168.5 (+/- 3)
82.5	172.5 (+/- 3)
90	176 (+/- 3)
100	178 (+/- 3)
110	181 (+/- 3)
110+	185 (+/- 3)

Table 7-2. Anthropometric data for Olympic-style weightlifting, older weight classes (From Medvedyev, A.S. 1989)

Models can also help provide physical preparation data. This information can provide benchmarks to help you understand if the athlete is at the correct level of physical preparation and can aid in the selection process.

Table 7-3 lists physical preparation data for a 100-meter sprinter. It provides the physical preparation data that should be present to be able to achieve the desired level of performance. For a 100-meter sprinter, the physical preparation data gives you an idea about the sprinter's lower body strength requirements (standing long jump and triple jump), single-leg strength and explosiveness (triple jump and bounds), and total body explosiveness (medicine ball throws). If you determine that any of these qualities are deficient, then you may design your conditioning program to address those needs.

100m Performance	Standing Long Jump (m)	Standing Triple Jump (m)	3 Bounds (m)	5 Bounds (m)	100m Bounds (#)	4kg Overhead MB Throw(m)	4kg Behind MB Throw (m)
10.70-11.10	2.70-3.00	8.20-8.80	8.50-9.10	14.90-15.60	35-37	15.40-16.00	14.40-15.00
11.10-11.30	2.60-2.90	7.90-8.50	8.20-8.80	14.10-14.80	37-39	14.80-15.60	14.00-14.60
11.30-11.70	2.50-2.80	7.60-8.20	8.00-8.60	13.30-14.00	38-40	14.40-15.20	16.60-14.20

Table 7-3. Sample physical preparation model for 100m sprinters (From USA Track and Field Coaching Education Program, Level II Course, Sprints)

You may also use a model to help analyze performance of a specific event. Table 7-4 provides a performance model for the 100-meter sprint to be performed in 10seconds. For a 100-meter sprint, Table 7-4 shows that the athlete should be accelerating through at least the 60-meter mark. At that point, he should maintain his speed for another 20 to 30 meters. Comparing an athlete's performance to the model could indicate a need to work on acceleration, maximum velocity running, or the ability to maintain speed.

	Start	10m	20m	30m	40m	50m	60m	70m	80m	90m	100m
Time(s)	0.39	1.8	2.9	3.8	4.7	5.6	6.5	7.4	8.4	9.2	10
Average Speed (m/sec)		7.2	10.2	10.4	10.6	10.9	11.6	11.4	11.6	11.4	10.9

Table 7-4. Performance model for 100-meter sprint (From Kutznyetsov, V.V., et al. 1983)

Understanding biomechanical and metabolic demands, as well as what the "ideal" should look like, will help you understand what qualities are required for success in the event or sport. Understanding those qualities that are required for success will help you understand what tests to employ. Testing can help you select athletes and can aid in determining if the athlete's training is achieving the desired effects. After completing the analysis thus far, you know:

•   What muscles and motions are involved in the sport

•   What energy system(s) are involved in the sport

- What types of speed and agility are required in the sport (acceleration, maximum velocity running, etc.)

- What physical preparation qualities, according to the model, are important for success in the sport or event

Understanding these factors, you can select the best tests to measure those qualities. For example, you know that a 100-meter sprinter will primarily use the muscles of the lower body and will perform single-leg motions. Since the activity takes around 10 seconds, the ATP-PC system will provide the bulk of the energy for the event. A 100-meter sprinter requires acceleration, maximum velocity running, and a limited amount of speed endurance. According to the model, a number of event-specific tests are correlated with success in the sprint (bounds, long jump, triple jump, etc.). With this knowledge, you should implement testing that stresses:

- Total body explosiveness (for example, medicine ball throws)

- Leg strength and explosiveness (for example, the long jump and triple jump)

- Single-leg strength and explosiveness (for example, triple jump and bounds)

- ATP-PC system (primarily tests that last under 10 seconds)

- Acceleration (for example, 20- to 40-meter sprints from blocks)

- Maximum velocity running (for example, 40- to 60-meter flying sprints)

Performing a needs analysis for an event or sport will help to ensure that the coach is familiar with those qualities that are necessary for success in the activity. It's important to consider the biomechanical and metabolic demands of a sport or position to address potential limitations to performance. It is also important to understand the sport's injury characteristics so that these may be prevented in the conditioning program. In addition, you should have an idea of what characteristics are necessary for success in the sport so that you understand what you are attempting to develop. Finally, once you realize the qualities you want to develop, you can select tests to evaluate those qualities.

Taken together, this information will provide a powerful tool towards understanding the conditioning requirements for a given sport or activity. It can also be used to help determine whether an athlete possesses the qualities necessary to make him successful in a sport. If the athlete is deficient in certain qualities, those can be determined and addressed as a result of the information gathered during the needs analysis. This process will help make your conditioning program more effective.

Analyzing the Athlete

As a result of performing a needs analysis for a sport, you will understand what biomechanical demands, metabolic demands, and injury characteristics the sport has. You will also understand what type of physical preparation, event performance, and anthropometric characteristics an athlete in a given sport should possess. Based upon all this information, you are able to select those tests that will give both the best information about selecting/evaluating athletes and feedback about the effectiveness of the training program.

Once you understand what qualities need to be developed for success in a given sport, you can examine the athlete and determine if he possesses those qualities. When examining an athlete, consider:

- What is the athlete's training age?

- What level is the athlete competing at?

- What is the athlete's injury status?

- How did the athlete perform last year?

- Based upon the testing, what kind of shape is the athlete in?

An athlete's training age refers to how long an athlete has been training. An athlete that is just beginning his training will need to spend a great deal of time mastering fundamental exercises and skills, as well as developing a fitness base. An athlete with many years of training under his belt can be expected to understand how to perform fundamental exercises, which will allow more advanced exercises and drills to be performed in his training. Training age is one reason why one conditioning program does not fit all athletes.

The level an athlete is competing at is another important consideration in program design. International- or professional-caliber athletes tend to have a longer competition season, more time for training (becasue sport is the primary focus of their lives), and an advanced training age. All of those things will require a very different approach to programming than a developmental-level athlete who will have a shorter competition season; may be in school, working, or participating in other sports; and may have a low training age.

An athlete's injury status is another important consideration when designing programs. Is the athlete currently healthy? If the athlete is not currently healthy, then you should determine what the injury is and if it can be trained around. Another consideration is to determine if the athlete has a history of injury to a specific joint or muscle. If so, you should determine why. Perhaps the athlete's technique is poor, he may have a strength imbalance, poor mobility, etc. Considering not only an athlete's current health level but also his history of injuries will allow you to design a program to help keep the athlete healthy and maximize his performance.

The athlete's performance during the previous year should be considered when designing a conditioning program. This will help you understand how effective your program was last year. For example, did the athlete peak at the right time? If the athlete did not peak at the right time, then you should determine when the athlete peaked and why, so you can modify this year's program accordingly. Was the athlete overtrained? If so, you should determine if it was due to the conditioning program or to outside factors (e.g., breakup with a significant other, death in the family, school, etc.). If overtraining was due to the conditioning program, why did it occur? Volume may have been increased too much, the intensity might have been too high, etc. Examining the athlete's performance during the previous year will tell you what you did correctly and provide instruction in what you should change this year.

Finally, based upon the testing, what shape is the athlete currently in? Testing will not necessarily predict how an athlete will perform on the field. It will reveal an athlete's current level of physical preparation. In other words, it will tell you if the athlete possesses the physical tools necessary to give him the best chance at success. Testing will also give you feedback about the effectiveness of your conditioning program. If the athlete's testing results are getting worse during the conditioning program, it would indicate that the program is missing the mark.

Understanding a sport's needs, the qualities that are important for success in the sport, and whether or not an athlete possesses those qualities is key to determining what should be included in a conditioning program. Once you understand what qualities need to be developed, you should examine the sport's competition season before setting up the program because the season will dictate how the annual program is organized.

Examining the Sport's Competition Season

The sport's competition season is going to dictate how you organize the annual plan. When examining the competition season, consider:

- When is the competition season?

- What days of the week do competitions take place?

- Are all of the competitions equally important?

It is important to understand when the sport's competitive season occurs to determine when the athlete should be peaked and how long that peak should be maintained. The competitive season will also usually signal a time of reduced emphasis on training, as more focus is being placed upon the event itself.

In some sports, competitions will occur on certain days. For example, in professional football, games will be on Sundays or Mondays, with an occasional Thursday thrown in. If you know that competitions will occur on specific days, then you can organize an athlete's annual training around peaking on that day.

Are all of the competitions equally important? Granted, the won/loss record is important, but in some sports the competition season is so long, with so many competitions, that not all of them can realistically be peaked for. For example, professional baseball has 162 games a season. While the won/loss record is important in that sport, it's impossible to peak athletes for every game. Therefore, competitions must be evaluated and prioritized, so that the athletes are peaked for the important ones and trained through the others.

Putting Everything Together

Athlete A is a college sophomore who specializes in the 100-meter sprint. From performing the needs analysis on the 100-meter sprint, you know a number of things:

- Biomechanical demands: The 100-meter sprint involves running. During this action, the athlete is emphasizing a high knee lift combined with dorsiflexion at the ankle. The activity includes periods of time when one foot is exerting force against the ground. In addition to lower body action, the athlete must keep his hips tall (i.e. core stability), trunk upright, and arms swinging.

- Metabolic demands: As the 100-meter sprint takes place in 10 to 12 seconds, performance will be limited by the muscles' ability to break down and utilize ATP for fuel. An additional limiting factor to performance will be the muscles' ability to tolerate lactic acid.

- Injury characteristics: 100-meter sprinters are prone mainly to hamstring injuries and shin splints. Hamstring injuries may be the result of a number of factors, including poor flexibility, poor strength, or poor sprinting technique. Shin splints may result from overtraining, lack of strength in the anterior shank muscles, poor footwear, etc.

- Model: The 100-meter performance model in Table 7-4 showed that a 100-meter sprinter should be able to accelerate for six to seven seconds and then slow minimally for the rest of the race.

In summary, 100-meter sprinters must train their hip flexors/extensors, ankle plantar/dorsiflexors, core muscles, and upper body. These muscles must be trained in a way that involves exerting force against the ground and enhances the ability to break down and utilize ATP for fuel. In addition, one-legged strength work should be performed to help simulate the leg drive in the sprinting stride. Hamstring strength and flexibility, as well as shin strength, are important for injury prevention. Additionally, according to the model's characteristics, a 100-meter sprinter should accelerate for the first six to seven seconds and then slow minimally for the last three to four seconds.

Besides actual 100-meter performance, a number of tests can measure many of these qualities. To measure lower body strength and power, have the athlete perform the standing long jump and the behind-the-body 4kg medicine ball throw. To evaluate one-legged strength, have the athlete perform bounding drills of different distances and the standing triple jumps. All of these tests will also evaluate the athlete's ability to store and use ATP for fuel.

Now that you understand what qualities are important for a successful 100-meter sprinter, it's time to look for those qualities in Athlete A.

Athlete A runs the 100-meter sprint in 11.28 seconds. The breakdown of his performance in the 100 meter shows that he accelerates for the first four seconds, maintains his speed for two seconds, then begins to slow down during the remainder of the race. He is currently healthy and has no history of injuries. The results of his testing are as follows:

- Standing long jump: 3.01 meters

- 4kg behind medicine ball throw: 14.6 meters

- Standing triple jump: 8.60 meters

- 5 bounds: 15.05 meters

According to the testing, Athlete A has the strength and power to run the 100-meter sprint in under 11.10 seconds. He is not achieving this time because he has two major deficiencies: he is having trouble with his acceleration, and he is having trouble maintaining his speed. Knowing these weaknesses allows you to design a training program to do the following:

- Prioritize acceleration training through a combination of starts, stick drills, and resisted running.

- Prioritize speed endurance training through a combination of longer runs combined with incomplete recoveries.

- Continue working to maintain and increase strength and power levels through a combination of strength training and plyometric exercises.

- Continue working to prevent injuries through a combination of flexibility and strength training, especially for the hamstrings and shins.

The 100-meter sprinter's season, in college, lasts from roughly February through June (approximately 20 weeks). Competitions will occur just about every Saturday during the season and on some Sundays and Fridays. Working backwards, March through mid-June will make up the competition phase (14 weeks). Technical work is maintained unless it is a deficiency. Acceleration drills are performed mostly from starting blocks. Maximum velocity training is emphasized and uses all of the types of exercises available to the coach. Speed endurance is still performed, though it is only once every other week or so.

The precompetition phase will take up January and February (eight weeks). This phase is frequently the most intense of all the phases. Technical work is maintained unless it is a deficiency. Acceleration work is emphasized, and most drills are performed from blocks. Maximum velocity running is emphasized and all exercise types are used. Speed endurance is maintained.

The special preparation phase will take up November and December (eight weeks). The sprinter is seeking to apply the physical qualities developed in the general preparation phase directly to sprinting. As a result, technical exercises are continued. Acceleration work is beginning to be performed from blocks in this phase, though multiple types of acceleration drills are still performed. Maximum velocity running is emphasized, though several types of exercises are performed (varied pace, resisted, assisted, etc.). Speed endurance is maintained.

The general preparation phase will take up July through October and will last 16 weeks. The 100-meter sprinter will be seeking to build his fitness base during this period. The emphasis would be on technical exercises, acceleration work from different positions (i.e., standing, crouching, falling, etc., no block work yet), some maximum velocity work, and speed endurance work.

The transition phase will take up the last two weeks of June. The idea of this phase is to keep athletes in shape, while varying the training and giving them a chance to rest and recover. A 100-meter sprinter might run in the pool, play basketball, swim, climb, etc. to keep in shape during this phase.

Taking the time to gain an understanding of the qualities necessary for success in a given sport or position is important for successful program design. By understanding what qualities are important and by applying the principles of exercise, you can organize the program around developing those qualities. Failure to understand the sport and address its needs leaves the success of the program to chance.

Part II:
Sport-Specific Training

Chapters 8 to 13 present speed and agility training programs for baseball/softball, basketball, football, ice hockey, rugby, and soccer. Each event chapter is organized into several parts:

- background information about the sport and its unique needs

- speed and agility programs

- drills (agility and speed) specific to that sport

Background Information

The background information section presents the information that makes the sport unique from a conditioning standpoint. Information may include specific (and unique) movement patterns, work:rest ratios, lengths of an average game/play, etc. This information is important because it is used to determine the speed and agility program.

Speed and Agility Programs

Training programs are organized into beginner and advanced programs. The beginner program is geared towards high school athletes. With modifications, it could also be used with collegiate athletes that do not have much training experience. The advanced program is geared towards collegiate athletes. With modifications, it could be performed by more senior-level athletes.

The high school athlete needs to develop fitness and movement skills. He should be instructed on fundamentals. The high school athlete is not yet prepared to endure more intensive training. While fundamentals are important at the college level, sports-specificity takes on even greater importance. Unlike in high school, at the college level, only part of the year should focus on fundamentals, while the rest of the year should focus on more sports-specific drills. A collegiate athlete will have more training experience and, in general, will be better prepared for the game. The training can be more intense and the athlete should be able to handle a greater volume of training. After a fitness and technique base has been established, the collegiate athlete's program should be faster and feature more complex drills than the high school athlete's.

Each program is periodized—i.e., divided into the following phases:

- General preparation

- Special preparation

- Precompetition

- Competition

- Transition

Exact dates for each phase of training are not provided. In other words, nothing in the sample program indicates that on August 15 the athlete should be performing a specific workout. Instead, recommended lengths of each phase are provided for each level of training program, for a number of reasons. First, it would be inappropriate to design "cookie cutter" programs with too much detail without being familiar with an athlete's situation. Second, many schools (particularly at the high school level) do not have the same exact schedules—some may have seasons which start earlier, end later, etc.. Finally, athletes may participate in a sport outside of a school program (for example, in a city league). The recommended lengths of each phase should be reviewed carefully, as any of these situations may alter the length of each phase in a training program.

Each training phase has a different purpose and focus. During the general preparation phase, the athlete is preparing for the more intense training that will come as the season approaches. It is imperative that perfect technique is emphasized. If bad habits are reinforced in the general preparation phase, they will be more difficult to correct later in the training season.

The special preparation phase serves as a bridge between the all-around focus of the general preparation phase and the focused, event-specific training in the precompetition phase. During the special preparation phase, the fitness developed in the general preparation phase should be applied to the sport in a specific manner. This involves an emphasis on agility/sport-specific movement patterns. At this time during the training, it is also advisable to "open" the agility patterns to add a reactionary component, such as catching a ball or evading a defender.

With the precompetition phase, training is scaled back so that the athlete can focus more on game skills. Because the athlete is getting more rest, the complexity, intensity, and speed of the exercises is increased to ensure that the athlete continues to make improvements and to help peak the athlete for the competitive season.

Training is scaled back in the competition phase. Practicing and competition on a weekly schedule can be demanding on the body, no matter what level of play. The coach should approach the competition phase with a minimalist attitude—do as little as possible, but no less. Most of the time and energy should be directed toward practice and competition.

The transition phase is meant to allow the athlete to recover physically and psychologically from the previous year's training. Athletes should continue to exercise during this phase of training. However, exercise should be more general in nature and be relatively unstructured. Games such as basketball, soccer, and racquetball; activities such as climbing or swimming; medicine ball circuits, etc. are all great examples of transition phase training. Transition phase workouts are not detailed in this book. They should be heavily influenced by the athletes, their situation, the coach's preferences, and available resources. For example, a transition phase workout emphasizing swimming pool training would be irrelevant for a high school without a swimming pool.

Drills Specific to the Sport

Movement patterns for each sport covered in this book will vary from position to position. However, some common patterns are seen at almost every position. These common movement patterns are reflected in each chapter's drills.

Most positions in most sports require various changes of direction, the lateral shuffle, the ability to accelerate in all directions (both from a stop and at various speeds), and the ability to come to a stop quickly from multiple directions and movement patterns. In addition, to be successful, every position also has skill-specific movement patterns that the player must be proficient at.

In this book, work intervals in distance will remain the same for each position. Some variations exist between positions, but the essential movement elements are covered with the various drills. The drills selected will be executed for a specified distance that will coincide with an approximate time interval. Depending upon the particular situation, the coach may want to adjust some of the distances selected for each drill depending on the objective of the training session and the time of season.

Rest intervals of no more than three minutes should be used. A marginally conditioned athlete should be able to completely recover from an eight second work interval in two to three minutes. A shorter rest interval, as low as eight seconds, may be appropriate when metabolic-specific training is needed.

Increasing complexity is generally done by adding sensory information in the form of passing, kicking the ball, catching the ball, evading a defender, or reacting to a sport-specific cue. For instance, an athlete could run with the ball while weaving through a drill, elude a defender at the end of the pattern, and make a kick to finish the drill.

Each drill described in each chapter includes the following:

Purpose: reason for using the drill

Objective: what the drill is meant to accomplish

Description: how to perform the basic drill

Increasing Complexity/Difficulty: how to make the drill more advanced using sport-specific cues, or how to make the drill more difficult to perform for advanced athletes

Work Interval: general guidelines for how long the drill should take to execute. Note that this will vary with the level of the athlete.

Rest Interval: general guidelines for how much rest the athlete should get between work intervals

8

Baseball/Softball

Baseball and softball are sports of sudden starts, stops, and changes of direction. Therefore speed and agility are critical components to success. According to Szymanski and Fredrick (2001), speed gives teams an advantage in both offensive and defensive play. For the offense, speed is an advantage because the defense must get the ball to the base faster than the speed of the player in the batter's box or base paths. From a defense standpoint, a fast team is able to cover more ground and even to make up for mistakes.

Batters and runners need the ability to accelerate and stop suddenly; defensive players need quickness and lateral speed. Defensively, those players in the middle of the field (second base, shortstop, and center field) tend to be fastest, the players on the corners (first base, third base, right/left fields) tend to be the next fastest, and the pitchers and catchers tend to be the slowest players. These differences should be kept in mind as they indicate that different positions have slightly different conditioning needs.

While baseball and softball are usually played over nine and seven innings, respectively, the bulk of the energy for these sports is provided by the phosphagen energy system. The majority of speed and agility work should take place over short distances and emphasize complete recovery.

In general, a speed and agility program for baseball or softball should target the following:

- Acceleration: helps the athlete cover the distances between bases quickly.

- Ability to stop suddenly: an important skill for both base running and defensive play.

- Ability to change directions quickly: an important skill for base stealing and defensive play.

- Lateral speed: an important skill for base stealing and defensive play.

- Anaerobic conditioning: enables athletes to maintain their speed during a nine-inning game.

The program descriptions in this chapter will specifically refer to baseball, but softball players will also find these training programs helpful.

Beginning Program

The high school athlete's training will be organized around the following:

- 15- to 20-week general preparation phase

- 10-week special preparation phase

- 4-week precompetition phase

- 12- to 15-week competition phase

- 2-week transition phase

The high school athlete's training should focus on the development of running technique to help the athlete get to bases (or balls in play) more quickly, development of anaerobic conditioning to help them perform explosively throughout a nine-inning game, increasing strength and power to aid speed and agility, improving core conditioning to help with proper running and agility mechanics, and improving baseball-specific movement patterns.

General Preparation Phase

For the high school baseball player, the general preparation phase of training should emphasize fundamental running and agility technique in the form of drills and short sprints as well as anaerobic conditioning in the form of longer-distance sprints with short recovery periods. Table 8-1 provides an overview of the physical qualities that should be developed during this phase of training and the drills that should be used.

Physical Quality	Drills
Acceleration	• Starts • Stick drills
Sprinting technique	• High knee drills • Arm swing drills • Butt kicks
Agility	• Crossover step • Shuffle • Backpedal
Conditioning	• Interval training

Table 8-1. Physical qualities to develop and recommended drills for the high school baseball player during the general preparation phase

During the general preparation phase, the high school baseball player should be training two to four days per week. Table 8-2 provides a sample week of workouts from the early part of the general preparation phase. Note that each workout focuses on sprinting technique and agility. Although baseball does not require long-distance sprints, the sprinting technique is important for preventing injuries during conditioning.

In the sample in Table 8-2, the athlete is training three times per week. The first and third workouts emphasize acceleration and the middle workout emphasizes conditioning. As the athlete progresses through the general preparation phase, the volume, intensity, and complexity of the exercises should progressively increase.

Athletes should be allowed to fully recover for two to three minutes between sprinting technique, agility, and acceleration drills. The emphasis on drills should be on correct execution first and speed second.

Special Preparation Phase

Athletes should train two to four times per week during the special preparation phase. Conditioning becomes more difficult than the general preparation phase, with a greater volume and reduced recovery. Volume is greater on acceleration exercises. Agility exercises have become more difficult, with some patterns and drills being introduced. As this phase progresses, the ball should be introduced into the agility drills to help make the training more sport-specific. Sprinting technique drills should still be performed. Note that more complicated drills have been introduced. Table 8-3 describes the physical qualities that should be developed in this phase of training, along with the drills that should be used. The agility pattern drills mentioned in Table 8-3 (and subsequent tables) will be described later in this chapter.

Day	Primary Emphasis	Training Component	Drills
Mon.	Acceleration	Warm-up	Dynamic flexibility exercises (10-15 minutes)
		Sprinting technique	Arm swing drills, 2x20 yards High knee walks, 2x20 yards Butt kicks, 2x20 yards
		Agility	Shuffle right/left, 3x5-10 yards Crossover step plus sprint, 3-5x10 yards
		Acceleration	3-5x20 yards, standing start
Wed.	Conditioning	Warm-up	Dynamic flexibility exercises (10-15 minutes)
		Sprinting technique	Arm swing drills, 1x20 yards High knee skips, 3x20 yards Butt kicks, 3x20 yards
		Agility	Shuffle, 3-5x5-10 yards Backpedal, 3-5x10 yards
		Conditioning	Sprint 1x200 yards (3' rest), 1x100 yards (3' rest), 1x50 yards (2' rest), 2x25 yards (1' rest)
Fri.	Acceleration	Warm-up	Dynamic flexibility exercises (10-15 minutes)
		Sprinting technique	Arm swing drills, 2x20 yards High knee walks, 2x20 yards Butt kicks, 2x20 yards
		Agility	Shuffle right/left, 3x5-10 yards Crossover step plus sprint, 3-5x10 yards
		Acceleration	3-5x20 yards, standing start Stick drills, 3-5x

Table 8-2. Sample general preparation phase workouts for high school baseball players.

Physical Quality	Drills
Acceleration	• Starts from various positions • Stick drills
Sprinting technique	• High knee drills • Arm swing drills • Butt kicks • A drills
Agility	• Crossover step • Shuffle • Backpedal • Agility patterns, drills #1-3
Conditioning	• Interval training

Table 8-3. Physical qualities to be developed and recommended drills for the high school baseball player during the special preparation phase

Table 8-4 provides a sample week of workouts from the early part of the special preparation phase of training. The workouts cover three days per week and the emphasis of each session remains similar to the general preparation program, although the training variables and exercises may be different.

Precompetition Phase

Due to the reduction in training sessions during the precompetition phase, intensity and complexity will increase. Agility drills should be sport-specific, with the ball being integrated wherever possible. Acceleration and conditioning should be emphasized, with less sprinting mechanic work being performed in each training session (although sprinting drills should become progressively more complex). Table 8-5 provides an overview of the drills that should be used in the precompetition phase of training.

During the precompetition phase, athletes should train between two and three times per week, depending upon time availability. As the phase progresses and games begin, the amount of time available for training will decrease. Table 8-6 provides a sample week of late precompetition phase workouts for an athlete who is training twice a week.

Each training session includes acceleration, agility, and conditioning exercises. The first training session has a greater volume of acceleration exercises and the second has a greater volume of conditioning exercises. All training sessions include agility exercises.

Day	Primary Emphasis	Training Component	Drills
Mon.	Acceleration	Warm-up	Dynamic flexibility exercises (10-15 minutes)
		Sprinting technique	Arm swing drills, 2x20 yards High knee skips, 2x20 yards Butt kicks, 2x20 yards
		Agility	Shuffle right/left, 1x5-10 yards Crossover step plus sprint, 1-5x10 yards Agility pattern, drill #2, 3-5x
		Acceleration	3-5x20 yards, standing start 3-5x20 yards, prone start
Wed.	Conditioning	Warm-up	Dynamic flexibility exercises (10-15 minutes)
		Sprinting technique	Arm swing drills, 1x20 yards High knee skips, 1x20 yards Butt kicks, 1x20 yards A walks, 3x20 yards
		Agility	Shuffle, 1x5-10 yards Backpedal, 1x10 yards Agility pattern, drill #2, 3-5x
		Conditioning	Sprint 3x200 yards (3' rest), 2x100 yards (2' rest), 2x50 yards (1' rest), 2x25 yards (30" rest)
Fri.	Acceleration	Warm-up	Dynamic flexibility exercises (10-15 minutes)
		Sprinting technique	High knee skips, 2x20 yards Butt kicks, 2x20 yards A walks, 2x20 yards
		Agility	Shuffle right/left, 1x5-10 yards Crossover step plus sprint, 1x10 yards Agility pattern, drill #3, 3-5x
		Acceleration	2x3-5x20 yards Stick drills, 3-5x

Table 8-4. Sample special preparation phase workouts for high school baseball players

Physical Quality	Drills
Acceleration	• Starts from various positions
Sprinting technique	• A drills
	• B drills
Agility	• Agility patterns, drills #1-6
Conditioning	• Interval training

Table 8-5. Physical qualities to be developed and recommended drills for the high school baseball player during the precompetition phase

Day	Primary Emphasis	Training Component	Drills
Day One	Acceleration	Warm-up	Dynamic flexibility exercises (10-15 minutes) A skips, 3x20 yards Shuffle right/left, 1x5-10 yards Crossover step plus sprint, 1-5x10 yards
		Agility	Agility pattern, drills #2, 3, 5 (3-5x each)
		Acceleration	3-5x20 yards, standing start 3-5x20 yards, prone start 2-3x20 yards, push-up start
		Conditioning	Sprint 2x200 (3'), 2x100 (2'), 2x50 (1'), 4x25 (30")
Day Two	Conditioning	Warm-up	Dynamic flexibility exercises (10-15 minutes) B walks, 3x20 yards Shuffle, 1x5-10 yards Backpedal, 1x10 yards
		Agility	Agility pattern, drills #1, 4, 6 (3-5x each)
		Acceleration	2-3x 20 yards, standing start
		Conditioning	Sprint 3x200 yards (3' rest), 3x100 yards (2' rest), 3x50 yards (1' rest), 4x25 yards (30" rest)

Table 8-6. Sample precompetition phase workouts for high school baseball players

Competition Phase

During the competition phase, the focus is on maintaining speed, agility, and fitness, while winning baseball games. Training will often be reduced due to travel, games, and practices. As a result, training must be organized so that exercises may develop multiple qualities. For example, agility pattern drill #1 develops acceleration, stopping, change of direction, and conditioning. Agility pattern drills #5 and 6 develop acceleration, change of direction, and lateral acceleration. Table 8-7 describes how various exercises may be used to develop multiple physical qualities during the competition phase.

Physical Quality	Drills
Acceleration/Agility	• Agility patterns, drills #3, 4, 5, 6
Acceleration/Conditioning	• Agility patterns, drill #1

Table 8-7. Physical qualities to be developed and recommended drills for the high school baseball player during the competition phase

Table 8-8 provides a sample week of workouts during the competition phase. Ideally, athletes should train two to three times per week during the season. Each training session will focus on reinforcing sprinting technique and developing acceleration, agility, and conditioning. Whenever possible, the ball should be integrated with the drills to enhance the transfer of the training to the sport.

Day	Primary Emphasis	Training Component	Drills
Day One	All	Warm-up	Dynamic flexibility exercises (10-15 minutes) A skips, 3x20 yards
		Acceleration/Agility	Agility pattern, drills #3, 5 (5-10x each)
		Acceleration/Conditioning	Agility pattern, drill #1, 10-15x
Day Two	All	Warm-up	Dynamic flexibility exercises (10-15 minutes) B skips, 3x20 yards
		Acceleration/Agility	Agility pattern, drills #4, 6 (5-10x each)
		Conditioning	Sprint 3x200 yards (3' rest), 3x100 yards (2' rest), 3x50 yards (1' rest), 4x25 yards (30" rest)

Table 8-8. Sample competition phase workouts for high school baseball players

High school baseball players should focus on developing and refining movement fundamentals. By learning good skills early, they will have a more solid base to build on as they become more advanced athletes.

Advanced Program

The advanced program presented in this section is appropriate for collegiate-level athletes and beyond. The collegiate athlete's training will be organized around the following:

- 15- to 20-week general preparation phase

- 10-week special preparation phase

- 4-week precompetition phase

- 12- to 16-week competition phase

- 2-week transition phase

The training of collegiate baseball players should primarily focus on developing the following:

- Acceleration: The ability to run to the base after hitting the ball and the ability to run to balls that are in play is extremely important. Collegiate athletes will use a wide variety of tools (short sprints, resistance, stick drills, etc.) to enhance acceleration.

- Conditioning: While baseball is a sport that primarily uses the phosphagen energy system, players may have to perform maximal speed and agility tasks repeatedly during a game. As a result, anaerobic conditioning will be important to develop throughout the year.

- Agility: Stopping, starting, and changing directions rapidly are important tasks both for baserunning and for making defensive plays. The collegiate player will spend some time on fundamental skills, but the majority of training should be focused around sport-specific skills.

General Preparation Phase

As with the beginning program, the general preparation phase of the advanced program focuses on laying the foundation in terms of fitness and skills that the athlete will need the rest of the training year. At the collegiate level, this phase is a mixture of fundamental skills (sprinting and agility), conditioning, and sport-specific drills and patterns.

When programming for this phase, keep in mind that during parts of this phase, training may be unsupervised. As a result, the beginning portions of this phase should be restricted to drills and skills the athlete is already familiar with. As the phase progresses, more complicated drills and exercises should be integrated. Table 8-9 provides a breakdown of the qualities the athlete should develop in this phase and the exercises that could be used to develop those qualities.

Physical Quality	Drills
Acceleration	• Starts from a variety of positions • Stick drils
Sprinting technique	• High knee drills • Butt kicks • Arm swing drills
Agility	• A drills • Shuffles • Backpedals • Crossover step
Conditioning	• Agility patterns, drills #2, 3, 4, 5, 6 • Interval training

Table 8-9. Physical qualities to be developed and recommended drills for the collegiate baseball player during the general preparation phase

Table 8-10 provides a sample week of workouts for a collegiate baseball player in this phase of training. Ideally, the athlete should be training two to four times per week. The example in Table 8-10 has the athlete training four times per week. In this scheme, two sessions focus primarily on acceleration and two sessions focus primarily on conditioning. Due to its importance, some limited acceleration work is performed during every workout. Dynamic flexibility, sprinting technique, and agility training are performed during every training session. The workouts in Table 8-10 are intended for use towards the end of this phase of training. Therefore, more complicated exercises and higher training volumes are being employed. These factors will need to be adjusted when using this program earlier in the phase.

Special Preparation Phase

The special preparation phase continues the athlete's development while integrating more complex skills and more difficult drills, and increasing the sport-specific nature of the training. Fundamental skills are still trained, but they are done so in conjunction with baseball cues (for example: shuffle, perform a crossover step, sprint to second

Day	Primary Emphasis	Training Component	Drills
Mon.	Acceleration	Warm-up	Dynamic flexibility exercises (10-15 minutes)
		Sprinting technique	Arm swing drills, 2x20 yards
			High knee skips, 2x20 yards
			Butt kicks, 2x20 yards
		Agility	Shuffle right/left 5 yards plus sprint 10 yards, 2-3x Crossover step plus sprint 10 yards, 2-3x
			Agility pattern, drills #2, 3 (3-5x)
		Acceleration	3-5x20 yards, standing start
			3-5x20 yards, prone start
Tue.	Conditioning	Warm-up	Dynamic flexibility exercises (10-15 minutes)
		Sprinting technique	Arm swing drills, 1x20 yards
			High knee skips, 1x20 yards
			Butt kicks, 1x20 yards
			A walks, 3x20 yards
		Agility	Agility pattern, drills #3, 4, 5 (3-5x)
		Acceleration	3x5 yards, standing start
		Conditioning	Sprint 3x200 yards (3' rest), 2x100 yards (2' rest), 2x50 yards (1' rest), 2x25 yards (30" rest)
Thurs.	Acceleration	Warm-up	Dynamic flexibility exercises (10-15 minutes)
		Sprinting technique	Arm swing drills, 2x20 yards
			High knee skips, 2x20 yards
			Butt kicks, 2x20 yards
		Agility	Shuffle right/left 5 yards plus sprint
			10 yards, 2-3x Crossover step plus sprint 10 yards, 2-3x Agility pattern, drill #6, 3-5x
		Acceleration	2x3-5x20 yards
			Stick drills, 3-5x
Fri.	Conditioning	Warm-up	Dynamic flexibility exercises (10-15 minutes)
		Sprinting technique	Arm swing drills, 1x20 yards
			High knee skips, 1x20 yards
			Butt kicks, 1x20 yards
			A walks, 3x20 yards
		Agility	Agility pattern, drills #3, 4, 5 (3-5x)
		Acceleration	3x5 yards, standing start
		Conditioning	Sprint 1x200 yards (3' rest), 4x100 yards (2' rest), 4x50 yards (1' rest), 4x25 yards (30" rest)

Table 8-10. Sample general preparation phase workouts for collegiate baseball players

base before the ball arrives, etc.). As the phase progresses, training should emphasize baseball specificity more, and general training less. Table 8-11 provides an example of the qualities that should be developed in this phase and what tools should be used to develop those qualities.

Physical Quality	Drills
Acceleration	• Starts from a variety of positions • Resisted starts • Stick drills
Sprinting technique	• High knee drills • Butt kicks • Arm swing drills • A drills • B drills
Agility	• Agility patterns, drills #1-7
Conditioning	• Interval training

Table 8-11. Physical qualities to be developed and recommended drills for the collegiate baseball player during the special preparation phase

Ideally, an athlete should train two to four times per week during this phase. Table 8-12 provides a sample week of workouts from the beginning of this phase. The organization of the training sessions has not been altered from the general preparation phase. Remember that training should become more baseball-specific as the phase progresses (i.e., agility drills should be performed using the ball, etc.).

Precompetition Phase

Beginning with the precompetition phase, less time will be available for speed and agility work, as more time will need to be spent on sports practices, exhibition games, etc. Because less time is available for training, the training must be more focused and more intense to continue to carry a training effect. For the most part, general training will be greatly reduced in favor of training that will have a more significant transfer to the playing field. Some qualities, such as conditioning, will simply be maintained during this phase. Table 8-13 highlights those qualities that should be developed during this phase and the types of exercises that could be used. Note that, whenever possible, sport-specific elements (such as bases, reacting to the ball, reacting to the sound of the bat, etc.) should be included in the drills.

Day	Primary Emphasis	Training Component	Drills
Mon.	Acceleration	Warm-up	Dynamic flexibility exercises (10-15 minutes)
		Sprinting technique	Arm swing drills, 1x20 yards
			High knee skips, 1x20 yards
			Butt kicks, 1x20 yards
			A skips, 3x20 yards
		Agility	Agility pattern, drills #1, 2, 3 (3-5x)
		Acceleration	3x3-5x20 yards, standing start
			2x3-5x20 yards, prone start
Tue.	Conditioning	Warm-up	Dynamic flexibility exercises (10-15 minutes
		Sprinting technique	A skips, 3x20 yards
			B walks, 3x20 yards
		Agility	Agility pattern, drills #4, 5, 7 (3-5x)
		Acceleration	2x5x5 yards, standing start
		Conditioning	Sprint 3x200 yards (3' rest), 3x100 yards (2' rest), 3x50 yards (1' rest), 4x25 yards (30" rest)
Thurs.	Acceleration	Warm-up	Dynamic flexibility exercises (10-15 minutes)
		Sprinting technique	Arm swing drills, 1x20 yards
			High knee skips, 1x20 yards
			Butt kicks, 1x20 yards
			A walks, 3x20 yards
		Agility	Agility pattern, drill #6, 3x3-5x
		Acceleration	3x3-5x20 yards
			3x10 yards resisted sprints, standing start
			Stick drills, 3-5x
Fri.	Conditioning	Warm-up	Dynamic flexibility exercises (10-15 minutes)
		Sprinting technique	A skips, 3x20 yards
			B walks, 3x20 yards
		Agility	Agility pattern, drills #3, 4, 5 (3-5x)
		Acceleration	2x5x5 yards, standing start
		Conditioning	Sprint 1x200 yards (3' rest), 4x100 yards (2' rest), 4x50 yards (1' rest), 4x25 yards (30" rest)

Table 8-12. Sample special preparation phase workouts for collegiate baseball players

Physical Quality	Drills
Acceleration	• Starts from a variety of positions • Resisted starts
Sprinting technique	• A drills • B drills
Agility	• Agility patterns, drills #1-10
Conditioning	• Interval training

Table 8-13. Physical qualities to be developed and recommended drills for the collegiate baseball player during the precompetition phase

Due to the increased sport practice demands, training will be scaled back during this phase, ideally to two or three training sessions per week. Table 8-14 provides a sample week of workouts during the precompetition phase. All physical qualities are trained during each session. However, the goal behind sprinting technique and conditioning is maintenance of those qualities.

Day	Primary Emphasis	Training Component	Drills
Day One	N/A	Warm-up	Dynamic flexibility exercises (10-15 minutes)
		Sprinting technique	A skips, 2x20 yards B walks, 2x20 yards
		Agility	Agility pattern, drills #2, 3, 5, 7, 8 (3-5x)
		Acceleration	3x3-5x20 yards, standing start 3-5x20 yards, prone start
Day Two	N/A	Warm-up	Dynamic flexibility exercises (10-15 minutes)
		Sprinting technique	A walks, 2x20 yards B skips, 2x20 yards
		Agility	Agility pattern, drills #4, 5, 6, 9, 10 (3-5x)
		Acceleration	3x5x5 yards, standing start 3x10 yards resisted sprints, standing start
		Conditioning	Sprint 2x200 yards (3' rest), 2x100 yards (2' rest), 2x50 yards (1' rest), 4x25 yards (30" rest) Agility pattern, drill #1, 3-5x (2' rest)

Table 8-14. Sample precompetition phase workouts for collegiate baseball players

Competition Phase

Between competitions, the need for sport-specific practices, and travel, little time is available for speed and agility training during the competition phase. As training is scaled back, the coach should search for exercises that develop several qualities in order to make efficient use of training time (see Table 8-15 for an example). Remember to include sport-specific stimuli during the execution of many of these drills.

Physical Quality	Drills
Acceleration/Agility	• Agility patterns, drills #3-10
Acceleration/Conditioning	• Agility patterns, drill #1

Table 8-15. Physical qualities to be developed and recommended drills for the collegiate baseball player during the competition phase

Ideally, the athlete should train one to three times per week during the competition phase. Because of the length of the season, training should be carefully periodized to ensure that athletes maintain their fitness levels. Table 8-16 provides a sample week of competition phase workouts , with the athlete training twice a week. Dynamic flexibility exercises are included in each session. However, whenever possible, exercises that train multiple physical qualities are used.

Day	Primary Emphasis	Training Component	Drills
Day One	N/A	Warm-up	Dynamic flexibility exercises (10-15 minutes)
		Acceleration/Agility	Agility pattern, drills #3, 5, 7, 9, 10 (3-5x)
		Conditioning/Agility	Agility pattern, drill #1, 5-10x (2' rest)
Day Two	N/A	Warm-up	Dynamic flexibility exercises (10-15 minutes)
		Acceleration/Agility	Agility pattern, drills #2, 4, 6, 8 (5-10x)
		Conditioning/Agility	Agility pattern, drill #1, 8-15x (3' rest)

Table 8-16. Sample competition phase workouts for collegiate baseball players

Agility Drills

The remainder of this chapter will cover sample agility drills that may be used to help meet baseball's unique demands. Although different positions have somewhat different needs, the fundamental movement skills that apply to all positions are included in these drills. With the exception of drill #1 (which may also be used as a conditioning drill), full recovery should be emphasized on each drill, along with correct execution.

Agility Pattern: Drill #1

Purpose: Develop acceleration and stopping ability.

Objectives:

- Maintain body control.
- Develop specific rate of force production.
- Lower center of gravity when decelerating.

Description:

Begin at the start line and run to the five-yard line, run back to the start, run to the 10-yard line, run back to the start, run to the 15-yard line, run back to the start, run to the 20-yard line, run back to the start.

- The athlete should accelerate with 100% effort.
- The athlete should maximize the forward lean when initially accelerating.
- The athlete should use a forceful, high knee lift when initially accelerating.
- The athlete should drop his center of gravity while decelerating.
- The athlete should use short, choppy steps to decelerate quickly.
- The athlete should maintain a neutral spine at all times.

Increasing Complexity/Difficulty:

- Stagger the distance of the cones.
- Increase the number of cones.
- Perform the drill with a ball.
- Use two identical patterns of cones and have athletes race each other through the drill.

Work Interval: Will vary on distance of cones and ability of the athlete, but should be between 20 and 40 seconds.

Rest Interval: Once mastery of the drill has been reached, the rest intervals may be brought down to 3:1 rest to work interval.

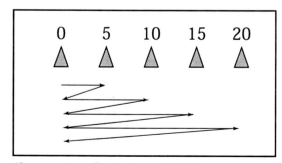

Figure 8-1. Agility Pattern: Drill #1

Agility Pattern: Drill #2

Purpose: Develop a lateral acceleration, lateral stopping ability, and body control.

Objectives:

- Simulate movement patterns seen at all positions.
- Reduce unnecessary body movements.
- Train eye-hand-foot coordination.

Description:

- Place two cones two to three yards apart for shuffling.
- Place two cones six to twelve yards apart for running.
- The athlete should not cross over his feet during the drill if shuffling.
- The athlete should maintain a low center of gravity, keeping the knees and hips bent while shuffling.
- The athlete should move his feet as quickly as possible while shuffling.
- The athlete should lower his center of gravity as he turns through the cones while running.
- The athlete should drop the inside shoulder and extend the arm toward the ground while turning when running.
- The athlete should emphasize a high knee lift while accelerating off the turn while running.

Increasing Complexity/Difficulty:

- The coach can pass a ball back and forth to the athlete while shuffling.
- The coach can have the athlete run for a ball off the end of the drill.
- The cones can be spread further apart to emphasize stopping mechanics while running.
- The coach can time the drill for completed cycles through the pattern.

Work Interval: Will vary on distance of cones and ability of the athlete, but should be between eight and twelve seconds.

Rest Interval: Once mastery of the drill has been reached, the rest intervals may be brought down to 3:1 rest to work interval.

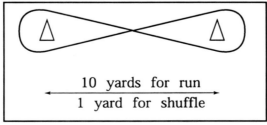

Figure 8-2. Agility Pattern: Drill #2

Agility Pattern: Drill #3

Purpose: Develop acceleration, stopping ability, and body control.

Objectives:

- Simulate movement patterns seen at all positions.
- Reduce unnecessary body movements.
- Train eye-hand-foot coordination.

Description:

- Place three cones in an upside-down triangle.
- Run from cone number one to cone number two.
- Touch cone number two and run back to cone number one.
- Touch cone number one and run to cone number three.
- Touch cone number three and run back to cone number one.

Increasing Complexity/Difficulty:

- The drill may be performed using shuffling, backpedaling, or some combination thereof.
- The coach can pass a ball back and forth to the athlete.
- The coach can have the athlete run for a ball off the end of the drill.
- The cones can be spread further apart to emphasize stopping mechanics while running.
- The coach can time the drill for completed cycles through the pattern.
- The coach can set up two courses and have athletes run against each other.

Work Interval: Will vary on distance of cones and ability of the athlete, but should be between eight and twelve seconds.

Rest Interval: Once mastery of the drill has been reached, the rest intervals may be brought down to 3:1 rest to work interval.

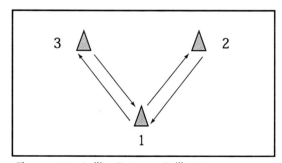

Figure 8-3. Agility Pattern: Drill #3

Agility Pattern: Drill #4

Purpose: Develop acceleration, stopping ability, lateral acceleration, and body control.

Objectives:

- Simulate movement patterns seen at all positions.
- Reduce unnecessary body movements.
- Train eye-hand-foot coordination.

Description:

- Place four cones in a "T" shape (see Figure8-4).
- Run from cone number one to cone number two.
- Touch cone number two and shuffle to cone number three.
- Touch cone number three and shuffle to cone number four.
- Shuffle from cone number four to cone number two.
- Touch cone number two and backpedal to cone number one.
- The athlete should maintain a low center of gravity, keeping the knees and hips bent while shuffling.
- The athlete should move his feet as quickly as possible while shuffling.
- The athlete should emphasize a high knee lift as he accelerates off the turn while running.

Increasing Complexity/Difficulty:

- The direction the athlete runs may be changed.
- The coach can pass a ball back and forth to the athlete.
- The coach can have the athlete run for a ball off the end of the drill.
- The cones can be spread further apart to emphasize stopping mechanics while running.
- The coach can time the drill for completed cycles through the pattern.
- The coach can set up two courses and have athletes run against each other.

Work Interval: Will vary on distance of cones and ability of the athlete, but should be between eight and twelve seconds.

Rest Interval: Once mastery of the drill has been reached, the rest intervals may be brought down to 3:1 rest to work interval.

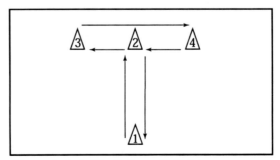

Figure 8-4. Agility Pattern: Drill #4

Agility Pattern: Drill #5

Purpose: Develop acceleration, stopping ability, lateral acceleration, and body control.

Objectives:

- Simulate movement patterns seen at all positions.
- Reduce unnecessary body movements.
- Train eye-hand-foot coordination.

Description:

- On command, sprint forward.
- When the coach signals, the athlete should begin shuffling to the right or to the left.
- When the coach signals, the athlete should stop shuffling and sprint straight ahead.
- The athlete should maintain a low center of gravity, keeping the knees and hips bent while shuffling.
- The athlete should move his feet as quickly as possible while shuffling.
- The athlete should emphasize a high knee lift while accelerating.

Increasing Complexity/Difficulty:

- The coach can pass a ball back and forth to the athlete.
- The coach can have the athlete run for a ball off the end of the drill.
- The coach can time the drill for completed cycles through the pattern.
- The coach can set up two courses and have athletes run against each other.

Work Interval: Will vary on distance of cones and ability of the athlete, but should be between eight and twelve seconds.

Rest Interval: Once mastery of the drill has been reached, the rest intervals may be brought down to 3:1 rest to work interval.

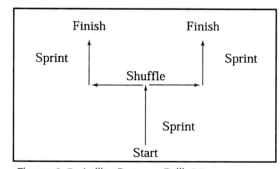

Figure 8-5. Agility Pattern: Drill #5

Agility Pattern: Drill #6

Purpose: Develop acceleration, stopping ability, lateral acceleration, the crossover step, and body control.

Objectives:

- Simulate movement patterns seen at all positions.
- Reduce unnecessary body movements.
- Train eye-hand-foot coordination.

Description:

- The athlete should backpedal.
- On command, the athlete should shuffle to the left or right.
- On command, the athlete should execute the crossover step and then sprint.
- The athlete should maintain a low center of gravity, keeping the knees and hips bent while shuffling.
- The athlete should move his feet as quickly as possible while shuffling.
- The athlete should emphasize a high knee lift while accelerating.

Increasing Complexity/Difficulty:

- The coach can have the athlete performing the drill by reacting to the crack of the bat.
- The coach can have the athlete backpedal, shuffle, and sprint for longer or shorter distances.
- The coach can time the drill for completed cycles through the pattern.
- The coach can set up two courses and have athletes run against each other.

Work Interval: Will vary on distance of cones and ability of the athlete, but should be between eight and twelve seconds.

Rest Interval: Once mastery of the drill has been reached, the rest intervals may be brought down to 3:1 rest to work interval.

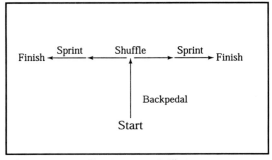

Figure 8-6. Agility Pattern: Drill #6

Agility Pattern: Drill #7

Purpose: Develop acceleration, stopping ability, lateral acceleration, and body control.

Objectives:

- Simulate movement patterns seen at all positions.
- Reduce unnecessary body movements.
- Train eye-hand-foot coordination.

Description:

- Place four cones in a box (see Figure 8-7).
- Sprint from cone number one to cone number two.
- Run around cone number two and sprint to cone number three.
- Run around cone number three and sprint to cone number four.
- Run around cone number four and sprint to cone number one.
- The athlete should lower his center of gravity as he turns through the cones while running.
- The athlete should drop the inside shoulder and extend the arm toward the ground while turning when running.
- The athlete should emphasize a high knee lift while accelerating off the turn when running.

Increasing Complexity/Difficulty:

- The direction the athlete runs may be changed.
- Backpedaling, crossover steps, and shuffling may be incorporated.
- The coach can pass a ball back and forth to the athlete.
- The coach can have the athlete run for a ball off the end of the drill.
- The cones can be spread further apart to emphasize stopping mechanics while running.
- The coach can time the drill for completed cycles through the pattern.
- The coach can set up two courses and have athletes run against each other.

Work Interval: Will vary on distance of cones and ability of the athlete, but should be between 15 and 20 seconds.

Rest Interval: Once mastery of the drill has been reached, the rest intervals may be brought down to 3:1 rest to work interval.

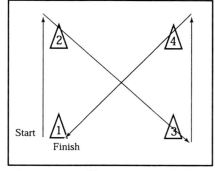

Figure 8-7. Agility Pattern: Drill #7

Agility Pattern: Drill #8

Purpose: Develop reactive and change-of-direction ability.

Objectives:

- Incorporate decision-making.
- Reduce unnecessary body movements.

Description:

- Start in an athletic stance.
- The athlete should accelerate with 100% effort.
- The athlete should cut sharply and sprint in the instructed direction.
- The athlete should maximize the forward lean when initially accelerating.
- The athlete should use a forceful, high knee lift when initially accelerating.
- The athlete should drop his center of gravity while decelerating.
- The athlete should use short, choppy steps to decelerate quickly.
- The athlete should maintain a neutral spine at all times.

Increasing Complexity/Difficulty:

- Instead of running, the athlete can shuffle.
- Vary the distances.
- Change the cutting angle.
- Perform the drill with a ball.
- Use two identical patterns of cones and have athletes race each other through the drill.

Work Interval: Will vary on distance of cones and ability of the athlete, but should be between eight and twelve seconds.

Rest Interval: Once mastery of the drill has been reached, the rest intervals may be brought down to 3:1 rest to work interval.

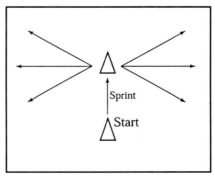

Figure 8-8. Agility Pattern: Drill #8

Agility Pattern: Drill #9

Purpose: Develop reactive and change-of-direction ability.

Objectives:

*   Incorporate decision-making.
*   Reduce unnecessary body movements.

Description:

*   Start in an athletic stance.
*   Backpedal on command, cut sharply, and sprint in the designated direction.
*   The athlete should maintain a neutral spine at all times.

Increasing Complexity/Difficulty:

*   Instead of running, the athlete shuffles.
*   Vary the distances.
*   Change the cutting angle.
*   Perform the drill with a ball.
*   Use two identical patterns of cones and have athletes race each other through the drill.

Work Interval: Will vary on distance of cones and ability of the athlete, but should be between eight and twelve seconds.

Rest Interval: Once mastery of the drill has been reached, the rest intervals may be brought down to 3:1 rest to work interval.

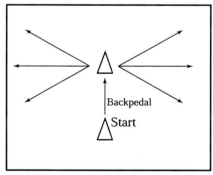

Figure 8-9. Agility Pattern: Drill #9

Agility Pattern: Drill #10

Purpose: Develop reactive and change-of-direction ability.

Objectives:

- Incorporate decision-making.
- Reduce unnecessary body movements.

Description:

- Start in an athletic stance.
- Run around the first two cones.
- Upon reaching the third cone, the athlete will react to the coach's command by:
- Sprinting/shuffling to the right or left.
- Sprinting/shuffling to the right or left diagonally.
- Backpedaling.
- The athlete should maintain a neutral spine at all times.

Increasing Complexity/Difficulty:

- Instead of running past the first two cones, the athlete shuffles or backpedals.
- Vary the distances.
- Change the cutting angle (i.e., move the first two cones closer together or further apart).
- Perform the drill with a ball.
- Use two identical patterns of cones and have athletes race each other through the drill.

Work Interval: Will vary on distance of cones and ability of the athlete, but should be between eight and twelve seconds.

Rest Interval: Once mastery of the drill has been reached, the rest intervals may be brought down to 3:1 rest to work interval.

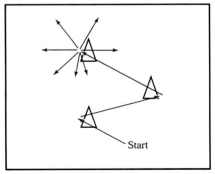

Figure 8-10. Agility Pattern: Drill #10

9

Basketball

Basketball is a team sport that is played and enjoyed by millions worldwide. Variations of the game are observed at various levels. Playing with five people per team and full court, basketball is 80 to 85% anaerobic. This high level of anaerobic demand should be reflected in training by sprint and interval training.

Each position has specialized skills or characteristics that are conducive for success. The center is usually the tallest person on the team and most likely possesses baseline offensive and defensive moves. The point guard needs to be proficient at ballhandling and acceleration. All players on the court should be able to defend using various techniques, such as a defensive slide with the knees and hips bent.

Many movements in basketball are observed at all the positions. Some of the common movements are accelerating forward and running the length of the court quickly, moving backwards with varying techniques, and stopping effectively. These movements are reflected in the sample program in this chapter.

A speed and agility program for basketball should target the following:

• Sprinting technique: helps with speed and helps prevent injuries.

- Anaerobic conditioning: helps the athlete recover from high-intensity sprints and helps them perform for the entire game.

- Agility training and its subcomponents: teach how to change directions to help prevent injuries and develop agility to improve performance.

- Using an appropriate rest interval that will vary on goals of training during each phase.

Beginning Program

The high school athlete's training will be organized around the following:

- 16-week general preparation phase
- 8-week special preparation phase
- 4-week precompetition phase
- 15-week competition phase

The high school athlete's training should focus on the following:

- Building anaerobic metabolic efficiency
- Developing strength and power
- Developing running technique
- Improving speed
- Developing sport specific-agility

General Preparation Phase

During the general preparation phase, the high school athlete should focus on developing anaerobic endurance, learning running technique, and learning agility technique. As a guideline, at this level, athletes should train two to four times per week. Each session should focus on dynamic flexibility exercises, running technique drills, and basic agility technique. Table 9-1 shows the types of drills that a high school basketball player should focus on in the general preparation phase.

An active rest interval is very important. Rarely, if ever, during the game of basketball is the athlete at rest. The game is a series of sprints with active rest, positioning to either offend or defend the opposing team.

Physical Quality	Drills
Sprinting technique	• Arm swing drills • High knee drills • A drills • B drills
Speed	• Half- and full-court sprints for technique
Acceleration	• Position-specific starts • Stick drills
Agility	• Agility patterns for basketball
Conditioning	• Conditioning patterns for basketball

Table 9-1. Physical qualities to be developed and recommended drills for the high school basketball player during the general preparation phase

Table 9-2 outlines a sample workout for a high school athlete training four times per week during the general preparation phase. Because the sample athlete is a beginner, the focus is on fundamental basketball agility and running skills. The workouts are completed four days per week. Two of the days are dedicated to anaerobic endurance and two days to agility training. Sprinting technique focuses on arm swing, the high knee movement, and pulling the heel to the hip. Athletes should be allowed to fully recover for two to three minutes between sprinting technique, agility, and acceleration drills. The quality of these drills is imperative. The emphasis on drills should be on correct execution first and speed second.

An indoor basketball court is the preferred place to train for basketball. The court offers several advantages, including a surface that the players will compete on, a defined space in which they can simulate competitive movement patterns and easily incorporate a basketball, and protection from environmental conditions.

Special Preparation Phase

During the special preparation phase, the high school basketball player should focus on applying anaerobic endurance/capacity developed in the general preparation phase in a sport-specific manner by emphasizing agility/sport-specific movement patterns. During this phase of training, it is also advisable to "open" the agility patterns to add a reactionary component such as passing, catching, dribbling, and/or evading a defender.

Athletes should train three to four times per week. Each session must include dynamic flexibility exercises, running technique drills, sport-specific agility technique drills, and/or anaerobic conditioning. Table 9-3 shows the types of drills that a high school athlete should focus on in the special preparation phase.

Day	Primary Emphasis	Training Component	Drills
Mon.	Anaerobic endurance	Warm-up	Dynamic flexibility exercises for 10-15 minutes
		Sprinting technique	Arm swing drills, 2x half court High knee walks, 2x half court Butt kicks, 2x half court
		Anaerobic endurance	Eight repetitions completing conditioning pattern 1 with a 45-second active rest interval
Tues.	Agility	Warm-up	Dynamic flexibility exercises for 10-15 minutes
		Sprinting technique	Arm swing drills, 1x half court High knee walks, 1x half court High knee skips, 3x half court Butt kicks, 1x half court A walks, 3x half court
		Agility technique	Agility patterns 1, 3, 7. Two reps each drill with a one-minute rest interval. Two-minute rest interval between patterns
Thurs.	Anaerobic endurance	Warm-up	Dynamic flexibility exercises for 10-15 minutes
		Sprinting technique	Arm swing drills, 2x half court High knee walks, 2x half court Butt kicks, 2x half court A walks, 2x half court
		Anaerobic endurance	Eight repetitions completing conditioning pattern 1 with a 45-second active rest interval
Fri.	Agility	Warm-up	Dynamic flexibility exercises for 10-15 minutes
		Sprinting technique	Arm swing drills, 1x half court High knee walks, 1x half court High knee skips, 3x half court Butt kicks, 1x half court A walks, 3x half court
		Agility technique	Agility patterns 5, 9, 10. Two reps each drill with a one-minute rest interval. Two-minute rest interval between patterns.

Table 9-2. Sample general preparation workout for high school basketball player

Physical Quality	Drills
Sprinting technique	• Arm swing drills • High knee drills • A drills • B drills
Sport-specific agility for basketball	• All agility patterns • Add reactionary component (i.e., passing, catching, evading) • Use a 20- to 25-second active rest interval
Anaerobic conditioning	• Conditioning patterns • Interval training with active rest

Table 9-3. Physical qualities to be developed and recommended drills for the high school basketball player during the special preparation phase

Day	Primary Emphasis	Training Component	Drills
Mon.	Conditioning	Warm-up	Dynamic flexibility exercises for 10-15 minutes
		Sprinting technique	High knee skips, 2x half court Butt kicks, 2x half court A skips, 2x half court B walks, 2x half court
		Agility	Basketball agility patterns 1, 3, 5, 9. Three reps per pattern. 20- to 25-second active rest between repetitions. Two-minute rest between sets.
		Anaerobic conditioning	10 repetitions completing conditioning pattern 2 with a 30-second active rest interval
Tues.	Conditioning	Warm-up	Dynamic flexibility exercises for 10-15 minutes
		Sprinting technique	Arm swing drills, 1x half court High knee walks, 1x half court High knee skips, 3x half court Butt kicks, 1x half court
		Agility technique	Basketball agility patterns 2, 4, 6, 8. Three reps per pattern. 20- to 25-second active rest between repetitions. Three-minute rest between sets.
		Anaerobic conditioning	10 repetitions completing conditioning pattern 2 with a 30-second active rest interval

Table 9-4. Sample special preparation workout for high school basketball player

Table 9-4 describes a sample week of workouts for the special preparation phase. Dynamic flexibility exercises are still performed at the beginning of each workout as a warm-up. Sprinting technique drills are performed at a faster pace and begin integrating more complicated A and B drills. While agility training still focuses on fundamentals, the fundamentals are now being incorporated into movement patterns that are seen during the game.

Precompetition Phase

With the precompetition phase, training is scaled back so that the high school basketball player can focus more on game skills. Table 9-5 highlights the physical qualities and exercises that should be used in the precompetition phase.

In this phase of training, dynamic flexibility drills are still performed as a warm-up for each workout. Sprinting technique is trained daily; however, remedial exercises such as arm swings and high knee drills have been removed in favor of more complex

Day	Primary Emphasis	Training Component	Drills
Thurs.	Agility	Warm-up	Dynamic flexibility exercises for 10-15 minutes
		Sprinting technique	High knee skips, 1x half court Butt kicks, 2x half court A skips, 3x half court B walks, 1x half court B skips, 3x half court
		Agility technique	Basketball agility patterns 1, 3, 5, 7. Three reps per pattern. 20- to 25-second active rest between repetitions. Two-minute rest between sets.
Fri.	Conditioning	Warm-up	Dynamic flexibility exercises for 10-15 minutes
		Sprinting technique	Arm swing drills, 1x half court High knee walks, 3x half court High knee skips, 3x half court Butt kicks, 1x half court A walks, 3x half court
		Agility technique	Basketball agility patterns 2, 4, 6, 9. Three reps per pattern. 20- to 25-second active rest between repetitions. Three-minute rest between sets.
		Anaerobic conditioning	10 repetitions completing conditioning pattern 2 with a 30-second active rest interval

Table 9-4. Cont'd

Physical Quality	Drills
Sprinting technique	• A drills • B drills
Speed	• Half- and full-court sprints
Acceleration	• Position-specific starts • Stick drills • Agility patterns
Conditioning	• Agility patterns • Sprint intervals with a 20- to 25-second active rest interval

Table 9-5. Physical qualities to be developed and recommended drills for the high school basketball player during the precompetition phase

Day	Primary Emphasis	Training Component	Drills
Mon.	Speed	Warm-up	Dynamic flexibility exercises for 10-15 minutes
		Sprinting technique	A skips, 2x half court B walk, 2x half court
		Agility	Basketball agility patterns 2, 6, 8, 10. Three reps per pattern. 20- to 25-second active rest interval.
		Speed	3x full court sprints, flying. 2-3 full court sprints
Wed.	Acceleration	Warm-up	Dynamic flexibility exercises for 10-15 minutes
		Sprinting technique	A walk, 2x half court B skips, 2x half court
		Agility	Basketball agility patterns 1, 3, 5, 9. Three reps per pattern. 20- to 25-second active rest interval.
		Acceleration	Standing starts, 3-5x Resisted starts, 3x
Fri.	Agility	Warm-up	Dynamic flexibility exercises for 10-15 minutes
		Sprinting technique	A skips, 2x20 yards B walks, 2x20 yards
		Agility	Basketball agility patterns 2, 3, 7, 9, 10. Three reps per pattern. 20- to 25-second active rest interval.

Table 9-6. Sample precompetition workout for high school basketball player

movements such as A and B drills. Agility work focuses on movement patterns that are likely to occur in game situations—especially patterns emphasizing a reactionary component. Speed training is balanced between acceleration movements and speed. Finally, conditioning uses interval training to make the conditioning more metabolically basketball-specific. At this time during training, other components of training, such as plyometrics and resistance, should also be considered.

Competition Phase

Training is scaled back in the competition phase so that most of the athlete's time and energy can be directed towards practice and competition. Training speed and agility twice a week during the competition phase is enough to maintain peak levels.

In the competition phase, dynamic flexibility exercises are still performed at the beginning of each training session. Sprinting technique is still considered important; however, the drills are minimized with this phase. Acceleration and speed training is combined. For example, a coach might emphasize an explosive start from a defensive stance. Agility training will focus exclusively on movement patterns that may be seen during the sport, with the emphasis being on correct execution and quality of movement. Finally, conditioning will continue to be focused around interval training with active rest.

The high school athlete needs to develop fitness and movement skills. These athletes should be instructed on fundamentals. The high school athlete is not yet prepared to endure more intensive training.

Physical Quality	Drills
Sprinting technique	• A drills • B drills
Speed	• Half- and full-court sprints
Acceleration	• Position-specific starts
Agility	• Pattern runs
Conditioning	• Interval training with active rest interval

Table 9-7. Physical qualities to be developed and recommended drills for the high school basketball player during the competition phase

Day	Primary Emphasis	Training Component	Drills
Day One	Speed	Warm-up	Dynamic flexibility exercises for 10-15 minutes
		Sprinting technique	A skips, 2x20 yards
		Agility	Agility patterns 3, 4, 8 with active rest interval
		Speed	3-5x full-court sprints
Day Two	Conditioning	Warm-up	Dynamic flexibility exercises for 10-15 minutes
		Sprinting technique	B skips, 2x20 yards
		Agility	Agility patterns 2, 9, 10 with active rest interval
		Conditioning	12 full-court sprints with a 1:3 work to rest interval

Table 9-8. Sample competition phase workout for high school basketball player

Advanced Program

While fundamentals are still important at the college level, sports-specificity takes on even greater importance. The collegiate athlete's training will be organized around the following:

*   20-week general preparation phase

*   12-week special preparation phase

*   4-week precompetition phase

*   12-week competition phase

In general, the collegiate athlete's training should focus on the following:

*   Basketball-specific conditioning

*   Perfecting running technique

*   Improving acceleration

*   Improving speed

*   Improving basketball-specific agility

Unlike the high school athlete, the college athlete should spend only part of the year focusing on fundamentals, and should spend the rest of the year focusing on more sport-specific drills. A collegiate athlete will have more training experience than a high school athlete and in general will be better prepared for the game. Therefore, the training can be more intense and athletes should be able to handle a higher volume of training. After a fitness and technique base has been established, the collegiate athlete's program should be more intense and feature more complex drills than the high school athlete's.

General Preparation Phase

During the general preparation phase, the collegiate player should focus on developing an anaerobic endurance base, learning running technique, and improving agility technique. Athletes should train four to fives times per week. Each session should focus on dynamic flexibility exercises, running technique drills, and basic agility technique. Table 9-9 shows the types of drills that a collegiate athlete should focus on in the general preparation phase.

Physical Quality	Drills
Sprinting technique	• Arm swing drills • High knee drills • A drills • B drills
Speed	• Half- and full-court sprints for technique
Acceleration	• Position-specific starts • Stick drills
Agility	• Agility patterns for basketball
Conditioning	• Conditioning patterns for basketball

Table 9-9. Physical qualities to be developed and recommended drills for the collegiate basketball player during the general preparation phase

Table 9-10 outlines a sample workout for a collegiate basketball player training four times per week during the general preparation phase. The athlete's level of training and experience is intermediate to advanced. The athlete's level can be accelerated by increasing the intensity and volume of training. The workouts are divided into two days with a primary focus on anaerobic endurance and two days with a primary focus on quality movement patterns. Agility, sprinting technique, and dynamic flexibility are trained daily. Sprinting technique focuses on arm swing, the high knee movement, and pulling the heel to the hip. Agility technique focuses primarily on acceleration, stopping ability, and change of direction. Athletes should be allowed to fully recover for two to three minutes between sprinting technique, agility, and acceleration drills. The emphasis of the agility patterns and speed drills should be on correct execution first and speed second.

Day	Primary Emphasis	Training Component	Drills
Mon.	Anaerobic endurance	Warm-up	Dynamic flexibility exercises for 10-15 minutes
		Sprinting technique	Arm swing drills, 2x half court High knee walks, 2x half court Butt kicks, 2x half court
		Anaerobic endurance	10 repetitions completing conditioning pattern 1 with a 45-second active rest interval
Tues.	Sport-specific agility	Warm-up	Dynamic flexibility exercises for 10-15 minutes
		Sprinting technique	Arm swing drills, 1x half court High knee walks, 1x half court High knee skips, 3x half court Butt kicks, 1x half court A walks, 3x half court
		Agility technique	Agility patterns 1, 3, 7. Three reps each drill with a one-minute rest interval. Two-minute rest interval between patterns
Thurs.	Anaerobic endurance	Warm-up	Dynamic flexibility exercises for 10-15 minutes
		Sprinting technique	Arm swing drills, 2x half court High knee walks, 2x half court Butt kicks, 2x half court A walks, 2x half court
		Anaerobic endurance	10 repetitions completing conditioning pattern 1 with a 45-second active rest interval
Fri.	Sport-specific agility	Warm-up	Dynamic flexibility exercises for 10-15 minutes
		Sprinting technique	Arm swing drills, 1x half court High knee walks, 1x half court High knee skips, 3x half court Butt kicks, 1x half court A walks, 3x half court
		Agility technique	Agility patterns 5, 9, 10. Three reps each drill with a one-minute rest interval. Two-minute rest interval between patterns.

Table 9-10. Sample general preparation workout for collegiate basketball player

Special Preparation Phase

During the special preparation phase, the rest intervals will be adjusted to reflect the demands of the game at its most intense times. At the collegiate level, the most metabolically demanding time in a game will resemble an eight-play drive with a 20-second rest interval. The agility patterns are biomechanically and metabolically designed to reflect basketball movement patterns. Therefore, the coach can simply move the rest interval down to 20 to 25 seconds to reflect the time clock in a basketball game.

Athletes should train four to five times per week. Each session should focus on dynamic flexibility exercises, running technique drills, sport-specific agility technique drills, and/or anaerobic conditioning. Table 9-11 shows the types of drills that a collegiate player should focus on in the special preparation phase.

Physical Quality	Drills
Sprinting technique	• Arm swing drills • High knee drills • A drills • B drills
Sport-specific agility for basketball	• All agility patterns • Add reactionary component (i.e., passing, catching, evading) • Use a 20- to 25-second active rest interval
Anaerobic conditioning	• Conditioning patterns • Interval training with active rest

Table 9-11. Physical qualities to be developed and recommended drills for the collegiate basketball player during the special preparation phase

Table 9-12 describes a sample week of workouts for the special preparation phase. Dynamic flexibility exercises are still performed at the beginning of each workout as a warm-up. Sprint technique drills are performed at a faster pace and begin integrating more complicated A and B drills. Agility training emphasizes perfect execution by adding varied and additional patterns.

Precompetition Phase

During the precompetition phase, the overall volume of training is reduced in an effort to focus on position-specific skills. In this phase of training, dynamic flexibility drills are still performed as a warm-up for each workout. Sprinting technique is trained daily.

Day	Primary Emphasis	Training Component	Drills
Mon.	Conditioning	Warm-up	Dynamic flexibility exercises for 10-15 minutes
		Sprinting technique	High knee skips, 2x half court Butt kicks, 2x half court A skips, 2x half court B walks, 2x half court
		Agility	Basketball agility patterns 1, 3, 5, 9. Three reps per pattern. 20- to 25-second active rest between repetitions. Two-minute rest between sets.
		Anaerobic conditioning	10 repetitions completing conditioning pattern 2 with a 30-second active rest interval
Wed.	Conditioning	Warm-up	Dynamic flexibility exercises for 10-15 minutes
		Sprinting technique	Arm swing drills, 1x half court High knee walks, 1x half court High knee skips, 3x half court Butt kicks, 1x half court
		Agility technique	Basketball agility patterns 2, 4, 6, 8. Three reps per pattern. 20- to 25-second active rest between repetitions. Three-minute rest between sets.
		Anaerobic conditioning	10 repetitions completing conditioning pattern 2 with a 30-second active rest interval
Fri.	Agility	Warm-up	Dynamic flexibility exercises for 10-15 minutes
		Sprinting technique	High knee skips, 1x half court Butt kicks, 2x half court A skips, 3x half court B walks, 1x half court B skips, 3x half court
		Agility technique	Basketball agility patterns 1, 3, 5, 7. Three reps per pattern. 20- to 25-second active rest between repetitions. Two-minute rest between sets.

Table 9-12. Sample special preparation workout for collegiate basketball player

However, remedial exercises such as arm swings and high knee drills have been removed in favor of more complex movements such as A and B drills. Agility work focuses on movement patterns that are likely to occur in game situations—especially movements emphasizing a reactionary component. Speed training is balanced between acceleration from a position-specific stance and speed (as appropriate for position). Finally, conditioning uses interval training with active rest intervals to make the conditioning more metabolically basketball-specific. At this time during training, other training components (such as plyometrics and resistance) that add to the overall training stress should also be considered.

Competition Phase

As with the beginning program, training is scaled back in the competition phase of the advanced program. Table 9-15 highlights the qualities that should be developed and the exercises that should be used to develop those qualities.

Physical Quality	Drills
Sprinting technique	• A drills • B drills
Speed	• Half- and full-court sprints
Acceleration	• Position-specific starts • Stick drills
Agility	• Agility patterns
Conditioning	• Agility patterns • Sprint intervals with a 20- to 25-second active rest interval

Table 9-13. Physical qualities to be developed and recommended means for the collegiate basketball player during the precompetition phase.

In the competition phase, dynamic flexibility exercises are still performed at the beginning of each training session. Sprinting technique is still considered important; however, the drills are minimized in this phase. Acceleration and speed training is combined. For example, a coach might emphasize an explosive, position-specific start as part of a 40-yard sprint. Agility training will focus exclusively on movement patterns that may be seen during the sport, with the emphasis being on correct execution and quality of movement. Finally, conditioning will continue to be focused around interval training.

Day	Primary Emphasis	Training Component	Drills
Mon.	Speed	Warm-up	Dynamic flexibility exercises for 10-15 minutes
		Sprinting technique	A skips, 2x half court B walk, 2x half court
		Agility	Basketball agility patterns 2, 6, 8, 10. Three reps per pattern. 20- to 25-second active rest interval.
		Speed	2-3 full court sprints
Wed.	Acceleration	Warm-up	Dynamic flexibility exercises for 10-15 minutes
		Sprinting technique	A walk, 2x half court B skips, 2x half court
		Agility	Basketball agility patterns 1, 3, 5, 9. Three reps per pattern. 20- to 25-second active rest interval.
		Acceleration	3-5 standing starts
Fri.	Agility	Warm-up	Dynamic flexibility exercises for 10-15 minutes
		Sprinting technique	A skips, 2x20 yards B walks, 2x20 yards
		Agility	Basketball agility patterns 2, 3, 7, 9, 10. Three reps per pattern. 20- to 25-second active rest interval.

Table 9-14. Sample precompetition workout for a collegiate basketball player

Physical Quality	Drills
Sprinting technique	• A drills • B drills
Speed	• Half- and full-court sprints
Acceleration	• Position-specific starts
Agility	• Pattern runs
Conditioning	• Interval training with active rest interval

Table 9-15. Physical qualities to be developed and recommended drills for the collegiate basketball player during the competition phase

Day	Primary Emphasis	Training Component	Drills
Day One	Speed	Warm-up	Dynamic flexibility exercises for 10-15 minutes
		Sprinting technique	A skips, 2x half court
		Agility	Agility patterns 3, 4, 8 with active rest interval. Three reps per pattern. 20- to 25-second rest interval. Two minutes between patterns.
		Speed	3-5x full-court sprints
Day Two	Conditioning	Warm-up	Dynamic flexibility exercises for 10-15 minutes
		Sprinting technique	B skips, 2x20 yards
		Agility	Agility patterns 2, 9, 10 with active rest interval
		Conditioning	12 full-court sprints with a 1:3 work to rest interval

Table 9-16. Sample competition phase workout for collegiate basketball player

Agility Drills

Agility Pattern: Drill #1

Purpose: Develop a low athletic stance; move effectively in the open court by transitioning from movement to movement.

Objectives:

- Maintain body control.
- Move feet quickly.
- Maintain a low center of gravity at all times.

Description:

- The athlete assumes a low defensive stance with the knees and hips bent, a flat back, the arms extended at the sides, and the eyes up.

- The athlete starts at the baseline and shuffles laterally across.
- The athlete then transitions into two angled shuffles until midcourt.
- Once at midcourt, the athlete turns and runs until reaching the opposite baseline.
- At the far baseline, the drill is finished with a final lateral shuffle.
- The athlete should make quick turns at each cone.
- The athlete should maintain a neutral spine at all times.

Increasing Complexity/Difficulty:

- Have the athlete mirror another player at the baselines.
- Have the athlete take a jump shot when running forward toward the second baseline.
- Have the athlete pick up a ball placed midcourt and dribble down to the far baseline.

Work Interval: Will vary on distance of cones and ability of athlete but should be between 8 and 12 seconds.

Rest Interval: Once mastery of the drill has been reached, the rest interval can be brought down to 2:1 rest to work interval. Another option is to have the athlete run at a moderate intensity back to the start of the drill and repeat the pattern to emphasize conditioning. (Note: This option will compromise true movement/agility acquisition.)

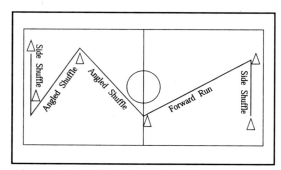

Figure 9-1. Agility Pattern: Drill #1

Agility Pattern: Drill #2

Purpose: Develop controlled change of direction.

Objectives:

- Develop effective transitions from different movement patterns.
- Control unnecessary body movements.

Description:

- Have the athlete start at the baseline and side shuffle across the paint.

- The athlete then backpedals, transitions to a forward run, backpedals, and finally finishes the drill with a forward run.
- Quality of movement is emphasized.
- The athlete should maintain a low center of gravity.
- The athlete should keep the corners "tight" when passing cones.

Increasing Complexity/Difficulty:

- Have the athlete mirror another player at the baseline.
- Have the athlete receive a passed ball and take a jump shot at the top two cones of the free-throw line.
- Have the athlete dribble a ball through the pattern.

Work Interval: Will vary on distance of cones and ability of athlete but should be between 5 and 10 seconds.

Rest Interval: Once mastery of the drill has been reached, the rest interval can be brought down to 2:1 rest to work interval.

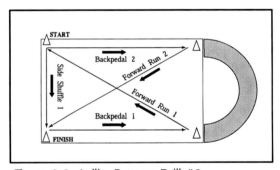

Figure 9-2. Agility Pattern: Drill #2

Agility Pattern: Drill #3

Purpose: Develop lateral acceleration, stopping ability, and a low athletic stance.

Objectives:

- Simulate movement patterns often seen while defending an opponent.
- Reduce unnecessary body movements.

Description:

- The athlete starts with his back to the drill.
- The athlete should keep his head up and eyes forward and use peripheral vision to locate the cones.

- The athlete should touch the top of the cones with the outside hand to ensure that he stays low.

Increasing Complexity/Difficulty:

- The coach can pass a ball back and forth to the athlete.
- At the end of the drill, the athlete can receive a passed ball and take a jump shot.
- The distance between the cones can be increased.
- Use two identical patterns of cones and have athletes race each other through the drill.

Work Interval: Will vary on distance of cones and ability of athlete, but should be between 8 and 12 seconds.

Rest Interval: Once mastery of the drill has been reached, the rest interval can be brought down to 2:1 rest to work interval. Another option is to have the athlete run at a moderate intensity back to the start of the drill and repeat the pattern to emphasize conditioning. (Note: This option will compromise true movement/agility acquisition.)

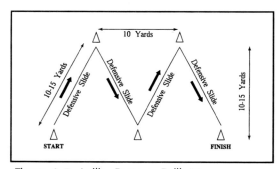

Figure 9-3. Agility Pattern: Drill #3

Agility Pattern: Drill #4

Purpose: Develop effective transitions between movements and body control.

Objectives:

- Simulate movement patterns often seen in games.
- Reduce unnecessary body movements.

Description:

- The athlete starts at the baseline and uses an angled slide, opens the hips to go into a forward run, transfers back into a defensive slide, and finishes the drill with a forward run.

- The athlete should make quick turns at each cone.
- The athlete should maintain a neutral spine at all times.

Increasing Complexity/Difficulty:

- The cones can be spread further apart.
- The athlete can receive a passed ball and dribble during the last forward run.

Work Interval: Will vary on distance of cones and ability of athlete, but should be between five and eight seconds.

Rest Interval: Once mastery of the drill has been reached, the rest interval can be brought down to 2:1 rest to work interval. Another option is to have the athlete run at a moderate intensity back to the start of the drill and repeat the pattern to emphasize conditioning. (Note: This option will compromise true movement/agility acquisition.)

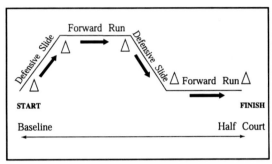

Figure 9-4. Agility Pattern: Drill #4

Agility Pattern: Drill #5

Purpose: Develop effective transitions between movements and body control.

Objectives:

- Simulate movement patterns often seen in games.
- Reduce unnecessary body movements.

Description:

- The athlete starts at the baseline and backpedals, then transitions into an angled defensive slide, goes to a backpedal, and finishes with a defensive slide.
- The athlete should make quick turns at each cone.
- The athlete should maintain a neutral spine at all times.

Increasing Complexity/Difficulty:

- The cones can be spread further apart.
- The athlete can receive a passed ball and dribble.

Work Interval: Will vary on distance of cones and ability of athlete, but should be between five and eight seconds.

Rest Interval: Once mastery of the drill has been reached, the rest interval can be brought down to 2:1 rest to work interval. Another option is to have the athlete run at a moderate intensity back to the start of the drill and repeat the pattern to emphasize conditioning. (Note: This option will compromise true movement/agility acquisition.)

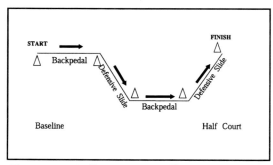

Figure 9-5. Agility Pattern: Drill #5

Agility Pattern: Drill #6

Purpose: Develop acceleration and stopping ability.

Objectives:

- Simulate movement patterns often seen at various positions.
- Reduce unnecessary body movements.

Description:

- Have the athlete start at the baseline or at a cone and sprint forward 10 yards, backpedal five yards, sprint forward 10 yards, and so on, until completing the drill.
- The athlete should accelerate with 100% effort.
- The athlete should maximize the forward lean when initially accelerating.
- The athlete should use a forceful, high knee lift when initially accelerating.
- The athlete should minimize braking distance by quickly dropping the center of gravity.
- The athlete should use short choppy steps to minimize stopping distance.

Increasing Complexity/Difficulty:

- A coach can pass a ball back and forth with the athlete during the drill.
- The athlete can dribble a ball during the drill.
- The drill can be positioned close enough to a basket to make jump shots at various stages during the drill.

- Have athletes perform the drill at the same time to increase competition.
- Stagger the distance of the cones.

Work Interval: Will vary on distance of cones and ability of athlete, but should be between 10 and 18 seconds.

Rest Interval: Once mastery of the drill has been reached, the rest interval can be brought down to 2:1 rest to work interval.

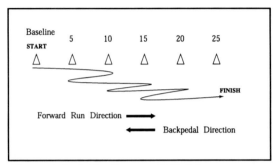

Figure 9-6. Agility Pattern: Drill #6

Agility Pattern: Drill #7

Purpose: Develop lateral acceleration, lateral stopping ability, and body control.

Objectives:

- Simulate movement patterns seen at various positions.
- Reduce unnecessary body movements.
- Train eye-hand-foot coordination.

Description:

- Place two cones one to two yards apart for shuffling or place two cones up to 10 yards apart for running.
- The athlete should not cross over the feet during the drill if shuffling.
- The athlete should maintain a low center of gravity, keeping the knees and hips bent while shuffling.
- The athlete should move the feet as quickly as possible while shuffling.
- The athlete should lower the center of gravity as he turns through the cones while running.
- The athlete should drop the inside shoulder and extend the arm toward the ground while turning when running.
- The athlete should emphasize a high knee lift while accelerating off the turn when running.

Increasing Complexity/Difficulty:

- The coach can toss a ball back and forth to the athlete while shuffling.
- The coach can have the athlete receive a passed ball and take a jump shot at the end of the drill.
- The cones can be spread further apart to emphasize stopping mechanics while running.
- The coach can time the drill for completed cycles through the pattern.

Work Interval: Will vary on distance of cones and ability of athlete, but should be between 10 and 30 seconds. If the drill is done with shuffling, the coach can toss a ball for completed catches to dictate the completion of the drill.

Rest Interval: Once mastery of the drill has been reached, the rest interval can be brought down to 2:1 rest to work interval.

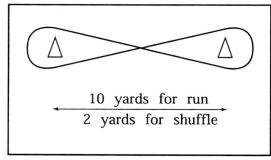

Figure 9-7. Agility Pattern: Drill #7

Agility Pattern: Drill #8

Purpose: Develop stopping ability with a reactionary component.

Objectives:

- Simulate movement patterns seen at various positions.
- Reduce unnecessary body movements.

Description:

- The coach and athlete use a wall about 15 feet in front of them to rebound a ball off of.
- The coach stands slightly behind the athlete and bounces a ball off the wall at various angles.
- The athlete returns the ball by rebounding the ball off the wall back to the coach.
- The athlete uses a lateral shuffle to perform the drill.

Increasing Complexity/Difficulty: The drill can be moved closer to the wall to reduce the reaction time to the ball.

Work Interval: The coach can vary the time of the drill up to 30 seconds.

Rest Interval: Once mastery of the drill has been reached, the rest interval can be brought down to a 2:1 rest to work interval.

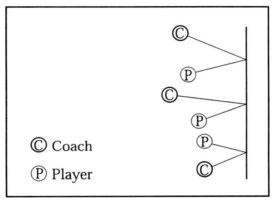

Figure 9-8. Agility Pattern: Drill #8

Agility Pattern: Drill #9

Purpose: Develop movement patterns seen at various positions.

Objective: Develop an effective change of direction.

Description:

- The athlete runs forward through the cone pattern as shown in Figure 9-9.
- The athlete should keep the center of gravity low.
- The athlete should emphasize a high knee lift out of each turn.
- The athlete should reduce stopping distance by lowering the center of gravity and use short, choppy steps while decelerating.

Increasing Complexity/Difficulty:

- The cones can be set up further apart to increase the work interval.
- Two identical sets of cones can be set up to allow athletes to compete against each other.

Work Interval: Will vary on distance of the cones and ability of the athlete, but should be between 5 and 10 seconds.

Rest Interval: Once mastery of the drill has been reached, the rest interval can be brought down to a 2:1 rest to work interval.

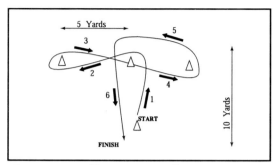

Figure 9-9. Agility Pattern: Drill #9

Agility Pattern: Drill #10

Purpose: Develop acceleration, stopping ability, and body control.

Objectives:

- Simulate movement patterns at various positions.
- Reduce unnecessary body movements.

Description:

- Have the athlete start at a cone and make a crossover step, moving forward five yards. The athlete turns 180 degrees and runs 10 yards. The athlete then turns 180 degrees and finishes the drill with a five-yard sprint.
- The athlete should accelerate with 100% effort.
- The athlete should maximize the forward lean when initially accelerating from each turn.
- When the athlete turns, he should drop the inside shoulder and reach toward the ground with the same hand.
- The athlete should use a forceful, high knee lift when initially accelerating.
- The athlete should minimize braking distance by quickly dropping the center of gravity.
- The athlete should use short choppy steps to minimize stopping distance.

Increasing Complexity/Difficulty:

- The coach can indicate which direction the athlete should start in.
- Have athletes perform the drill at the same time to increase competition.

Work Interval: Will vary on distance of cones and ability of athlete, but should be between five and eight seconds.

Rest Interval: Once mastery of the drill has been reached, the rest interval can be brought down to 2:1 rest to work interval.

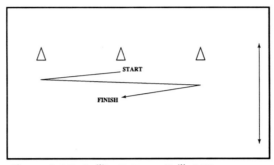

Figure 9-10. Agility Pattern: Drill #10

10

Football

Each position in football has specialized skills or characteristics that are conducive for success. Defensive backs are proficient at backpedaling and transitioning directions. Offensive linemen must be able to shuffle their feet and coordinate upper-body blocking technique. The receiver must be able to accelerate forward, decelerate quickly, change direction, and catch the ball, to name just a few demands of the position.

Many movements in football are observed at all the positions. Some of the common movements are accelerating forward, lateral shuffling, decelerating in all directions, and moving backwards with varying techniques. These movements are reflected in the sample programs in this chapter.

A speed and agility program for football should target the following:

- Sprinting technique: helps with speed and helps prevent injuries.

- Anaerobic conditioning: helps the athlete recover from high-intensity sprints and helps them perform for the entire game.

- Agility training and its subcomponents: teach how to change directions to help prevent injuries and develop agility to improve performance.

- Using an appropriate rest interval that will vary on goals of training during each phase.

Beginning Program

The high school athlete's training will be organized around the following:

- 16-week general preparation phase

- 8-week special preparation phase

- 4-week precompetition phase

- 15-week competition phase

- 2-week transition phase following the season

The high school athlete's training should focus on the following:

- Building anaerobic metabolic efficiency

- Developing strength and power

- Developing running technique

- Improving speed

- Developing sport-specific agility

General Preparation Phase

During the general preparation phase, the high school athlete should focus on developing anaerobic endurance, learning running technique, and learning agility technique. As a guideline, at this level athletes should train two to four times per week. Each session should focus on dynamic flexibility exercises, running technique drills, and basic agility technique. Table 10-1 shows the types of drills that a high school football player should focus on in the general preparation phase.

Physical Quality	Drills
Sprinting technique	• Arm swing drills • High knee drills • A drills • B drills
Speed	• 40-yard sprints for sprint technique
Acceleration	• Position-specific starts • Stick drills
Agility	• Agility patterns for football
Conditioning	• 40- to 100-yard sprints

Table 10-1. Physical qualities to be developed and recommended drills for the high school football player during the general preparation phase

Day	Primary Emphasis	Training Component	Drills
Mon.	Anaerobic endurance	Warm-up	Dynamic flexibility exercises for 10-15 minutes
		Sprinting technique	Arm swing drills, 2x20 yards High knee walks, 2x20 yards Butt kicks, 2x20 yards A walks, 2x20 yards Shuffle (right, then left), 2x5 yards Backpedal, 2x20 yards
		Anaerobic endurance	12x100 yards with a 45-second rest interval
Tues.	Agility	Warm-up	Dynamic flexibility exercises for 10-15 minutes
		Sprinting technique	Arm swing drills, 1x20 yards High knee walks, 1x20 yards High knee skips, 3x20 yards Butt kicks, 1x20 yards A walks, 3x20 yards 12 40-yard sprints
		Agility technique	Agility patterns 1, 5. Three reps each drill with a one-minute rest interval. Three-minute rest interval between patterns
Thurs.	Anaerobic endurance	Warm-up	Dynamic flexibility exercises for 10-15 minutes
		Sprinting technique	Arm swing drills, 2x20 yards High knee walks, 2x20 yards Butt kicks, 2x20 yards A walks, 2x20 yards
		Anaerobic endurance	12x100 yards with a 45-second rest interval
Fri.	Agility	Warm-up	Dynamic flexibility exercises for 10-15 minutes
		Sprinting technique	Arm swing drills, 1x20 yards High knee walks, 1x20 yards High knee skips, 3x20 yards Butt kicks, 1x20 yards A walks, 3x20 yards 12 40-yard sprints
		Agility technique	Agility patterns 2, 6. Three reps each drill with a one-minute rest interval. Three-minute rest interval between patterns

Table 10-2. Sample general preparation workout for high school football player

Table 10-2 outlines a sample workout for a high school athlete training four times per week during the general preparation phase. Because the sample athlete is a beginner, the focus is on fundamental agility and running skills. The workouts are divided into two days with a primary focus on anaerobic endurance and two days with a primary focus on quality movement patterns. Agility, sprinting technique, and dynamic flexibility are trained daily. Sprinting technique focuses on arm swing, the high knee movement, and pulling the heel to the hip. Agility technique focuses primarily on shuffling and backpedaling. Athletes should be allowed to fully recover for two to three minutes between sprinting technique, agility, and acceleration drills. The emphasis of the drills should be on correct execution first and speed second.

Special Preparation Phase

During the special preparation phase, the rest intervals will be adjusted to reflect the demands of the game at its most intense times. At the high school level, it is likely that the most metabolically demanding time in a game will resemble an eight-play drive with a 20-second rest interval. The agility patterns are biomechanically and metabolically designed to reflect football movement patterns. Therefore, the coach can simply move the rest interval down to 20 to 25 seconds to reflect the time clock in a football game.

Athletes should train three to four times per week. Each session should focus on dynamic flexibility exercises, running technique drills, sport-specific agility technique drills, and/or anaerobic conditioning. Table 10-3 shows the types of drills that a high school athlete should focus on in the special preparation phase.

Table 10-4 describes a sample week of workouts for the special preparation phase. Dynamic flexibility exercises are still performed at the beginning of each workout as a warm-up. Sprinting technique drills are performed at a faster pace and begin integrating more complicated A and B drills. While agility training still focuses on fundamentals, the fundamentals are now being incorporated into movement patterns that are seen during the game.

Physical Quality	Drills
Sprinting technique	• Arm swing drills • High knee drills • A drills • B drills
Sport-specific agility for footbal	• All agility patterns • Add reactionary component (i.e., throwing, catching, evading) • Use a 20- to 25-second rest interval
Anaerobic conditioning	• Sprint distances for 60-100 yards • Interval training (1:3 work/rest)

Table 10-3. Physical qualities to be developed and recommended drills for the high school football player during the special preparation phase

Day	Primary Emphasis	Training Component	Drills
Mon.	Agility	Warm-up	Dynamic flexibility exercises for 10-15 minutes
		Sprinting technique	High knee skips, 2x20 yards Butt kicks, 2x20 yards A skips, 2x20 yards B walks, 2x20 yards
		Agility technique	Football agility patterns 1, 3, 5, 9. Three reps per pattern. 20- to 25-second rest between repetitions. Three-minute rest between sets.
Tues.	Conditioning	Warm-up	Dynamic flexibility exercises for 10-15 minutes
		Sprinting technique	Arm swing drills, 1x20 yards High knee walks, 1x20 yards High knee skips, 3x20 yards Butt kicks, 1x20 yards
		Agility technique	Football agility patterns 2, 4, 6, 8. Three reps per pattern. 20- to 25-second rest between repetitions. Three-minute rest between sets.
		Interval training	10- to 60-yard sprints (10-15x)
Thurs.	Agility	Warm-up	Dynamic flexibility exercises for 10-15 minutes
		Sprinting technique	High knee skips, 1x20 yards Butt kicks, 2x20 yards A skips, 3x20 yards B walks, 1x20 yards B skips, 3x20 yards
		Agility technique	Football agility patterns 1, 3, 5, 9. Three reps per pattern. 20- to 25-second rest between repetitions. Three-minute rest between sets.
Fri.	Conditioning	Warm-up	Dynamic flexibility exercises for 10-15 minutes
		Sprinting technique	Arm swing drills, 1x20 yards High knee walks, 3x20 yards High knee skips, 3x20 yards Butt kicks, 1x20 yards A walks, 3x20 yards
		Agility technique	Football agility patterns 2, 4, 6, 10. Three reps per pattern. 20- to 25-second rest between repetitions. Three-minute rest between sets.
		Interval training	10- to 60-yard sprints (10-15x)

Table 10-4. Sample special preparation workout for high school football player

Precompetition Phase

Training is scaled back during the precompetition phase so that the high school football player can focus more on game skills. Table 10-5 highlights some of the exercises that should be used in this phase.

Physical Quality	Drills
Sprinting technique	• A drills • B drills
Speed	• Flying sprints • 40- to 100-yard sprints
Acceleration	• Position-specific starts • Stick drills
Agility	• Agility patterns
Conditioning	• Agility patterns • Sprint intervals with a 20- to 25-second rest interval

Table 10-5. Physical qualities to be developed and recommended drills for the high school football player during the precompetition phase

In this phase of training, dynamic flexibility drills are still performed as a warm-up for each workout. Sprinting technique is trained daily. However, remedial exercises such as arm swings and high knee drills have been removed in favor of more complex movements such as A and B drills. Agility work focuses on movement patterns that are likely to occur in game situations—especially patterns emphasizing a reactionary component. Speed training is balanced between acceleration movements from a position-specific stance and speed (as appropriate for position). Finally, conditioning uses interval training to make the conditioning more metabolically football-specific. At this time during training, other components of training, such as plyometrics and resistance, should also be considered.

Competition Phase

Training is scaled back in the competition phase so that most of the athlete's time and energy can be directed towards practice and competition. Training speed and agility twice a week during the competition phase is enough to maintain peak levels.

In the competition phase, dynamic flexibility exercises are still performed at the beginning of each training session. Sprinting technique is still considered important; however, the drills are minimized with this phase. Acceleration and speed training is combined. For example, a coach might emphasize an explosive position-specific start

Day	Primary Emphasis	Training Component	Drills
Mon.	Speed	Warm-up	Dynamic flexibility exercises for 10-15 minutes
		Sprinting technique	A skips, 2x20 yards B walk, 2x20 yards
		Agility	Football agility patterns 2, 6, 8, 10. Three reps per pattern. 20- to 25-second rest interval.
		Speed	3x40 yards, flying 2-3x60 yards, standing start
Wed.	Acceleration	Warm-up	Dynamic flexibility exercises for 10-15 minutes
		Sprinting technique	A walk, 2x20 yards B skips, 2x20 yards
		Agility	Football agility patterns 1, 3, 5, 9. Three reps per pattern. 20- to 25-second rest interval.
		Acceleration	Standing starts, 3-5x Resisted starts, 3x
Fri.	Conditioning	Warm-up	Dynamic flexibility exercises for 10-15 minutes
		Sprinting technique	A skips, 2x20 yards B walks, 2x20 yards
		Agility	Football agility patterns 2, 6, 8, 10. Three reps per pattern. 20- to 25-second rest interval.
		Conditioning	12-15x 1' sprints followed by 3' jog

Table 10-6. Sample precompetition workout for high school football player

as part of a 40-yard sprint. Agility training will focus exclusively on movement patterns that may be seen during the sport, with the emphasis being on correct execution and quality of movement. Finally, conditioning will continue to be focused around interval training.

Physical Quality	Drills
Sprinting technique	• A drills • B drills
Speed	• Flying sprints
Acceleration	• Position-specific starts
Agility	• Pattern runs
Conditioning	• Interval training (1:3 work:rest)

Table 10-7. Physical qualities to be developed and recommended drills for the high school football player during the competition phase

Day	Primary Emphasis	Training Component	Drills
Day One	Speed	Warm-up	Dynamic flexibility exercises for 10-15 minutes
		Sprinting technique	A skips, 2x20 yards
		Agility	Agility patterns 3, 6, 9 with a 1:3 work to rest interval
		Speed	3-5x40 yards, position-specific start
Day Two	Conditioning	Warm-up	Dynamic flexibility exercises for 10-15 minutes
		Sprinting technique	B skips, 2x20 yards
		Agility	Agility patterns 1, 4, 8 with a 1:3 work to rest interval
		Conditioning	10x60-yard sprints with a 1:3 work to rest interval

Table 10-8. Sample competition phase workout for high school football player

Advanced Program

The collegiate athlete's training will be organized around the following:

- 20-week general preparation phase
- 12-week special preparation phase

- 4-week precompetition phase

- 12-week competition phase

- 2-week transition phase following the season

The collegiate athlete's training should focus on the following:

- Football-specific conditioning

- Perfecting running technique

- Improving acceleration

- Improving speed

- Improving football-specific agility

General Preparation Phase

During the general preparation phase, the collegiate player should focus on developing an anaerobic endurance base, learning running technique, and improving agility technique. Athletes should train four to fives times per week. Each session should focus on dynamic flexibility exercises, running technique drills, and basic agility technique. Table 10-9 shows the types of drills that a collegiate athlete should focus on in the general preparation phase.

Physical Quality	Drills
Sprinting technique	• Arm swing drills • High knee drills • A drills • B drills
Speed	• 40-yard sprints for sprint technique
Acceleration	• Position-specific starts • Stick drills
Agility	• Agility patterns for football
Conditioning/anaerobic endurance	• 40- to 100-yard sprints

Table 10-9. Physical qualities to be developed and recommended drills for the collegiate football player during the general preparation phase

Table 10-10 outlines a sample workout for a collegiate football player training four times per week during the general preparation phase. The athlete's level of training and experience is intermediate to advanced. The athlete's level can be accelerated by increasing the intensity and volume of training. The workouts are divided into two days

Day	Primary Emphasis	Training Component	Drills
Mon.	Anaerobic endurance	Warm-up	Dynamic flexibility exercises for 10-15 minutes
		Sprinting technique	Arm swing drills, 2x20 yards High knee walks, 2x20 yards Butt kicks, 2x20 yards A walks, 2x20 yards Shuffle (right, then left), 2x5 yards Backpedal, 2x20 yards
		Anaerobic endurance	14x100 yards with a 45-second rest interval
Tues.	Sport-specific agility	Warm-up	Dynamic flexibility exercises for 10-15 minutes
		Sprinting technique	Arm swing drills, 1x20 yards High knee walks, 1x20 yards High knee skips, 3x20 yards Butt kicks, 1x20 yards A walks, 3x20 yards 12 40-yard sprints
		Agility technique	Agility patterns 1, 3, 6. Three reps each drill with a one-minute rest interval. Three-minute rest interval between patterns.
		Anaerobic endurance	14x100 yards with a 45-second rest interval
Thurs.	Sprinting technique	Warm-up	Dynamic flexibility exercises for 10-15 minutes
		Sprinting technique	Arm swing drills, 2x20 yards High knee walks, 2x20 yards Butt kicks, 2x20 yards A walks, 2x20 yards
Fri.	Anaerobic endurance	Warm-up	Dynamic flexibility exercises for 10-15 minutes
		Sprinting technique	Arm swing drills, 1x20 yards High knee walks, 1x20 yards High knee skips, 3x20 yards Butt kicks, 1x20 yards A walks, 3x20 yards 12 40-yard sprints
		Agility technique	Football agility patterns 1, 7, 9. Three reps per pattern. Three-minute rest interval between patterns
		Anaerobic endurance	14x100 yards with a 45-second rest interval

Table 10-10. Sample general preparation workout for collegiate football player

with a primary focus on anaerobic endurance and two days with a primary focus on quality movement patterns. Agility, sprinting technique, and dynamic flexibility are trained daily. Sprinting technique focuses on arm swing, the high knee movement, and pulling the heel to the hip. Agility technique focuses primarily on acceleration, stopping ability, and change of direction. Athletes should be allowed to fully recover for two to three minutes between sprinting technique, agility, and acceleration drills. The emphasis of the agility patterns and speed drills should be on correct execution first and speed second.

Special Preparation Phase

During the special preparation phase, the rest intervals will be adjusted to reflect the demands of the game at its most intense times. At the collegiate level, the most metabolically demanding time in a game will resemble an eight-play drive with a 20-second rest interval. The agility patterns are biomechanically and metabolically designed to reflect football movement patterns. Therefore, the coach can simply move the rest interval down to 20 to 25 seconds to reflect the time clock in a football game.

Athletes should train four to five times per week. Each session should focus on dynamic flexibility exercises, running technique drills, sport-specific agility technique drills, and/or anaerobic conditioning. Table 10-11 shows the types of drills that a collegiate player should focus on in the special preparation phase.

Physical Quality	Drills
Sprinting technique	• Arm swing drills • High knee drills • A drills • B drills
Sport-specific agility for football	• All agility patterns • Add reactionary component (i.e., throwing, catching, evading) • Use a 20- to 25-second rest interval
Anaerobic conditioning	• Sprint distances for 60-100 yards • Interval training (1:3 work:rest)

Table 10-11. Physical qualities to be developed and recommended drills for the collegiate football player during the special preparation phase

Table 10-12 describes a sample week of workouts for the special preparation phase. Dynamic flexibility exercises are still performed at the beginning of each workout as a warm-up. Sprinting technique drills are performed at a faster pace and begin integrating more complicated A and B drills. Agility training emphasizes perfect execution by adding varied and additional patterns.

Day	Primary Emphasis	Training Component	Drills
Mon.	Agility	Warm-up	Dynamic flexibility exercises for 10-15 minutes
		Sprinting technique	High knee skips, 2x20 yards Butt kicks, 2x20 yards A skips, 2x20 yards B walks, 2x20 yards
		Agility	Football agility patterns 2, 4, 6, 8, 10. Three reps per pattern. 20- to 25-second rest interval
Tues.	Anaerobic endurance	Warm-up	Dynamic flexibility exercises for 10-15 minutes
		Sprinting technique	Arm swing drills, 1x20 yards High knee walks, 1x20 yards High knee skips, 3x20 yards Butt kicks, 1x20 yards
		Agility technique	Football agility patterns 1, 3, 5, 7, 9. Three reps per pattern. 20- to 25-second rest interval. Two minutes rest between sets.
		Interval training	10- to 60-yard sprints (10-15x)
Thurs.	Agility	Warm-up	Dynamic flexibility exercises for 10-15 minutes
		Sprinting technique	High knee skips, 1x20 yards Butt kicks, 2x20 yards A skips, 3x20 yards B walks, 1x20 yards B skips, 3x20 yards
		Agility technique	Football agility patterns 2, 4, 6, 8, 10. Three reps per pattern. 20- to 25-second rest interval. Three reps per pattern. Two-minute rest between sets.
Fri.	Anaerobic endurance	Warm-up	Dynamic flexibility exercises for 10-15 minutes
		Sprinting technique	Arm swing drills, 1x20 yards High knee walks, 3x20 yards High knee skips, 3x20 yards Butt kicks, 1x20 yards A walks, 3x20 yards
		Agility technique	Football agility patterns 2, 4, 6, 8, 10. Three reps per pattern. 20- to 25-second rest interval. Two minutes rest between sets.
		Interval training	10- to 60-yard sprints (10-15x)

Table 10-12. Sample special preparation workout for collegiate football player

Precompetition Phase

During the precompetition phase, training is scaled back so that the athlete can focus more on game skills. The overall volume of training is reduced in an effort to focus on position-specific skills.

Physical Quality	Drills
Sprinting technique	• A drills • B drills
Speed	• 20- to 60-yard sprints
Acceleration	• Standing starts • Stick drills
Agility	• Agility patterns
Conditioning	• Agility patterns • Sprint intervals (1:3 work:rest)

Table 10-13. Physical qualities to be developed and recommended drills for the collegiate football player during the precompetition phase

In this phase of training, dynamic flexibility drills are still performed as a warm-up for each workout. Sprinting technique is trained daily. However, remedial exercises such as arm swings and high knee drills have been removed in favor of more complex movements such as A and B drills. Agility work focuses on movement patterns that are likely to occur in game situations—especially movements emphasizing a reactionary component. Speed training is balanced between acceleration from a position-specific stance and speed (as appropriate for position). Finally, conditioning uses interval training to make the conditioning more metabolically football-specific. At this time during training, other training components (such as plyometrics and resistance) that add to the overall training stress should also be considered.

Competition Phase

In the competition phase, dynamic flexibility exercises are still performed at the beginning of each training session. Sprinting technique is still considered important; however, the drills are minimized with this phase. Acceleration and speed training is combined. For example, a coach might emphasize an explosive position-specific start as part of a 40-yard sprint. Agility training will focus exclusively on movement patterns that may be seen during the sport, with the emphasis being on correct execution and quality of movement. Finally, conditioning will continue to be focused around interval training.

Day	Primary Emphasis	Training Component	Drills
Mon.	Anaerobic conditioning	Warm-up	Dynamic flexibility exercises for 10-15 minutes
		Sprinting technique	A skips, 2x20 yards B walk, 2x20 yards
		Agility	Football agility patterns 2, 4, 6, 8, 10. Three reps per pattern. 20- to 25-second rest interval. Two-minute rest interval between sets.
		Interval training	10-15 x 10- to 60-yard sprint with a 1:3 work to rest interval
Wed.	Anaerobic conditioning	Warm-up	Dynamic flexibility exercises for 10-15 minutes
		Sprinting technique	A walk, 2x20 yards B skips, 2x20 yards
		Agility	Football agility patterns 2, 4, 6, 8, 10. Three reps per pattern. 20- to 25-second rest interval. Three reps per pattern. Two-minute rest interval between sets.
		Interval training	10-15 x 10- to 60-yard sprint with a 1:3 work to rest interval
Fri.	Anaerobic conditioning	Warm-up	Dynamic flexibility exercises for 10-15 minutes
		Sprinting technique	A skips, 2x20 yards B walks, 2x20 yards
		Agility	Football agility patterns 2, 4, 6, 8, 10. Three reps per pattern. 20- to 25-second rest interval. Two-minute rest interval between sets.
		Interval training	10-15 x 10- to 60-yard sprint

Table 10-14. Sample precompetition workout for a collegiate football player

Physical Quality	Drills
Sprinting technique	• A drills • B drills
Speed	• Flying sprints
Acceleration	• Standing starts
Agility	• Pattern runs
Conditioning	• Interval training (1:3 work:rest)

Table 10-15. Physical qualities to be developed and recommended drills for the collegiate football player during the competition phase

Day	Primary Emphasis	Training Component	Drills
Day One	Speed	Warm-up	Dynamic flexibility exercises for 10-15 minutes
		Sprinting technique	A skips, 2x20 yards
		Agility	Agility patterns 3, 6, 9 with a 20- to 25-second rest interval.
		Speed	10x20-yard position-specific start with a 1:3 work to rest interval
Day Two	Conditioning	Warm-up	Dynamic flexibility exercises for 10-15 minutes
		Sprinting technique	B skips, 2x20 yards
		Agility	Agility patterns 1, 4, 8 with a 20- to 25-second rest interval
		Conditioning	14x20-yard position-specific start with a 1:3 work to rest interval

Table 10-16. Sample competition phase workout for collegiate football player

Agility Drills

Agility Pattern: Drill #1

Purpose: Develop acceleration and stopping ability.

Objectives:

- Maintain body control.
- Develop specific rate of force production.
- Lower center of gravity when decelerating.

Description:

- The athlete starts at one end and runs forward to each cone in the series.
- The athlete can use a position-specific start (i.e., two- or three-point).
- The athlete should concentrate on running in straight lines.
- The athlete should make "tight" corners.
- The athlete should keep the elbows relatively close to the body.
- The athlete should drop the center of gravity while decelerating.
- The athlete should use short choppy steps to decelerate quickly.
- The athlete should maintain a neutral spine at all times.

Increasing Complexity/Difficulty:

- Combine a forward run with side shuffling.
- Use shuffling only.
- Have the athlete run off the end of the drill to catch a thrown ball.
- Ball-carrying positions can hold a ball for the duration of the drill.
- Use two identical patterns of cones and have athletes race each other through the drill.

Work Interval: Will vary on distance of cones and ability of athlete but should be between 8 and 12 seconds.

Rest Interval: Once mastery of the drill has been reached, the rest interval can be brought down to 2:1 rest to work interval.

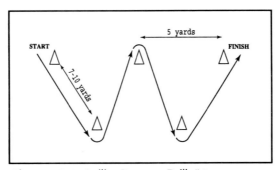

Figure 10-1. Agility Pattern: Drill #1

Agility Pattern: Drill #2

Purpose: Develop controlled running at maximal or near maximal running speed.

Objectives:

- Simulate special teams movement patterns.
- Incorporate decision-making.
- Control unnecessary body movements.

Description:

- Have the athlete use a "rolling" start for this drill.
- Once the athlete reaches the first cone, he should be at a maximal controlled speed.
- The athlete should keep the corners "tight" when passing cones.
- The athlete should keep the elbows relatively close to the sides of the body.

Increasing Complexity/Difficulty:

- Stagger the distance of the cones.
- Stagger the width of the cones.
- The coach can direct the athlete which direction to run (left or right) at the end of the drill.
- Ball-carrying positions can hold a ball for the duration of the drill.
- Use two identical patterns of cones and have athletes race each other through the drill.

Work Interval: Will vary on distance of cones and ability of athlete but should be between 8 and 12 seconds.

Rest Interval: Once mastery of the drill has been reached, the rest interval can be brought down to 2:1 rest to work interval.

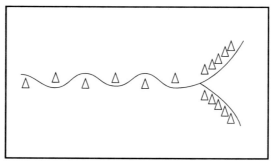

Figure 10-2. Agility Pattern: Drill #2

Agility Pattern: Drill #3

Purpose: Develop acceleration and stopping ability.

Objectives:

- Simulate movement patterns often seen at defensive back and the receiver position.
- Incorporate decision-making.
- Reduce unnecessary body movements.

Description:

- Have the athlete start on a yard line or at a cone and sprint forward 10 yards, backpedal five, sprint forward 10, back five again, then finish with a sprint forward to complete the drill.
- The athlete should accelerate with 100 percent effort.
- The athlete should maximize the forward lean when initially accelerating.
- The athlete should use a forceful, high knee lift when initially accelerating.
- The athlete should minimize braking distance by quickly dropping the center of gravity.
- The athlete should use short choppy steps to minimize stopping distance.

Increasing Complexity/Difficulty:

- Receivers, defensive backs, and running backs can catch a ball thrown from a coach in the forward direction and toss it back.
- Linemen and linebackers can add shuffles and pass sets (either right or left) to the backward directions.
- Quarterbacks can use drop steps in the backward direction.
- Ball-carrying positions can hold a ball for the duration of the drill.
- Use two identical patterns of cones and have athletes race each other through the drill.

Work Interval: Will vary on distance of cones and ability of athlete but should be between 8 and 12 seconds.

Rest Interval: Once mastery of the drill has been reached, the rest interval can be brought down to 2:1 rest to work interval.

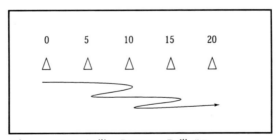

Figure 10-3. Agility Pattern: Drill #3

Agility Pattern: Drill #4

Purpose: Develop acceleration, stopping ability, and body control.

Objectives:

- Simulate movement patterns often seen at running back and linebacker.
- Reduce unnecessary body movements.

Description:

- Have the athlete straddle a yard line or a cone and make a crossover step, moving forward five yards. The athlete turns 180 degrees and runs 10 yards. The athlete then turns 180 degrees and finishes the drill with a 15-yard sprint to finish.
- The athlete should accelerate with 100% effort.
- The athlete should maximize the forward lean when initially accelerating from each turn.
- When the athlete turns, he should drop the inside shoulder and reach toward the ground with the same hand.
- The athlete should use a forceful, high knee lift when initially accelerating.
- The athlete should minimize braking distance by quickly dropping the center of gravity.
- The athlete should use short choppy steps to minimize stopping distance.

Increasing Complexity/Difficulty: The coach can indicate which direction the athlete should start in.

Work Interval: Will vary on distance of cones and ability of athlete but should be between five and eight seconds.

Rest Interval: Once mastery of the drill has been reached, the rest interval can be brought down to 2:1 rest to work interval.

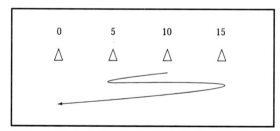

Figure 10-4. Agility Pattern: Drill #4

Agility Pattern: Drill #5

Purpose: Develop lateral acceleration, lateral stopping ability, and body control.

Objectives:

- Simulate movement patterns often seen at linebacker, offensive line, and quarterback, and in blocking of receivers and tight ends.
- Reduce unnecessary body movements.

Description:

- The athlete begins in an athletic stance at the start position of the cones as defined in Figure 10-5. The athlete side shuffles through the cone pattern. Once the athlete completes the initial series of cones, he sprints toward the last cone in the drill.
- The athlete should not cross over the feet during the drill.
- The athlete should maintain a low center of gravity, keeping the knees and hips bent while shuffling.
- The athlete should accelerate with 100% effort.
- The athlete should lower the center of gravity further when transitioning from the shuffle to the forward run.
- The athlete should emphasize a forward lean when accelerating toward the last cone of the drill.

Increasing Complexity/Difficulty:

- The coach can toss a ball to the athlete while he is shuffling.
- The coach can have the athlete run for a thrown ball off the end of the drill.
- The athlete can backpedal instead of running forward after completing the shuffle.
- The athlete can complete the drill by facing the opposite direction.
- The last cone of the drill can be placed further away to increase the running distance.
- Set up an identical series of cones to have athletes race against each other.

Work Interval: Will vary on distance of cones and ability of athlete but should be between 8 and 12 seconds.

Rest Interval: Once mastery of the drill has been reached, the rest interval can be brought down to 2:1 rest to work interval.

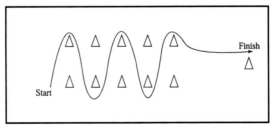

Figure 10-5. Agility Pattern: Drill #5

Agility Pattern: Drill #6

Purpose: Develop lateral acceleration, lateral stopping ability, and body control.

Objectives:

- Simulate movement patterns seen at all positions.
- Reduce unnecessary body movements.
- Train eye-hand-foot coordination.

Description:

- Place two cones two to three yards apart for shuffling.
- Place two cones 6 to 12 yards apart for running.
- The athlete should not cross over the feet during the drill if shuffling.
- The athlete should maintain a low center of gravity, keeping the knees and hips bent while shuffling.
- The athlete should move the feet as quickly as possible while shuffling.
- The athlete should lower the center of gravity as he turns through the cones while running.
- The athlete should drop the inside shoulder and extend the arm toward the ground while turning when running.
- The athlete should emphasize a high knee lift while accelerating off the turn when running.

Increasing Complexity/Difficulty:

- The coach can toss a ball back and forth to the athlete while he is shuffling.
- The coach can have the athlete run for a thrown ball off the end of the drill.
- Two coaches can toss two balls to the athlete.
- The cones can be spread further apart to emphasize stopping mechanics while running.
- The coach can time the drill for completed cycles through the pattern.
- The coach can toss a ball for completed catches if shuffling which will dictate the completion of the drill

Work Interval: Will vary on distance of cones and ability of athlete but should be between 6 and 15 seconds. If the drill is done with shuffling, the coach can toss a ball for completed catches to dictate the completion of the drill.

Rest Interval: Once mastery of the drill has been reached, the rest interval can be brought down to 2:1 rest to work interval.

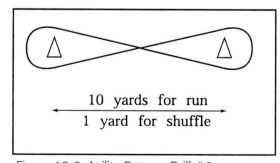

Figure 10-6. Agility Pattern: Drill #6

Agility Pattern: Drill #7

Purpose: Develop acceleration, stopping ability, and body control.

Objectives:

- Simulate movement patterns seen predominately at receiver and defensive back.
- Reduce unnecessary body movements.
- Train eye-hand coordination.

Description:

- Place two cones 10 to 15 yards away from a third cone as depicted in Figure 10-7.
- This drill is performed while running.
- The athlete should start in a position-specific stance.
- The athlete should accelerate and decelerate at 100% effort.
- The athlete should lower the center of gravity while turning through the cones.
- The athlete should drop the inside shoulder and extend the arm toward the ground while turning when running.
- The athlete should emphasize a high knee lift while accelerating off the turn when running.
- If using a ball, the athlete should have the hands in a ready position to catch the ball when turning through the cone.

Increasing Complexity/Difficulty:

- The coach can serve as a starting cone and throw a ball to the athlete after he has completed turning around the other cones. (The ball should be handed back to the coach.)
- Increasing the distance between cones can increase the acceleration and stopping mechanics.
- Pop-up bags can be used instead of cones to limit the athlete's sight of the ball if throwing between coach and athlete.

Work Interval: Will vary on distance of cones and ability of athlete but should be between 10 and 20 seconds. The coach can time the drill for completed cycles through the pattern or the coach can have the athlete complete a prescribed number of catches.

Rest Interval: Once mastery of the drill has been reached, the rest interval can be brought down to 2:1 rest to work interval.

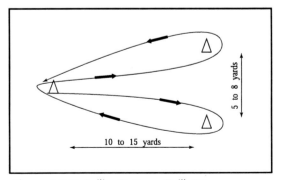

Figure 10-7. Agility Pattern: Drill #7

Agility Pattern: Drill #8

Purpose: Develop athletic stance, hand-eye-foot coordination, reactive ability, and lateral agility.

Objectives:

- Simulate movement patterns seen in all football positions.
- Reduce unnecessary body movements.

Description:

- The essence of this drill is to have the athlete react to the random movements of the football.
- The athlete starts in an athletic stance.
- The coach lightly tosses the football to the ground in the direction of the athlete.
- The athlete reacts to the direction of the ball by shuffling.
- With two hands, the athlete tossed the ball back to the coach.
- The coach redirects the ball in the desired direction.

Increasing Complexity/Difficulty:

- The coach can toss the ball a little harder to get the athlete to react more quickly.
- The coach can toss the ball further away from the athlete to increase the shuffling distance.
- A sprint out to catch the ball can be incorporated at the end of the drill.

Work Interval: The coach can use a determined number of tosses to complete the drill. The coach can also use an approximate time of the drill, ranging from 5 to 15 seconds.

Rest Interval: Once mastery of the drill has been reached, the rest interval can be brought down to a 2:1 rest to work interval.

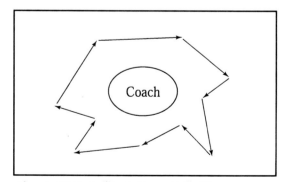

Figure 10-8. Agility Pattern: Drill #8

Agility Pattern: Drill #9

Purpose: Develop acceleration and stopping ability.

Objectives:

- Simulate movement patterns seen predominately at defensive back.
- Reduce unnecessary body movements.

Description:

- The athlete starts on a yard line and accelerates forward at an angle.
- Once a predetermined distance is reached, the athlete backpedals and repeats the cycle in a W-pattern as depicted in Figure 10-9.
- The athlete should accelerate forward as quickly as possible by emphasizing a high knee lift.
- The athlete reduces stopping distance by using short choppy steps to transition from forward running to the backpedal.
- The athlete should transition from the backpedal to the forward direction by slightly opening their hips, using full foot contact on the ground.

Increasing Complexity/Difficulty:

- The coach can throw a ball to the athlete while the athlete transitions from the backward to forward direction. The ball is tossed back to the coach in each backward-to-forward direction change.
- Increasing the distance from 5 to 10 yards can increase the difficulty of the drill by emphasizing acceleration and stopping ability mechanics.

Work Interval: Will vary on distance of lines and ability of athlete but should be between 8 and 12 seconds.

Rest Interval: Once mastery of the drill has been reached, the rest interval can be brought down to a 2:1 rest to work interval.

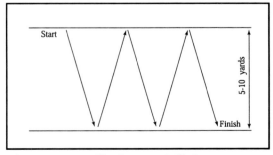

Figure 10-9. Agility Pattern: Drill #9

Agility Pattern: Drill #10

Purpose: Develop movement patterns (quick feet) specific to the offensive line.

Objectives:

- Position the body in a mechanically efficient position.
- Keep the vision focused in front of the athlete.

Description:

- The athlete starts on a yard line and rolls a stability ball behind him while backpedaling.
- The athlete should keep the center of gravity low.
- The athlete should maintain a flat neutral spine.
- The athlete should move the feet as quickly as possible without losing balance and efficiency of movement.

Increasing Complexity/Difficulty:

- The coach can act as a defensive lineman and attempt to run around the athlete in random movement patterns.
- The athlete should learn this drill in a straight line before moving through cones.
- Increasing the distance of the drill can increase the amount of work per repetition.

Work Interval: Will vary on predetermined distance and ability of athlete but should be between 8 and 12 seconds.

Rest Interval: Once mastery of the drill has been reached, the rest interval can be brought down to a 2:1 rest to work interval.

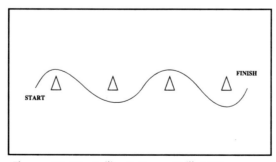

Figure 10-10. Agility Pattern: Drill #10

11

Ice Hockey

Hockey has been referred to as the fastest team game in the world. It is played on a surface that is 200 x 85 feet and presents a number of unique conditioning demands. First, hockey is played on a slippery surface with skating as the mode of locomotion. Speed and agility training on dry land will be difficult to apply to the sport, so speed and agility work will have to be done on the ice. Second, hockey is a high-velocity sport requiring acceleration, deceleration, abrupt starts, and explosive starts. Third, a hockey player may play in 12 to 22 shifts per game, each lasting up to a minute with varying degrees of high and moderate intensity during the shift. During a shift, players will predominately use slow to moderate skating that accelerates rapidly into a short sprint followed by a turn or stop.

Different positions in hockey will have different conditioning demands. Goaltenders perform quick, explosive movements that are short in duration, mixed with periods of rest. Forwards may be on the ice for a third of the game during their high intensity shifts, whereas defensemen may be on the ice for half the game. Defensemen (on average) will skate slower than forwards, experiencing periods of both high intensity efforts and lower intensity activity.

In general, a speed and agility program for ice hockey should target the following:

- Skating skills.

- Speed training on the ice to focus on starting, accelerating, and stopping.

- Conditioning: helps the athlete recover from high intensity shifts and perform for the entire game.

- Agility training and its subcomponents: teach how to change directions to help prevent injuries and develop agility to improve performance on the ice.

Beginning Program

The high school athlete's training will be organized around the following:

- 15- to 20-week general preparation phase

- 10-week special preparation phase

- 4-week precompetition phase

- 12- to 15-week competition phase

- 2-week transition phase following the season

The high school athlete's training should focus on the following:

- Refining skating skills

- Developing conditioning

- Increasing strength and power

- Increasing core conditioning

- Improving speed

- Improving sport-specific agility

General Preparation Phase

During the general preparation phase, the high school athlete should be developing his conditioning base, focusing on dry land speed and agility training, and reinforcing fundamental skating skills. Dry land training is performed to give the athletes variety and to teach starting, stopping, and changing directions. As a guideline, at this level athletes should train two to four times per week. Each session should focus on dynamic flexibility exercises, speed and agility drills, and basic skating technique. Table 11-1 shows the types of drills that a high school hockey player should focus on in the general preparation phase.

Physical Quality	Drills
Physical quality drills	• Speed Fast feet • High knee drills • Butt kicks • Flying sprints
Acceleration	• Standing starts
Agility	• Agility patterns 1-3
Conditioning	• Interval training
Skating skills	• Starting, stopping, gliding forwards and backwards • Side-stepping • Turning from forward/backward skating to backward/forward skating

Table 11-1. Physical qualities to be developed and recommended drills for the high school hockey player during the general preparation phase

Table 11-2 outlines a sample workout for a high school athlete training four times per week during the general preparation phase. Because the sample athlete is a beginner, the focus is on conditioning and fundamental movement skills. Two sessions per week are devoted primarily to conditioning, one is devoted primarily to acceleration, and one is devoted primarily to on-ice training. Agility, speed training, and dynamic flexibility are trained daily. Note that during the on-ice day, dynamic flexibility training is hockey movement-specific. Athletes should be allowed to fully recover for two to three minutes between sprinting technique, agility, and acceleration drills. The emphasis of drills should be on correct execution first and speed second.

Special Preparation Phase

In the special preparation phase, training will be evenly divided between on-ice and off-ice training during the early stages and will progress to mostly on-ice training as the special preparation phase continues. Dry land training will focus mostly on conditioning. On-ice training will emphasize on-ice acceleration, speed, and agility. A major difference between training for hockey and training for other sports is that little carryover exists between dry land speed/agility training and on-ice game performance using skates. As a result, speed and agility training will become increasingly performed on the ice, in skates, for the rest of the training year. The on-ice speed and agility drills that will be employed are described at the end of this chapter. Note that dynamic flexibility exercises will be performed during each training session, whether it is on the ice or on land. Table 11-3 shows the types of drills that a high school hockey player should focus on in the special preparation phase.

Day	Primary Emphasis	Training Component	Drills
Mon.	Conditioning	Warm-up	Dynamic flexibility exercises (10-15 minutes)
		Speed	Fast feet, 1x5 yards High knee walks, 1x20 yards Butt kicks, 1x20 yards Flying 40-yard sprints, 3-5x
		Agility	Agility drill, pattern 3, 3-5x
		Conditioning	8-12 x 30" sprints, rest 90"
Tues.	Acceleration	Warm-up	Dynamic flexibility exercises (10-15 minutes)
		Speed	Fast feet, 3x5 yards High knee skips, 3x20 yards Butt kicks, 3x20 yards
		Acceleration	3-5x20 yards, standing starts
		Agility	Agility drills, patterns 1 & 2, 3x each
Thurs.	Conditioning	Warm-up	Dynamic flexibility exercises (10-15 minutes)
		Speed	Fast feet, 1x5 yards High knee walks, 1x20 yards Butt kicks, 1x20 yards Flying 40-yard sprints, 3-5x
		Agility	Agility drills, patterns 1-3, 3x each
		Conditioning	8-12x1' sprints, rest 3' in between
Fri.	Skating	Warm-up	On-ice dynamic flexibility exercises (10-15 minutes) (See the drill section of this chapter for a description.)
		Skating skills	20-30 minutes, integrate puckhandling, passing, and shooting drills

Table 11-2. Sample general preparation phase workouts for high school hockey players

Physical Quality	Drills
Speed	• Hockey speed drill #1 • Hockey speed drill #2
Acceleration	• Standing starts (dry land) • Hockey acceleration drill #1 (ice) • Hockey acceleration drill #2 (ice)
Agility	• Agility patterns #1-3 (dry land) • Agility patterns #4, 5, 7 (ice)
Conditioning	• Interval training (dry land) • Agility pattern #6 (ice)

Table 11-3. Physical qualities to be developed and recommended drills for the high school hockey player during the special preparation phase

Optimally, a hockey athlete should train three to four days per week in the special preparation phase. Towards the beginning of the phase, half of the training should be on dry land and half on ice. As the phase progresses, the ratio of dry land to on-ice sessions should change until no more than one session per week is performed on dry land.

Table 11-4 presents a sample workout from the later part of the special preparation phase, with only one of the four training sessions being performed on dry land. Workouts emphasize either acceleration or conditioning. Speed, agility, and dynamic flexibility are trained daily. Workouts should emphasize a 1:3 work:recovery ratio. Note that as the phase progresses, speed and agility training should be done with the puck to help emphasize sports specificity.

Day	Primary Emphasis	Training Component	Drills
Mon.	Acceleration (on-ice training)	Warm-up	On-ice dynamic flexibility exercises (10-15 minutes)
		Acceleration	Hockey acceleration drill #1, 10-15x
		Speed	Hockey speed drill #1, 6-10x1', 3' rest
		Agility	Agility pattern, drill #4, 6-10x, 1:3 work:recovery, with and without puck
Tues.	Conditioning (dry land training)	Warm-up	Dry land dynamic flexibility exercises (10-15 minutes)
		Agility	Agility pattern, drills #1-3, 3-5x each
		Conditioning	12-15x 1' sprints, 3' recovery
Thurs.	Acceleration (on-ice training)	Warm-up	On-ice dynamic flexibility exercises (10-15 minutes)
		Acceleration	Hockey acceleration drill #2, 12-15x
		Speed	Hockey speed drill #2, 6-10x
		Agility	Agility pattern, drill #5, 6-10x 1', 3' recovery
Fri.	Conditioning (on-ice training)	Warm-up	On-ice dynamic flexibility exercises (10-15 minutes)
		Agility	Agility pattern, drill #7, 6-10x
		Speed	Hockey speed drill #1, 3-5x1', 3' recovery
		Conditioning	Agility pattern, drill #6, 12-15x, 1:3 work: recovery, with and without puck

Table 11-4. Sample special preparation phase workouts for high school hockey players

Precompetition Phase

Beginning with the precompetition phase, training is scaled back to allow the hockey player to focus more on game situations, scrimmages, and preparing for games. Most training should take place on the ice in the precompetition phase, although some dry land training may be introduced for variety.

Sessions should focus primarily on acceleration, agility, and conditioning, with some speed work. Agility drills should be performed with the puck to help with transfer of the training to the sport. Table 11-5 describes the qualities to be developed and the exercises that will be used to develop them in the precompetition phase.

Physical Quality	Drills
Speed	• Hockey speed drill #1 • Hockey speed drill #2
Acceleration	• Hockey acceleration drill #1 (ice) • Hockey acceleration drill #2 (ice)
Agility	• Agility patterns #5, 7, 9-13
Conditioning	• Agility pattern #6 (ice)

Table 11-5. Physical qualities to be developed and recommended drills for the high school hockey player during the precompetition phase

Table 11-6 presents a sample week from the precompetition phase. Training has been scaled back to three times per week. Each session focuses on agility, acceleration or speed, conditioning, and dynamic flexibility exercises. Whenever possible, the puck should be integrated into the agility drills.

Competition Phase

In the competition phase, training is scaled back and focuses on maintaining conditioning and working on essential skills. Whenever possible, drills should attempt to train more than one quality to maximize the use of the athlete's training time (for example, agility pattern drill #6 trains conditioning, acceleration, and stopping). Between games and sport practices, athletes may become overtrained and injured if training is not scaled back in this phase. Table 11-7 describes the qualities to be developed in this phase of training and the exercises that will be used to develop those qualities.

Day	Primary Emphasis	Training Component	Drills
Mon.	N/A	Warm-up	On-ice dynamic flexibility exercises (10-15 minutes)
		Acceleration	Hockey acceleration drill #1, 8-12x 1', 3' recovery
		Agility	Agility pattern, drills #5, 9, 10, 13, 3-5x with and without puck
		Conditioning	Agility pattern, drill #6, 12-15x, without puck
Wed.	N/A	Warm-up	On-ice dynamic flexibility exercises (10-15 minutes)
		Speed	Hockey speed drill #1, 6-10x1', 3' recovery
		Agility	Agility pattern, drills #9, 11, 12, 3-5x with and without puck
		Conditioning	Agility pattern, drill #6, 8-12x with puck
Fri.	N/A	Warm-up	On-ice dynamic flexibility exercises (10-15 minutes)
		Acceleration	Hockey acceleration drill #2, 12-15x
		Agility	Agility pattern, drills #8, 9, 10, 13, 6-10x
		Conditioning	Agility pattern, drill #6, 6-10x with puck

Table 11-6. Sample precompetition phase workouts for high school hockey players

Physical Quality	Drills
Speed	• Hockey speed drill #1 • Hockey speed drill #2
Acceleration	• Agility patterns #6, 7, 11, 12, 13
Agility	• Agility patterns #5, 7-13
Conditioning	• Agility pattern #6 (ice)

Table 11-7. Physical qualities to be developed and recommended drills for the high school hockey player during the competition phase

Table 11-8 presents a sample week of workouts from the competition phase. Note that training has been scaled back to two sessions per week. Each session focuses on dynamic flexibility and speed, and then uses agility patterns that develop acceleration, agility, and conditioning. Wherever possible, the puck should be integrated into agility drills to assist with their transfer to the sport.

Day	Primary Emphasis	Training Component	Drills
Day One	N/A	Warm-up	On-ice dynamic flexibility exercises (10-15 minutes)
		Speed	Hockey speed drill #1, 6-10x1', 3' recovery, with puck
		Acceleration/agility	Agility pattern, drills #7, 11, 6-10x
		Agility	Agility pattern, drill #5, 6-10x, with puck
		Acceleration / conditioning	Agility pattern, drill #6, 12-15x, without puck
Day Two	N/A	Warm-up	On-ice dynamic flexibility exercises (10-15 minutes)
		Speed	Hockey speed drill #2, 6-10x
		Acceleration/agility	Agility pattern, drills #12, 13, 6-10x
		Agility	Agility pattern, drill #8, 6-10x, with puck
		Acceleration/ conditioning	Agility pattern, drill #6, 8-12x with puck

Table 11-8. Sample competition phase workouts for high school hockey players

The high school hockey player must develop a fitness and movement/skating skill base. As a result, the major focus behind the high school athlete's training is on fundamentals. While all these qualities are important at the college level and beyond, sports specificity takes on more importance as the game becomes faster and more complex. The next part of this chapter will cover conditioning for college and beyond.

Advanced Program

The collegiate athlete's training will be organized around the following:

- 12- to 18-week general preparation phase

- 8- to 14-week special preparation phase

- 4-week precompetition phase

- 20- to 24-week competition phase
- 2-week transition phase following the season

The collegiate athlete's training should focus on the following:

- Hockey-specific conditioning
- Improving acceleration
- Improving speed
- Improving hockey-specific agility

Unlike high school training, at the college level only part of the year should focus on fundamentals, while the rest of the year should focus on more sport-specific drills. After a fitness and technique base has been established, the collegiate athlete's program should be faster and feature more complex drills than the high school athlete's. In addition, collegiate hockey players will perform the bulk of their conditioning, speed, and agility training on the ice, even from the start of training.

General Preparation Phase

A collegiate athlete should train two to four times per week during the general preparation phase. The focus of training should be on developing a conditioning base, developing the ability to start and stop suddenly on the ice, improving skating speed, and working on agility on the ice. In this phase, half of the training sessions should be on dry land, focusing mostly on conditioning. The other half of the sessions should be on ice, focusing on speed, agility, acceleration, etc. Table 11-9 details the qualities that should be developed during this phase and the exercises that will be used.

Coaches should keep in mind that athletes may be unsupervised during part of this phase of training (i.e., during the summer). This fact should dictate when new drills are introduced (i.e., refrain from introducing drills during periods that athletes are unsupervised).

Table 11-10 presents a sample week of workouts from the general preparation phase of training. In these workouts, two sessions are dry land and focus primarily on conditioning, and two sessions are on ice. One of the on-ice sessions focuses on acceleration and one focuses on speed. Agility and dynamic flexibility are trained daily.

Special Preparation Phase

As the special preparation phase begins, some dry land training will still be conducted (one session out of every three or four); however, the amount of dry land training will decrease and then disappear as this phase of training progresses.

Physical Quality	Drills
Speed	• Hockey speed drill #1 • Hockey speed drill #2
Acceleration	• Hockey acceleration drill #1 • Hockey acceleration drill #2
Agility	• Agility patterns 1-5, 7
Conditioning	• Interval training

Table 11-9. Physical qualities to be developed and recommended drills for the collegiate hockey player during the general preparation phase

Day	Primary Emphasis	Training Component	Drills
Mon.	Conditioning (dry land)	Warm-up	Dynamic flexibility exercises (10-15 minutes)
		Agility	Agility pattern, drills #1-3, 6-10x
		Conditioning	Interval training, sprint 10-15x1', 3' recovery
Tues.	Speed (on ice)	Warm-up	Dynamic flexibility exercises (on ice, 10-15 minutes)
		Speed	Hockey speed drill #1, 6-10x30", 90" recovery Hockey speed drill #2, 3x3
		Agility	Agility pattern, drills #4 & 5, 3-5x each
Thurs.	Conditioning (dry land)	Warm-up	Dynamic flexibility exercises (10-15 minutes)
		Agility	Agility pattern, drills #1-3, 6-10x
		Conditioning	Interval training, sprint 12-18x30", 90" recovery
Fri.	Acceleration (on ice)	Warm-up	Dynamic flexibility exercises (on ice, 10-15 minutes)
		Acceleration	Hockey acceleration drill #1, 6-10x Hockey acceleration drill #2, 3-5x
		Agility	Agility pattern, drills #5 & 7, 3-5x each

Table 11-10. Sample general preparation phase workouts for collegiate hockey players

Speed and acceleration training should take place on the ice. Acceleration training should incorporate more drills that require more of the athlete (i.e., reaction time, starting, stopping, etc.). Agility training should also take place primarily on the ice and should incorporate use of the puck and interaction with other players whenever possible.

Athletes will be supervised in their workouts during much of this phase, so more complicated drills may be incorporated. Ideally, athletes should train three to four times per week during this phase. Table 11-11 presents a summary of the physical qualities to be developed and exercises that could be used in this phase of training.

Physical Quality	Drills
Speed	• Hockey speed drill #1 • Hockey speed drill #2
Acceleration	• Hockey acceleration drills #1-4
Agility	• Agility patterns #1-5, 7-9
Conditioning	• Interval training (dry land) • Agility pattern #6 (on ice)

Table 11-11. Physical qualities to be developed and recommended drills for the collegiate hockey player during the special preparation phase

Day	Primary Emphasis	Training Component	Drills
Mon.	Acceleration	Warm-up	Dynamic flexibility exercises (on ice, 10-15 minutes)
		Acceleration	Hockey acceleration drills #1-2, 6-10x each
		Agility	Agility patterns, drills #3 (on ice) & 4, 6-10x each, with the puck
Tues.	Conditioning	Warm-up	Dynamic flexibility exercises (on ice, 10-15 minutes)
		Agility	Agility patterns, drills #5, 7, 8, 3-5x each, without the puck
		Conditioning	Agility pattern, drill #6, 8-12x
Thurs.	Acceleration	Warm-up	Dynamic flexibility exercises (on ice, 10-15 minutes)
		Acceleration	Hockey acceleration drills #3 & 4, 6-10x each
		Agility	Agility patterns, drills #3 (on ice) & 9, 6-10x each, with the puck
Fri.	Speed	Warm-up	Dynamic flexibility exercises (on ice, 10-15 minutes)
		Speed	Hockey speed drills #1 & 2, 6-10x each
		Agility	Agility patterns, drills #5, 7, 8, 3-5x each, with the puck

Table 11-12. Sample special preparation phase workouts for collegiate hockey players

Table 11-12 shows a sample week of special preparation workouts. Note that these take place late in the special prep phase and no dry land training is taking place. Agility and dynamic flexibility are trained on a daily basis. One day is devoted to speed training, one to conditioning, and two to acceleration. The focus of training is switching from foundational qualities (i.e., conditioning and basic skills) to a focus on maintaining/using the conditioning that was developed earlier and refining the ability to skate fast and change directions.

Precompetition Phase

During the precompetition phase, exhibition games have begun and more focus is being placed on team practices and game preparation. With regards to speed and agility training, this phase offers the final chance to peak the athletes for the upcoming competitive season. Because the intensity and complexity of the drills will be increased, training should be scaled back to two to three times per week. Training should take place on the ice and, whenever possible, should incorporate the puck and interaction with other players. Table 11-13 shows what qualities should be focused on and what exercises could be used to develop those qualities.

Physical Quality	Drills
Speed	• Hockey speed drill #1 • Hockey speed drill #2
Acceleration	• Hockey acceleration drills #1-6
Agility	• Agility patterns #1-5, 7-13
Conditioning	• Agility pattern #6

Table 11-13. Physical qualities to be developed and recommended drills for the collegiate hockey player during the precompetition phase

Table 11-14 shows a sample week of workouts from the precompetition phase. During this week, training has been reduced to three times per week. One session is oriented primarily towards acceleration, one to speed, and one to conditioning. Acceleration drills include resisted skating to help improve the athlete's explosiveness. Note that agility, dynamic flexibility, and acceleration are trained in every session. All workouts take place on ice.

Competition Phase

Unlike other collegiate sports, hockey has a long competitive season. It may last as long as six months for teams that make the NCAA finals. Therefore speed and agility training must be approached somewhat differently than with other sports. The length of the competitive season means that it will not be enough simply to maintain speed, acceleration, and agility—these qualities will have to be enhanced during training.

Day	Primary Emphasis	Training Component	Drills
Mon.	Acceleration	Warm-up	Dynamic flexibility exercises (on ice, 10-15 minutes)
		Acceleration	Hockey acceleration drills #1, 6, 2x4-5 each
		Agility	Agility patterns, drills #7, 8, 11, 6-10x each
Wed.	Conditioning	Warm-up	Dynamic flexibility exercises (on ice, 10-15 minutes)
		Acceleration	Hockey acceleration drills #2 & 4, 3-5x each
		Agility	Agility pattern, drills #5, 10, 12, with puck
		Conditioning	Agility pattern, drill #6, 15-20x
Fri.	Speed	Warm-up	Dynamic flexibility exercises (on ice, 10-15 minutes)
		Acceleration	Hockey acceleration drills # 3 & 5, 3-5x each
		Speed	Hockey speed drills, #1 & 2, 2x4-5 each
		Agility	Agility pattern, drills #4, 9, 13, 6-10x each, with puck

Table 11-14. Sample precompetition phase workouts for collegiate hockey players

A coach must carefully lay out training and periodize it (i.e., know when to back off with the training). A collegiate hockey player should train two to three times per week, depending upon the schedule. Training sessions should focus on enhancing speed, acceleration, and agility. Whenever possible, drills should be included that develop multiple qualities to help maximize the athlete's training time. Table 11-15 presents those physical qualities that should be developed and the drills that may be used to develop them.

Physical Quality	Drills
Speed/Agility	• Agility pattern, drill #3 (on ice) • Hockey speed drills #1 & 2
Acceleration/Agility	• Hockey acceleration drills #1-6 • Agility pattern, drills #4, 6, 7, 13
Agility	• Agility patterns #1-5, 7-13
Conditioning/Acceleration	• Agility pattern #6

Table 11-15. Physical qualities to be developed and recommended drills for the collegiate hockey player during the competition phase

Table 11-16 shows a sample week of workouts during the competition phase. Note that the athlete is training twice during this week. The first day focuses primarily on acceleration, agility, and conditioning. The second day focuses primarily on speed and agility. The second day has the lower volume of training because it will be closest to competitions. Whenever possible, drills are included that work on multiple qualities. All workouts take place on ice.

Day	Primary Emphasis	Training Component	Drills
Day One	Acceleration/Agility/Conditioning	Warm-up	Dynamic flexibility exercises (on ice, 10-15 minutes)
		Acceleration	Hockey acceleration drill #5, 3x3-5
		Acceleration/Agility	Agility pattern, drills #7 & 13, 6-10x each, with puck
		Acceleration/Conditioning	Agility pattern, drill #6, 10-15x
Day Two	Speed/Agility	Warm-up	Dynamic flexibility exercises (on ice, 10-15 minutes)
		Speed	Hockey speed drill #2, 3x3-5
		Speed/Agility	Agility pattern, drill #3 (ice), 2x6

Table 11-16. Sample competition phase workouts for collegiate hockey players

The remainder of this chapter will describe many of the drills that are unique to hockey speed and agility training. These drills will include on-ice dynamic flexibility drills, ice acceleration drills, ice speed drills, and both dry land and ice agility drills.

Drills

❏ Dynamic Flexibility Exercises

The following dynamic flexibility exercises may be performed on the ice. This list is by no means comprehensive, but it should be sufficient to get the strength and conditioning coach started. On-ice dynamic flexibility exercises will be used during on-ice workouts.

Groin Lunges

Purpose: To loosen the groin and develop balance and a long stride.

Start: Skate around the rink at a slow pace.

Action: While skating, squat down so that the weight is on one foot while the other foot drags along behind. The player should try to force the crotch towards the ice while in the lunge. Keeping the body close to the ice, push off the back leg and take a long stride forward. The leg that was in front will now be in the rear. Repeat with that leg in back.

Finish: This drill is completed after the desired number of repetitions has been performed.

Side Lunges

Purpose: To loosen the groin and develop balance.

Start: Skate around the rink at a slow pace.

Action: Spread the legs as far as possible, maintaining the forward pace. Flex the right knee and hip, placing the weight on the right leg. Hold this position for a few seconds, then switch sides. Stand up, take a few strides, and repeat.

Finish: This drill is completed after the desired number of repetitions has been performed.

Kick the Fence

Purpose: To loosen the hip joint and the muscles that act on it; to develop balance and ankle strength; and to enhance the ability to skate on one skate.

Start: Hold the hockey stick at shoulder height.

Action: Kick at the stick with a straight leg (i.e., from the hip). Repeat, then switch sides.

Finish: This drill is completed after the desired number of repetitions has been performed.

Leg Swings

Purpose: To loosen the hip joint and the muscles that act on it; to develop balance and agility; to enhance the ability to skate on one skate.

Start: Skate at a slow pace, then coast on one skate.

Action: Swing the free leg forward from the hip as far as possible, trying to kick higher than the waist, then (continuing the swing) swing it behind as far as possible. Repeat, then switch legs.

Finish: This drill is completed after the desired number of repetitions has been performed.

Strict Skates

Purpose: To loosen the muscles in the lower legs and strengthen the ankles.

Start: Feet should be placed shoulder-width apart.

Action: Keeping the skates on the ice at all times, skate forward by transferring body weight from one side to the other, while at the same time pushing off the inside edge of the skate blade.

Finish: This drill is completed after the desired amount of time has elapsed.

Twisters

Purpose: To loosen the muscles of the back and lower body.

Start: Feet should be placed shoulder-width apart. The hockey stick should be placed across the athlete's back, with the elbows hooked over the stick. The athlete should flex the trunk so that the upper body is parallel to the floor.

Action: The athlete will skate as described in the strict skates drill. As the athlete pushes off the inside edge of the skate blade, the athlete will rotate the upper body so that the end of the stick is facing the direction he is skating.

Finish: This drill is completed after the desired amount of time has elapsed.

Toe Touches

Purpose: To loosen the muscles of the hamstrings and lower back.

Start: Start skating, then coast. Hold the hockey stick overhead.

Action: Bend forward and touch the stick to the toes of the skate. Try to keep the arms and legs mostly straight (slight bend at the knees).

Finish: This drill is completed after the desired number of repetitions has been performed.

Skating High Knee Pulls

Purpose: To loosen the hamstrings and develop balance.

Start: Start skating, then coast.

Action: Pull the knee to the chest and hold it for a few seconds. Switch sides.

Finish: This drill is completed after the desired number of repetitions has been performed.

❑ Acceleration Drills

The following acceleration drills may be performed on the ice. They are important because a hockey player must learn to start, stop, and increase his speed on the ice in skates.

Acceleration Drill #1

Purpose: To develop acceleration and stopping ability.

Start: Athletes line up on the length of the rink against the boards, facing the other side.

Action: On command, athletes skate as fast as possible across the width of the hockey rink, stopping at the opposite side. They will then turn and skate back as fast as possible. They should then prepare for the next repetition.

Finish: This drill is completed after the desired number of repetitions has been performed.

Acceleration Drill #2

Purpose: To develop acceleration.

Start: Players should line up on the blue line with their skates on the line.

Action: On command, players should skate as fast as possible to the center line, then coast to the blue line, stop, and turn around, getting ready for the next repetition.

Finish: This drill is completed after the desired number of repetitions has been performed.

Acceleration Drill #3

Purpose: To develop acceleration and speed, and to improve reaction time.

Start: Players should skate around the rink at a slow pace.

Action: On command, players will change their pace and skate at a full sprint. Players should sprint until they hear the next command, at which time they should return to a slow pace.

Finish: This drill is completed after the desired number of repetitions has been performed.

Acceleration Drill #4

Purpose: To develop acceleration and stopping ability, and to enhance reaction time.

Start: Players skate around the rink at a slow pace.

Action: On command, athletes come to a stop. On the next command, they skate as hard as possible in the same direction. On the next command, they stop.

Finish: This drill is completed after the desired number of repetitions has been performed.

Acceleration Drill #5

Purpose: To provide resistance to acceleration.

Start: Two athletes line up, one behind the other. Each athlete holds the end of the other's stick.

Action: The front athlete should pull his partner around the rink, trying to move as quickly as possible. The rear athlete should not offer resistance, but should allow himself to be pulled. The athletes should switch places after a full lap has been completed.

Finish: This drill is completed after the desired number of repetitions has been performed.

Acceleration Drill #6

Purpose: To provide resistance to acceleration.

Start: Two athletes line up one behind the other, with the front athlete on the blue line. The rear athlete places his hands on the front athlete's hips.

Action: The rear athlete should push the front athlete to the opposing blue line as fast as possible. Players should then switch positions.

Finish: This drill is completed after the desired number of repetitions has been performed.

❏ Speed Drills

The following on-ice drills are designed to help enhance an athlete's top-end speed. These drills are critical because dry land drills will not have the same transfer to skating on ice, since dry land sprinting mechanics (i.e., lifting the knees, driving the leg towards the ground from the hip, landing on the ball of the foot) are irrelevant to hockey players.

Speed Drill #1

Purpose: To develop maximum speed and acceleration.

Start: Athletes should skate slowly around the rink.

Action: When the athlete crosses the blue line, he should skate as fast as possible to the opposite blue line. After crossing the second blue line, he should coast behind the net to the next blue line, at which point the drill repeats.

Finish: The drill is complete when the desired amount of time has elapsed.

Speed Drill #2

Purpose: To develop the ability to skate at different speeds and to change gears.

Start: Athletes should begin the drill with a slow skate.

Action: On the first signal, athletes should skate at half-speed. At the second signal, they should progress to three-quarters speed. At the third signal, they should skate at full speed. At the fourth signal, they should rest by coasting.

Finish: The drill is completed when the desired number of repetitions has been completed.

Agility Drills

The following agility drills may be performed for hockey. The first three are dry land drills (although drill #3 may also be performed on the ice, and is used in the collegiate program). Drills #4-13 are on-ice drills. The puck may be incorporated into any of the on-ice drills to make the exercises more complicated and more sport-specific.

Agility Pattern: Drill #1

Purpose: Develop acceleration and stopping ability.

Objectives:

- Maintain body control.
- Develop specific rate of force production.
- Lower center of gravity when decelerating.

Description:

- The athlete starts at one end and runs forward to each cone in the series.
- The athlete should concentrate on running in straight lines.
- The athlete should make "tight" corners.
- The athlete should keep the elbows relatively close to the body.
- The athlete should drop the center of gravity while decelerating.
- The athlete should use short choppy steps to decelerate quickly.
- The athlete should maintain a neutral spine at all times.

Increasing Complexity/Difficulty: Use two identical patterns of cones and have athletes race each other through the drill.

Work Interval: Will vary on distance of cones and ability of athlete but should be between 8 and 12 seconds.

Rest Interval: Once mastery of the drill has been reached, the rest interval can be brought down to 3:1 rest to work interval.

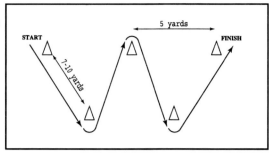

Figure 11-1. Agility Pattern: Drill #1

Agility Pattern: Drill #2

Purpose: Develop acceleration and stopping ability.

Objective: Reduce unnecessary body movements.

Description:

- The athlete starts on a yard line and accelerates forward at an angle.
- Once a predetermined distance is reached, the athlete backpedals and repeats the cycle in a W-pattern, as depicted in Figure 11-2.
- The athlete should accelerate forward as quickly as possible by emphasizing a high knee lift.
- The athlete reduces stopping distance by using short choppy steps to transition from forward running to the backpedal.
- The athlete should transition from the backpedal to the forward direction by slightly opening the hips, using full foot contact on the ground.

Increasing Complexity/Difficulty: Increasing the distance from 5 to 10 yards can increase the difficulty of the drill by emphasizing acceleration and stopping ability mechanics.

Work Interval: Will vary on distance of lines and ability of athlete but should be between 8 and 12 seconds.

Rest Interval: Once mastery of the drill has been reached, the rest interval can be brought down to a 3:1 rest to work interval.

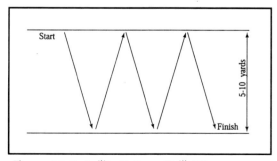

Figure 11-2. Agility Pattern: Drill #2

Agility Pattern: Drill #3

Purpose: Develop lateral acceleration, lateral stopping ability, and body control.

Objectives:

- Simulate movement patterns seen at all positions.
- Reduce unnecessary body movements.
- Train eye-hand-foot coordination.

Description:

- Place two cones 6 to 12 yards apart.
- The athlete should lower the center of gravity while turning through the cones when running.
- The athlete should drop the inside shoulder and extend the arm toward the ground while turning when running.
- The athlete should emphasize a high knee lift while accelerating off the turn when running.

Increasing Complexity/Difficulty:

- The cones can be spread further apart to emphasize stopping mechanics while running.
- The coach can time the drill for completed cycles through the pattern.

Work Interval: Will vary on distance of cones and ability of athlete but should be between 6 and 15 seconds.

Rest Interval: Once mastery of the drill has been reached, the rest interval can be brought down to 3:1 rest to work interval.

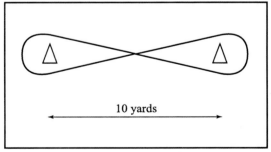

Figure 11-3. Agility Pattern: Drill #3

Agility Pattern: Drill #4

Purpose: Develop skating skill and improve conditioning.

Objectives:

- Simulate movement patterns seen at all positions.
- Reduce unnecessary body movements.
- Train eye-hand-foot coordination.

Description:

- Set up a square on the ice, with the cones 40 to 50 feet apart.
- The athlete should skate a predetermined circuit as fast as possible.
- Athletes should turn in both directions, not just to their "favorite" side.

Increasing Complexity/Difficulty:

- The cones can be brought closer together.
- The coach can time the drill for completed cycles through the pattern.
- The drill may be performed with the puck.
- Athletes may perform the drill while skating backwards.
- The drill may be set up to emphasize specific skating/handling weaknesses.

Work Interval: Will vary on distance of cones and ability of athlete but should be between 6 and 15 seconds. For conditioning, athletes may skate the square as fast as possible for 90 to 120 seconds, then rest for three to four minutes and repeat. Note that this variation will focus on conditioning more and agility less.

Rest Interval: Once mastery of the drill has been reached, the rest interval can be brought down to 3:1 rest to work interval. For conditioning, athletes may rest for three to four minutes between sessions.

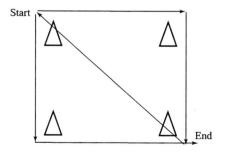

Figure 11-4. Agility Pattern: Drill #4

Agility Pattern: Drill #5

Purpose: Develop agility and balance.

Objectives:

- Develop skating control.
- Develop ability to skate backwards.

Description:

- Place two to three athletes on the circles.
- Athletes should skate backwards.
- On the coach's signal, players should turn around and continue skating backwards.
- Athletes should stay within the circle lines throughout the entire drill.

Increasing Complexity/Difficulty:

- Increase the speed with which the athletes perform the drill.
- Perform the drill for longer periods of time.
- Have the athlete execute the turns more frequently.
- Perform the drill with the puck.

Work Interval: Generally one minute, though this may be varied with the athlete's level of ability.

Rest Interval: Once mastery of the drill has been reached, the rest interval can be brought down to 3:1 rest to work interval.

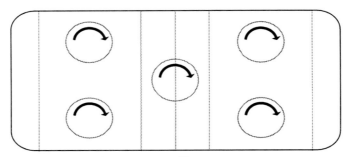

Figure 11-5. Agility Pattern: Drill #5

Agility Pattern: Drill #6

Purpose: Develop acceleration, stopping ability, body control, and conditioning.

Objectives:

- Simulate starting and stopping patterns seen at all positions.
- Enhance turning abilities.
- Reduce unnecessary body movements.
- Develop conditioning.

Description:

- Line players up on goal line.
- On command, have players sprint to the blue line, stop, then sprint back to the goal line. From there, sprint to center ice, stop, then sprint back to the goal line. Sprint to the far blue line, stop, sprint back to the goal line. Sprint to far red line, stop, sprint back to the goal line.
- Athlete should stop right on the line and turn each time he changes direction.
- Drill must be performed with maximum speed and precision.

Increasing Complexity/Difficulty:

- Perform additional repetitions.
- Perform with the puck.
- Perform following a zigzag course around pylons.

Work Interval: Will vary with the complexity of the course and the ability of the athlete, but should be between 20 and 40 seconds.

Rest Interval: Once mastery of the drill has been reached, the rest interval can be brought down to 3:1 rest to work interval.

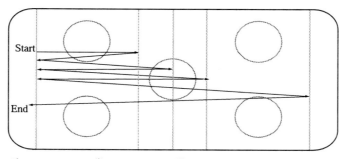

Figure 11-6. Agility Pattern: Drill #6

Agility Pattern: Drill #7

Purpose: Develop acceleration, stopping ability, and ability to change directions.

Objectives:

- Simulate movement patterns seen at all positions.
- Reduce unnecessary body movements.
- Develop players' reaction time.

Description:

- Athletes skate around the rink.
- On the whistle, they stop, then skate in the opposite direction as hard as possible.
- On the next whistle, they stop, then skate in the opposite direction as hard as possible.
- Continue this process until the drill is over.

Increasing Complexity/Difficulty:

- Blow the whistle closer together or further apart.
- Perform the drill for longer periods of time.
- Perform the drill with the puck.

Work Interval: Will vary on distance of cones and ability of athlete but should be between 20 and 40 seconds.

Rest Interval: Once mastery of the drill has been reached, the rest interval can be brought down to 3:1 rest to work interval.

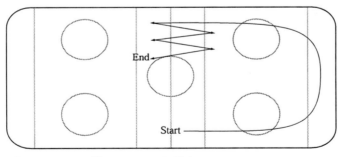

Figure 11-7. Agility Pattern: Drill #7

Agility Pattern: Drill #8

Purpose: Develop skating ability and puckhandling, and simulate offensive play.

Objectives:

- Simulate movement patterns seen at all positions.
- Reduce unnecessary body movements.
- Train eye-hand-foot coordination.

Description:

- Handling the puck, players begin on the goal line.
- Players skate as fast as possible to the far side of the nearest circle, then skate around the circle (staying on the circle) while handling the puck.
- After skating around the circle, players skate as fast as possible to the next circle and skate around that circle, keeping control of the puck the whole time.

Increasing Complexity/Difficulty:

- Time the drill and have players attempt to beat previous best times.
- Have players skate against defenders (i.e., complete the drill quickly, with the puck, while another player tries to take it away).
- Have two players perform the drill at the same time and make it a competition.

Work Interval: Will vary depending upon level of ability, but should take between 20 and 40 seconds.

Rest Interval: Once mastery of the drill has been reached, the rest interval can be brought down to 3:1 rest to work interval.

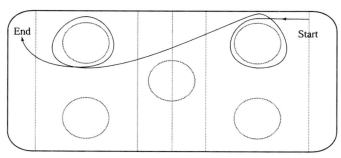

Figure 11-8. Agility Pattern: Drill #8

Agility Pattern: Drill #9

Purpose: Develop high speed cornering and body posture.

Objectives:

- Simulate movement patterns seen at all positions.
- Develop different types of turns.
- Enhance balance and agility.

Description:

- Stagger an uneven number of cones on one side of the rink.
- Athletes should skate a full circle around each cone, starting from the far side of the cone.
- The coach should designate the type of turn to do around each cone.

Increasing Complexity/Difficulty: The drill may be performed with the puck, emphasizing how to protect it during turns.

Work Interval: Will vary on distance of cones and ability of athlete but should be between 20 and 40 seconds.

Rest Interval: Once mastery of the drill has been reached, the rest interval can be brought down to 3:1 rest to work interval.

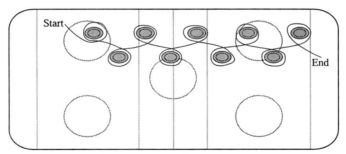

Figure 11-9. Agility Pattern: Drill #9

Agility Pattern: Drill #10

Purpose: Develop agility while reacting to an opponent.

Objectives:

- Simulate movement patterns seen at all positions.

- Reduce unnecessary body movements.
- Train eye-hand-foot coordination.

Description:

- Athletes line up facing each other.
- At the coach's signal, one player begins moving laterally from one side to the other while the other player tries to keep up with him.
- The drill continues until the coach signals, at which time the players change roles.

Increasing Complexity/Difficulty:

- The drill may be performed for longer periods of time.
- The drill may be performed with the puck.

Work Interval: Will vary on distance of cones and ability of athlete but should be between 6 and 15 seconds.

Rest Interval: Once mastery of the drill has been reached, the rest interval can be brought down to 3:1 rest to work interval.

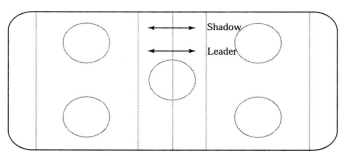

Figure 11-10. Agility Pattern: Drill #10

Agility Pattern: Drill #11

Purpose: Develop reaction time and agility.

Objectives:

- Simulate movement patterns seen at all positions.
- Reduce unnecessary body movements.
- Train eye-hand-foot coordination.

Description:

- Athletes line up on the goal line, facing the coach.
- At the coach's hand signal, players perform one of the following movements:

- Chopping to the right (i.e., crossover steps to the right)
- Chopping to the left
- Skating backward
- Skating forward
- Falling to the knees
- Each skill should be practiced at least twice during each session.

Increasing Complexity/Difficulty:

- The coach can vary the times between hand signals.
- The coach should randomly signal motions so that the athletes must react to the signal and not the pattern.
- Perform the drill with the puck.

Work Interval: Will vary on distance of cones and ability of athlete but should be between 20 and 40 seconds.

Rest Interval: Once mastery of the drill has been reached, the rest interval can be brought down to 3:1 rest to work interval.

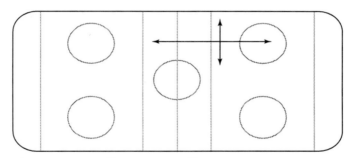

Figure 11-11. Agility Pattern: Drill #11

Agility Pattern: Drill #12

Purpose: Develop acceleration, stopping ability, and ability to turn.

Objectives:

- Simulate movement patterns seen at all positions.
- Reduce unnecessary body movements.
- Train eye-hand-foot coordination.

Description:

- Athlete should skate forward as fast as possible to center ice.
- Upon reaching center ice, the player should turn and skate backwards as fast as possible to the blue line.
- Upon reaching the blue line, the player should turn, cut, and skate towards the corner.

Increasing Complexity/Difficulty:

- Drill may be timed.
- Drill may be performed with the puck.
- Drill may be performed in a manner that forces the player to react to the coach's commands (i.e., instead of skating forward to center ice, skate forward until the coach signals, and then skate backwards).

Work Interval: Will vary on distance of cones and ability of athlete but should be between 6 and 15 seconds.

Rest Interval: Once mastery of the drill has been reached, the rest interval can be brought down to 3:1 rest to work interval.

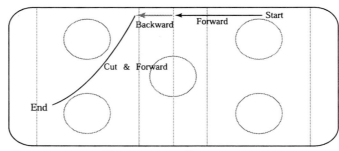

Figure 11-12. Agility Pattern: Drill #12

Agility Pattern: Drill #13

Purpose: Develop acceleration, body control, puckhandling, passing, and shooting.

Objectives:

- Simulate movement patterns seen at all positions.
- Reduce unnecessary body movements.
- Train eye-hand-foot coordination.

Description:

- Place several cones in a line in between the circles.
- Two players should skate next to each other, passing the puck back and forth between the pylons.
- At the last pylon, athletes should break for the goal.

Increasing Complexity/Difficulty:

- Increase the number of cones.
- Place the cones at irregular distances.

- Perform the drill skating backwards.
- Perform the drill against defenders.

Work Interval: Will vary on distance of cones and ability of athlete but should be between 20 and 40 seconds.

Rest Interval: Once mastery of the drill has been reached, the rest interval can be brought down to 3:1 rest to work interval.

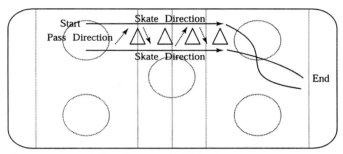

Figure 11-13. Agility Pattern: Drill #13

Hockey presents a number of unique challenges to the strength and conditioning professional. Because it is played on ice, in skates, dry land drills and techniques may not have much carryover to the sport. Therefore many of the drills must be performed on ice. Because hockey is a game of fast starts and sudden stops performed over extended periods of time, acceleration, agility, and conditioning will be critically important to develop.

12

Rugby

Many movements in rugby are observed at all the positions. Some of the common movements are accelerating forward, lateral shuffling, decelerating in all directions, and moving backwards with varying techniques. These movements are reflected in the sample programs in this chapter.

A speed and agility program for rugby should target the following:

- Sprinting technique: helps with speed and helps prevent injuries.

- Anaerobic conditioning: helps the athlete recover from high intensity sprints and helps them perform for the entire game.

- Agility training and its subcomponents: teach how to change directions to help prevent injuries and develop agility to improve performance.

- Using an appropriate rest interval that will vary on goals of training during each phase.

Beginning Program

The high school athlete's training will be organized around the following:

- 16-week general preparation phase

- 8-week special preparation phase
- 4-week precompetition phase
- 15-week competition phase

The high school athlete's training should focus on the following:

- Building anaerobic metabolic efficiency
- Developing strength and power
- Developing running technique
- Improving speed
- Developing sport-specific agility

General Preparation Phase

During the general preparation phase, the high school athlete should focus on developing anaerobic endurance, learning running technique, and learning agility technique. As a guideline, at this level athletes should train two to four times per week. Each session should focus on dynamic flexibility exercises, running technique drills, and basic agility technique. Table 12-1 shows the types of drills that a high school rugby player should focus on in the general preparation phase.

Physical Quality	Drills
Sprinting	• technique Arm swing drills • High knee drills • A drills • B drills
Speed	• 40-yard sprints for sprint technique
Acceleration	• Position-specific starts • Stick drills
Agility	• Agility patterns for rugby
Conditioning	• 40- to 100-yard sprints with an active rest interval

Table 12-1. Physical qualities to be developed and recommended drills for the high school rugby player during the general preparation phase

Rarely, if ever, during the game of rugby is the athlete at rest. Therefore, most of the rest intervals should reflect what is termed as active rest. Active rest means that the athlete is walking, jogging, or running at a moderate pace while recovering from a more intense effort. Many times in a match, the athlete cannot make it to the action around the ball to contribute. Therefore, the athletes position themselves to be prepared for future play. During this time, they are most likely to be running at a moderate pace to better position themselves. Metabolically, this movement is referred to as active rest.

Day	Primary Emphasis	Training Component	Drills
Mon.	Anaerobic endurance	Warm-up	Dynamic flexibility exercises (10-15 minutes)
		Sprinting technique	Arm swing drills, 2x20 yards High knee walks, 2x20 yards Butt kicks, 2x20 yards A walks, 2x20 yards Shuffle (right, then left), 2x5 yards Backpedal, 2x20 yards
		Anaerobic endurance	12x100 yards with a 30-second active rest interval
Tues.	Agility	Warm-up	Dynamic flexibility exercises for 10-15 minutes
		Sprinting technique	Arm swing drills, 1x20 yards High knee walks, 1x20 yards High knee skips, 3x20 yards Butt kicks, 1x20 yards A walks, 3x20 yards 12 40-yard sprints
		Agility technique	Agility patterns 2 and 6. Three reps each drill with a one-minute rest interval. Three-minute rest interval between patterns.
Thurs.	Anaerobic endurance	Warm-up	Dynamic flexibility exercises for 10-15 minutes
		Sprinting technique	Arm swing drills, 2x20 yards High knee walks, 2x20 yards Butt kicks, 2x20 yards A walks, 2x20 yards
		Anaerobic endurance	12x100 yards with a 30-second active rest interval
Friday	Agility	Warm-up	Dynamic flexibility exercises for 10-15 minutes
		Sprinting technique	Arm swing drills, 1x20 yards High knee walks, 1x20 yards High knee skips, 3x20 yards Butt kicks, 1x20 yards A walks, 3x20 yards 12 40-yard sprints
		Agility technique	Agility patterns 4 and 8. Three reps each drill with a one-minute rest interval. Three-minute rest interval between patterns.

Table 12-2. Sample general preparation workout for high school rugby player

Table 12-2 outlines a sample workout for a high school athlete training four times per week during the general preparation phase. Because this athlete is a beginner, the focus is on fundamental agility and running skills. The workouts are divided into two days with a primary focus on anaerobic endurance and two days with a primary focus on quality movement patterns. Agility, sprinting technique, and dynamic flexibility are trained daily. Sprinting technique focuses on arm swing, the high knee movement, and pulling the heel to the hip. Agility technique focuses primarily on shuffling and backpedaling. Athletes should be allowed to fully recover for two to three minutes between sprinting technique, agility, and acceleration drills. The emphasis of drills should be on correct execution first and speed second.

Special Preparation Phase

During the special preparation phase, the rest intervals will be adjusted to reflect the demands of the game at its most intense times, which occur while defending multiple phases of play. Metabolically, this intense time may last for more than one minute, with a blend of high intensity and short active rest intervals.

Athletes should train three to four times per week. Each session should focus on dynamic flexibility exercises, running technique drills, sport-specific agility technique drills, and/or anaerobic conditioning. Table 12-3 shows the types of drills that a high school athlete should focus on in the special preparation phase.

Physical Quality	Drills
Sprinting technique	• Arm swing drills • High knee drills • A drills • B drills
Sport-specific agility for rugby	• All agility patterns • Add reactionary component (i.e., passing, catching, evading) • Use a 20- to 25-second rest interval
Anaerobic conditioning	• Sprint distances for 10 to 60 yards • Interval training with active rest

Table 12-3. Physical qualities to be developed and recommended drills for the high school rugby player during the special preparation phase

Table 12-4 describes a sample week of workouts for the special preparation phase. Dynamic flexibility exercises are still performed at the beginning of each workout as a warm-up. Sprinting technique drills are performed at a faster pace and begin integrating more complicated A and B drills. While agility training still focuses on fundamentals, the fundamentals are now being incorporated into movement patterns that are seen during the game.

Day	Primary Emphasis	Training Component	Drills
Mon.	Agility	Warm-up	Dynamic flexibility exercises for 10-15 minutes
		Sprinting technique	High knee skips, 2x20 yards Butt kicks, 2x20 yards A skips, 2x20 yards B walks, 2x20 yards
		Agility	Rugby agility patterns 1, 3, 5, and 9. Three reps per pattern. 20- to 25-second rest between repetitions. Three-minute rest between sets.
Tues.	Anaerobic endurance	Warm-up	Dynamic flexibility exercises for 10-15 minutes
		Sprinting technique	Arm swing drills, 1x20 yards High knee walks, 1x20 yards High knee skips, 3x20 yards Butt kicks, 1x20 yards
		Agility technique	Rugby agility patterns 2, 4, 6, and 8. Three reps per pattern. 20- to 25-second rest between repetitions. Three-minute rest between sets.
		Interval training	10- to 60-yard sprints with active rest interval
Thurs.	Agility	Warm-up	Dynamic flexibility exercises for 10-15 minutes
		Sprinting technique	High knee skips, 1x20 yards Butt kicks, 2x20 yards A skips, 3x20 yards B walks, 1x20 yards B skips, 3x20 yards
		Agility technique	Rugby agility patterns 1, 3, 5, and 7. Three reps per pattern. 20- to 25-second rest between repetitions. Three-minute rest between sets.
Fri.	Anaerobic endurance	Warm-up	Dynamic flexibility exercises for 10-15 minutes
		Sprinting technique	Arm swing drills, 1x20 yards High knee walks, 3x20 yards High knee skips, 3x20 yards Butt kicks, 1x20 yards A walks, 3x20 yards
		Agility technique	Rugby agility patterns 2, 4, 6, and 9. Three reps per pattern. 20- to 25-second rest between repetitions. Three-minute rest between sets.
		Interval training	10- to 60-yard sprint intervals with active rest

Table 12-4. Sample special preparation workout for high school rugby player

Precompetition Phase

With the precompetition phase, training is scaled back so that the high school rugby player can focus more on game skills. In this phase of training, dynamic flexibility drills are still performed as a warm-up for each workout. Sprinting technique is trained daily; however, remedial exercises such as arm swings and high knee drills have been removed in favor of more complex movements such as A and B drills. Agility work focuses on movement patterns that are likely to occur in game situations—especially patterns emphasizing a reactionary component. Speed training is balanced between acceleration movements from a position-specific stance and speed (as appropriate for position). Finally, conditioning uses interval training to make the conditioning more metabolically rugby-specific. At this time during training, other components of training, such as plyometrics and resistance, should also be considered.

Physical Quality	Drills
Sprinting technique	• A drills • B drills
Speed	• Flying sprints • 40- to 100-yard sprints
Acceleration	• Position-specific starts • Stick drills
Agility	• Agility patterns
Conditioning	• Agility patterns • Sprint intervals with a 20- to 25-second rest interval

Table 12-5. Physical qualities to be developed and recommended drills for the high school rugby player during the precompetition phase

Competition Phase

Training is scaled back in the competition phase so that most of the athlete's time and energy can be directed towards practice and competition. Training speed and agility twice a week during the competition phase is enough to maintain peak levels.

In the competition phase, dynamic flexibility exercises are still performed at the beginning of each training session. Sprinting technique is still considered important; however, the drills are minimized with this phase. Acceleration and speed training is combined. For example, a coach might emphasize an explosive start as part of a 40-yard sprint. Agility training will focus exclusively on movement patterns that may be seen during the sport, with the emphasis being on correct execution and quality of movement. Finally, conditioning will continue to be focused around interval training with active rest.

Day	Primary Emphasis	Training Component	Drills
Mon.	Speed	Warm-up	Dynamic flexibility exercises for 10-15 minutes
		Sprinting technique	A skips, 2x20 yards B walk, 2x20 yards
		Agility	Rugby agility patterns 2, 6, 8, and 10. Three reps per pattern. 20- to 25-second rest interval.
		Speed	3x40 yards, flying 2-3x60 yards, standing start
Wed.	Acceleration	Warm-up	Dynamic flexibility exercises for 10-15 minutes
		Sprinting technique	A walk, 2x20 yards B skips, 2x20 yards
		Agility	Rugby agility patterns 1, 3, 5, and 9. Three reps per pattern. Active rest interval.
		Acceleration	Standing starts, 3-5x Resisted starts, 3x
Fri.	Conditioning	Warm-up	Dynamic flexibility exercises for 10-15 minutes
		Sprinting technique	A skips, 2x20 yards B walks, 2x20 yards
		Agility	Rugby agility patterns 2, 3, 7, 9, and 10. Three reps per pattern. 20- to 25-second rest interval.
		Conditioning	10- to 60-yard sprints with active rest (15-20x)

Table 12-6. Sample precompetition workout for high school rugby player

Physical Quality	Drills
Sprinting technique	• A drills • B drills
Speed	• Flying sprints
Acceleration	• Position-specific starts
Agility	• Pattern runs
Conditioning	• Interval training with active rest interval

Table 12-7. Physical qualities to be developed and recommended drills for the high school rugby player during the competition phase

Day	Primary Emphasis	Training Component	Drills
Day One	Speed	Warm-up	Dynamic flexibility exercises for 10-15 minutes
		Sprinting technique	A skips, 2x20 yards
		Agility	Agility patterns 3, 4, 8 with active rest interval
		Speed	3-5x40 yards, position-specific start
Day Two	Conditioning	Warm-up	Dynamic flexibility exercises for 10-15 minutes
		Sprinting technique	B skips, 2x20 yards
		Agility	Agility patterns 2, 9, 10 with active rest interval
		Conditioning	10 60-yard sprints with a 1:3 work to rest interval

Table 12-8. Sample competition phase workout for high school rugby player

Advanced Program

The collegiate athlete's training will be organized around the following:

- 20-week general preparation phase
- 12-week special preparation phase
- 4-week precompetition phase
- 12-week competition phase

The collegiate athlete's training should focus on the following:

- Rugby-specific conditioning
- Perfecting running technique
- Improving acceleration
- Improving speed
- Improving rugby-specific agility

General Preparation Phase

During the general preparation phase, the collegiate player should focus on developing an anaerobic endurance base, learning running technique, and improving agility technique. Athletes should train four to fives times per week. Each session should focus on dynamic flexibility exercises, running technique drills, and basic agility technique. Table 12-9 shows the types of drills that a collegiate athlete should focus on in the general preparation phase.

Physical Quality	Drills
Sprinting technique	• Arm swing drills • High knee drills • A drills • B drills
Speed	• 40-yard sprints for sprint technique
Acceleration	• Position-specific starts • Stick drills
Agility	• Agility pattern for rugby
Conditioning/Anaerobic endurance	• 40- to 100-yard sprints with active rest intervals

Table 12-9. Physical qualities to be developed and recommended drills for the collegiate rugby player during the general preparation phase

Table 12-10 outlines a sample workout for a collegiate rugby player training four times per week during the general preparation phase. The athlete's level of training and experience is intermediate to advanced. The athlete's level can be accelerated by increasing the intensity and volume of training. The workouts are divided into two days with a primary focus on anaerobic endurance and two days with a primary focus on quality movement patterns. Agility, sprinting technique, and dynamic flexibility are trained daily. Sprinting technique focuses on arm swing, the high knee movement, and pulling the heel to the hip. Agility technique focuses primarily on acceleration, stopping ability, and change of direction. Athletes should be allowed to fully recover for two to three minutes between sprinting technique, agility, and acceleration drills. The emphasis of the agility patterns and speed drills should be on correct execution first and speed second.

Special Preparation Phase

During the special preparation phase, the rest intervals will be adjusted to reflect the demands of the game at its most intense times. At the collegiate level, the most metabolically demanding time in a game will resemble a sustained multiple phase drive. The agility patterns are biomechanically and metabolically designed to reflect rugby movement patterns.

Day	Primary Emphasis	Training Component	Drills
Mon.	Anaerobic endurance	Warm-up	Dynamic flexibility exercises (10-15 minutes)
		Sprinting technique	Arm swing drills, 2x20 yards High knee walks, 2x20 yards Butt kicks, 2x20 yards A walks, 2x20 yards Shuffle (right, then left), 2x5 yards Backpedal, 2x20 yards
		Anaerobic endurance	14x100 yards with a 30-second active rest interval
Tues.	Sport-specific agility	Warm-up	Dynamic flexibility exercises (10-15 minutes)
		Sprinting technique	Arm swing drills, 1x20 yards High knee walks, 1x20 yards High knee skips, 3x20 yards Butt kicks, 1x20 yards A walks, 3x20 yards 12 40-yard sprints
		Agility technique	Agility patterns 1, 3, and 6. Three reps each drill with a one-minute rest interval. Three-minute rest interval between patterns.
Thurs.	Anaerobic endurance	Warm-up	Dynamic flexibility exercises (10-15 minutes)
		Sprinting technique	Arm swing drills, 2x20 yards High knee walks, 2x20 yards Butt kicks, 2x20 yards A walks, 2x20 yards
		Anaerobic endurance	14x100 yards with a 30-second active rest interval
Fri.	Anaerobic endurance	Warm-up	Dynamic flexibility exercises (10-15 minutes)
		Sprinting technique	Arm swing drills, 1x20 yards High knee walks, 1x20 yards High knee skips, 3x20 yards Butt kicks, 1x20 yards A walks, 3x20 yards 12 40-yard sprints
		Agility technique	Rugby agility patterns 1, 3, and 9. Three reps per pattern. Three-minute rest interval between patterns.
		Anaerobic endurance	14x100 yards with active rest intervals

Table 12-10. Sample general preparation workout for collegiate rugby player

Athletes should train four to five times per week. Each session should focus on dynamic flexibility exercises, running technique drills, sport-specific agility technique drills, and/or anaerobic conditioning. Table 12-11 shows the types of drills that a collegiate player should focus on in the special preparation phase.

Physical Quality	Drills
Sprinting technique	• Arm swing drills • High knee drills • A drills • B drills
Sport-specific agility for rugby	• All agility patterns • Add reactionary component (i.e., passing, catching, evading) • Use a 20- to 25-second rest interval
Anaerobic conditioning	• Sprint distances for 10 to 60 yards • Use active rest intervals

Table 12-11. Physical qualities to be developed and recommended drills for the collegiate rugby player during the special preparation phase

Table 12-12 describes a sample week of workouts for the special preparation phase. Dynamic flexibility exercises are still performed at the beginning of each workout as a warm-up. Sprinting technique drills are performed at a faster pace and begin integrating more complicated A and B drills. Agility training emphasizes perfect execution by adding varied and additional patterns.

Precompetition Phase

In the precompetition phase, the overall volume of training is reduced in an effort to focus on position-specific skills. In this phase of training, dynamic flexibility drills are still performed as a warm-up for each workout. Sprinting technique is trained daily; however, remedial exercises such as arm swings and high knee drills have been removed in favor of focusing on more complex movements such as A and B drills. Agility work focuses on movement patterns that are likely to occur in game situations—especially movements emphasizing a reactionary component. Speed training is balanced between acceleration from a position-specific stance and speed (as appropriate for position). Finally, conditioning uses interval training with active rest intervals to make the conditioning more metabolically rugby-specific. At this time during training, other training components (such as plyometrics and resistance) that add to the overall training stress should also be considered.

Day	Primary Emphasis	Training Component	Drills
Mon.	Agility	Warm-up	Dynamic flexibility exercises for 10-15 minutes
		Sprinting technique	High knee skips, 2x20 yards Butt kicks, 2x20 yards A skips, 2x20 yards B walks, 2x20 yards
		Agility	Rugby agility patterns 1, 3, 5, and 9. Three reps per pattern. 20- to 25-second active rest between repetitions. Two-minute rest between sets.
Tues.	Anaerobic endurance	Warm-up	Dynamic flexibility exercises for 10-15 minutes
		Sprinting technique	Arm swing drills, 1x20 yards High knee walks, 1x20 yards High knee skips, 3x20 yards Butt kicks, 1x20 yards
		Agility technique	Rugby agility patterns 2, 4, 6, and 8. Three reps per pattern. 20- to 25-second active rest between repetitions. Two-minute rest between sets.
		Interval training	10-15, 10-60 yard sprints
Thurs.	Agility	Warm-up	Dynamic flexibility exercises for 10-15 minutes
		Sprinting technique	High knee skips, 1x20 yards Butt kicks, 2x20 yards A skips, 3x20 yards B walks, 1x20 yards B skips, 3x20 yards
		Agility technique	Rugby agility patterns 1, 3, 5, and 7. Three reps per pattern. 20- to 25-second rest between repetitions. Two-minute rest between sets.
Fri.	Anaerobic endurance	Warm-up	Dynamic flexibility exercises for 10-15 minutes
		Sprinting technique	Arm swing drills, 1x20 yards High knee walks, 3x20 yards High knee skips, 3x20 yards Butt kicks, 1x20 yards A walks, 3x20 yards
		Agility technique	Rugby agility patterns 2, 4, 6, and 9. Three reps per pattern. 20- to 25-second rest between repetitions. Two-minute rest between sets.
		Interval training	15-20, 60-100 yard sprint intervals with active rest

Table 12-12. Sample special preparation workout for collegiate rugby player

Physical Quality	Drills
Sprinting technique	• A drills • B drills
Speed	• 20- to 60-yard sprints
Acceleration	• Standing starts • Stick drills
Agility	• Agility patterns • Active rest intervals
Conditioning	• Agility patterns • Active rest intervals

Table 12-13. Physical qualities to be developed and recommended drills for the collegiate rugby player during the precompetition phase

Day	Primary Emphasis	Training Component	Drills
Monday	N/A	Warm-up	Dynamic flexibility exercises for 10-15 minutes
		Sprinting technique	A skips, 2x20 yards B walk, 2x20 yards
		Agility	Rugby agility patterns 2, 6, 8, and 10. Three reps per pattern. 20- to 25-second active rest interval.
		Interval training	10- to 60-yard sprints with a 20- to 25-second rest interval (10-15x)
Wed.	N/A	Warm-up	Dynamic flexibility exercises for 10-15 minutes
		Sprinting technique	A walk, 2x20 yards B skips, 2x20 yards
		Agility	Rugby agility patterns 1, 3, 5, and 9. Three reps per pattern. Active rest interval.
		Interval training	10- to 60-yard sprints with a 20- to 25-second rest interval (10-15x)
Fri.	N/A	Warm-up	Dynamic flexibility exercises for 10-15 minutes
		Sprinting technique	A skips, 2x20 yards B walks, 2x20 yards
		Agility	Rugby agility patterns 2, 3, 7, 9, and 10. Three reps per pattern. 20- to 25-second rest interval.
		Interval training	10- to 60-yard sprints with active rest (15-20x)

Table 12-14. Sample precompetition workout for a collegiate rugby player

Competition Phase

Practicing and playing rugby games on a weekly schedule can be demanding on the body, no matter what level of play. Therefore, training is scaled back in the competition phase.

Physical Quality	Drills
Sprinting technique	• A drills • B drills
Speed	• Flying sprints
Acceleration	• Standing starts
Agility	• Pattern runs
Conditioning	• Interval training • Active rest interval

Table 12-15. Physical qualities to be developed and recommended drills for the collegiate rugby player during the competition phase

Day	Primary Emphasis	Training Component	Drills
Day One	N/A	Warm-up	Dynamic flexibility exercises for 10-15 minutes
		Sprinting technique	A skips, 2x20 yards
		Agility	Agility patterns 3, 6, 9 with a 20- to 25-second active rest interval.
		Conditioning	10 20-yard position-specific start with an active rest interval
Day Two	N/A	Warm-up Sprinting technique	Dynamic flexibility exercises for 10-15 minutes B skips, 2x20 yards
		Agility	Agility patterns 1, 4, 8 with a 20- to 25-second rest interval
		Conditioning	14 20-yard position-specific start with an active rest interval

Table 12-16. Sample competition phase workout for collegiate rugby player

In the competition phase, dynamic flexibility exercises are still performed at the beginning of each training session. Sprinting technique is still considered important; however, the drills are minimized with this phase. Acceleration and speed training is combined. For example, a coach might emphasize an explosive position-specific start as part of a 40-yard sprint. Agility training will focus exclusively on movement patterns that may be seen during the sport, with the emphasis being on correct execution and quality of movement. Finally, conditioning will continue to be focused around interval training.

Agility Drills

Agility Pattern: Drill #1

Purpose: Develop lateral acceleration, stopping ability, and a low athletic stance.

Objectives:

- Simulate movement patterns often seen while defending an opponent.
- Reduce unnecessary body movements.

Description:

- The athlete starts at the center cone and assumes a low defensive stance with the knees and hips bent, a flat back, and the eyes up.
- The athlete simply shuffles to one of the cones and proceeds around the pattern until all cones have been reached.
- The athlete then transitions from one cone to the next at the center cone.
- The athlete should touch each cone with the outside hand.
- The athlete should keep his head up and eyes forward, and use peripheral vision to locate the cones.

Increasing Complexity/Difficulty:

- Have the athlete move both clockwise and counter-clockwise around the pattern.
- Increase the distance between the cones to increase the work interval.
- Have the athlete pick up a ball each time he reaches the center cone and pass it to a coach/player at the outside of the drill.

Work Interval: Will vary on distance of cones and ability of athlete but should be between 8 and 20 seconds.

Rest Interval: Once mastery of the drill has been reached, the rest interval can be brought down to 2:1 rest to work interval.

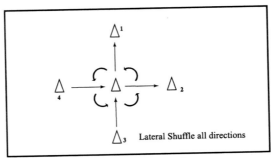

Figure 12-1. Agility Pattern: Drill #1

Agility Pattern: Drill #2

Purpose: Develop controlled change of direction, integrating two movement patterns.

Objectives:

- Develop controlled change of directions.
- Develop effective stopping ability.
- Develop effective transitions from different movement patterns.
- Control unnecessary body movements.

Description:

- The athlete starts at the first cone in the pattern and sprints out to the second cone. Once at the second cone, he laterally shuffles to the left, to the third cone. This process is repeated until the pattern is complete.
- The athlete should keep the head up and eyes forward and use peripheral vision to locate the cones.
- Quality of movement is emphasized.
- The athlete should maintain a low center of gravity.
- The athlete should keep the corners "tight" when passing cones.

Increasing Complexity/Difficulty:

- Have the athlete carry a ball through the pattern.
- Have the athlete receive a passed ball during the drill.
- Have the athlete make a kick off the end of the drill.
- The drill should be practiced in both directions, reversing the angled running and shuffling directions.

Work Interval: Will vary on distance of cones and ability of athlete but should be between 10 and 20 seconds.

Rest Interval: Once mastery of the drill has been reached, the rest interval can be brought down to 2:1 rest to work interval. Another option is to have the athlete run at a moderate intensity back to the start of the drill and repeat the pattern to emphasize conditioning. Note: This variation will compromise true movement/agility acquisition.

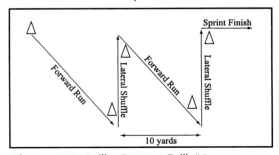

Figure 12-2. Agility Pattern: Drill #2

Agility Pattern: Drill #3

Purpose: Develop acceleration and stopping ability.

Objectives:

- Simulate movement patterns often seen at various positions.
- Reduce unnecessary body movements.

Description:

- Have the athlete start at a cone and sprint forward five yards, backpedal to the starting line, sprint forward 10 yards, and so on, backpedaling to the starting line each time and increasing the forward distance to 20 yards (in increments of five). See Figure 12-3.
- The athlete should accelerate with 100% effort.
- The athlete should maximize the forward lean when initially accelerating.
- The athlete should use a forceful, high knee lift when initially accelerating.
- The athlete should minimize braking distance by quickly dropping the center of gravity.
- The athlete should use short choppy steps to minimize stopping distance.

Increasing Complexity/Difficulty:

- A coach can pass a ball back and forth with the athlete during the drill.
- An athlete can hold a ball during the drill.
- Have athletes perform the drill at the same time to increase competition.
- Stagger the distance of the cones.

Work Interval: Will vary on distance of cones and ability of athlete but should be between 10 and 25 seconds.

Rest Interval: Once mastery of the drill has been reached, the rest interval can be brought down to 2:1 rest to work interval.

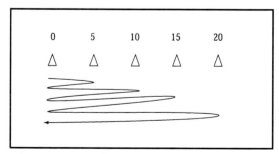

Figure 12-3. Agility Pattern: Drill #3

Agility Pattern: Drill #4

Purpose: Develop acceleration and stopping ability.

Objectives:

- Maintain body control.
- Develop specific rate of force production.
- Lower center of gravity when decelerating.

Description:

- The athlete starts (with his back to the pattern) at one end and shuffles backward to each cone in the series.
- The athlete can use a low athletic stance to start.
- The athlete should concentrate on shuffling in straight lines.
- The athlete should make "tight" corners.
- The athlete should keep the elbows relatively close to the body.
- The athlete should drop the center of gravity while changing directions at cones.
- The athlete should keep the eyes up and use peripheral vision to locate cones.
- The athlete should touch each cone with the outside hand.
- The athlete should maintain a neutral spine at all times.

Increasing Complexity/Difficulty:

- Combine a forward run with side shuffling.
- Use shuffling only.
- Have the athlete run off the end of the drill to catch a passed ball.
- The athlete can hold a ball for the duration of the drill.
- Use two identical patterns of cones and have athletes race each other through the drill.
- Increase the distance between cones to increase the work interval.

Work Interval: Will vary on distance of cones and ability of athlete but should be between 8 and 12 seconds.

Rest Interval: Once mastery of the drill has been reached, the rest interval can be brought down to 2:1 rest to work interval.

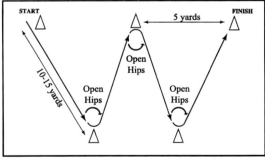

Figure 12-4. Agility Pattern: Drill #4

Agility Pattern: Drill #5

Purpose: Develop reactive capabilities to a defender in open space.

Objectives:

- Simulate movement patterns often seen in games.
- Familiarize the athlete with man-on-man situations.

Description:

- The athlete starts at the narrow end of a series as shown in Figure 12-5.
- The defending athlete starts at the opposite end.
- They both approach each other, either attempting to evade or defend.
- A rugby-specific tackle is attempted in the space between the cones.

Increasing Complexity/Difficulty: The cones can be spread apart further or narrowed, depending on objectives.

Work Interval: Will vary on distance of cones and ability of athlete but should be between three and eight seconds.

Rest Interval: Once mastery of the drill has been reached, the rest interval can be brought down to 2:1 rest to work interval.

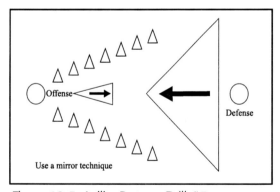

Figure 12-5. Agility Pattern: Drill #5

Agility Pattern: Drill #6

Purpose: Develop effective transitions between movements and body control.

Objectives:

- Simulate movement patterns often seen in games.
- Reduce unnecessary body movements.

Description:

- The athlete starts at the first cone and runs directly forward. Then he transitions into a side shuffle, transitions back to a forward run, goes back to the side shuffle, and finishes with a forward run.
- The athlete should make quick turns at each cone.
- The athlete should maintain a neutral spine at all times.

Increasing Complexity/Difficulty:

- The cones can be further spread apart.
- The athlete can run with a ball through the pattern.
- The athlete can either pass a ball or receive a passed ball during the drill.

Work Interval: Will vary on distance of cones and ability of athlete but should be between 8 and 12 seconds.

Rest Interval: Once mastery of the drill has been reached, the rest interval can be brought down to 2:1 rest to work interval. Another option is to have the athlete run at a moderate intensity back to the start of the drill and repeat the pattern to emphasize conditioning. Note: This variation will compromise true movement/agility acquisition.

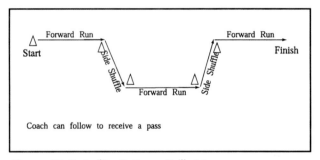

Figure 12-6. Agility Pattern: Drill #6

Agility Pattern: Drill #7

Purpose: Develop reactive ability to a specific stimulus/rugby ball.

Objectives:

- Develop acceleration.
- Reduce unnecessary body movements.
- Train eye-hand coordination.

Description:

- The coach stands five yards away from the athlete, holding a rugby ball at shoulder level.

- The coach drops the ball to the ground, which signals the athlete to accelerate toward the ball.
- The athlete attempts to pick up the ball, either in the air off the first bounce or from the ground, as quickly as possible.
- Once the ball is received, the athlete accelerates again to complete the drill.
- The athlete should accelerate as quickly as possible.
- The athlete should receive the ball in an athletic rugby-specific stance.

Increasing Complexity/Difficulty:

- The coach can toss a ball back to a second athlete.
- The coach can drop the ball to the ground to make a less predictable bounce.
- The athlete can move further away from the ball.
- The athlete can start with his back to the drill or start from the ground.

Work Interval: Will vary on distance of cones and ability of athlete but should be between four and eight seconds.

Rest Interval: Once mastery of the drill has been reached, the rest interval can be brought down to 2:1 rest to work interval.

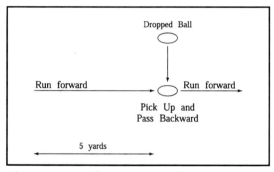

Figure 12-7. Agility Pattern: Drill #7

Agility Pattern: Drill #8

Purpose: Develop stopping ability and movements specific to rugby.

Objectives:

- Transition from running to lateral shuffling.
- Reduce unnecessary body movements.

Description:

- The athlete starts out by running toward the first set of cones. After reaching the first set of cones, he shuffles through and runs at an angle toward the second set of cones. He laterally shuffles through the second set of cones and sprints off the end to complete the pattern.

- The athlete should keep the head up and eyes forward and use peripheral vision to locate the cones.
- Quality of movement is emphasized.
- The athlete should maintain a low center of gravity.
- The athlete should keep the corners "tight" when passing cones.

Increasing Complexity/Difficulty:

- Have the athlete carry a ball through the pattern.
- Have the athlete receive a passed ball during the drill.
- Have the athlete make a kick in the middle or off the end of the drill.
- The drill should be practiced in both directions, reversing the angled running and shuffling directions.
- The cones can be set up further apart to increase the work interval.
- Additional sets of cones can be set up to increase the length of the pattern.

Work Interval: The coach can vary the time of the drill up to two minutes.

Rest Interval: Once mastery of the drill has been reached, the rest interval can be brought down to a 2:1 rest to work interval.

Note: The movements selected in this drill are basic and can be incorporated into rugby-specific conditioning.

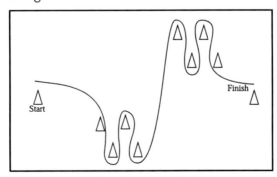

Figure 12-8. Agility Pattern: Drill #8

Agility Pattern: Drill #9

Purpose: Develop athletic stance, hand-eye-foot coordination, reactive ability, and lateral agility.

Objectives:

- Simulate movement patterns seen in all rugby positions.
- Reduce unnecessary body movements.

Description:

- The emphasis of this drill is to have the athlete react to the random movements of a rugby ball.
- The athlete starts in an athletic stance.
- The coach lightly tosses the ball to the ground in the direction of the athlete.
- The athlete reacts to the direction of the ball by shuffling.
- With two hands, the athlete passes the ball back to the coach.
- The coach redirects the ball in the desired direction.

Increasing Complexity/Difficulty:

- The coach can toss the ball a little harder to force the athlete to react more quickly.
- The coach can toss the ball further away from the athlete to increase the shuffling distance.
- A sprint out can be incorporated at the end of the drill.

Work Interval: The coach can use a determined number of tosses to complete the drill or an approximate time of the drill (5 to 15 seconds).

Rest Interval: Once mastery of the drill has been reached, the rest interval can be brought down to a 2:1 rest to work interval.

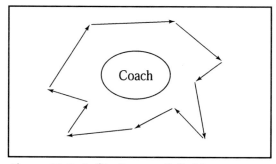

Figure 12-9. Agility Pattern: Drill #9

Agility Pattern: Drill #10

Purpose: Develop acceleration, stopping ability, and body control.

Objectives:

- Simulate movement patterns at various positions.
- Develop an effective integration of movements seen in rugby.
- Reduce unnecessary body movements.

Description:

- The athlete will run through a series of cones as shown in Figure 12-10.
- The athlete should maintain a low center of gravity.
- The athlete should maximize the forward lean when initially accelerating from each turn.
- The athlete should use a forceful, high knee lift when initially accelerating.
- The athlete should minimize braking distance by quickly dropping the center of gravity.
- The athlete should use short choppy steps to minimize stopping distance.

Increasing Complexity/Difficulty:

- The coach can indicate which direction the athlete should start in.
- The drill should be completed in both directions.

Work Interval: Will vary on distance of cones and ability of athlete but should be between 30 seconds and two to three minutes.

Rest Interval: Once mastery of the drill has been reached, the rest interval can be brought down to 2:1 rest to work interval.

Note: The movements selected in this drill are basic and can be incorporated into rugby-specific conditioning.

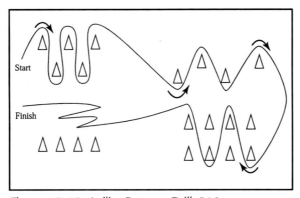

Figure 12-10. Agility Pattern: Drill #10

13

Soccer

Soccer is one of the fastest growing sports in the U.S. in terms of popularity and is the most popular sport in the world, with over 40 million estimated people participating in everything from pick-up games, to youth and adult leagues, to school teams at all levels, to professional soccer. Soccer is played on a field that is 120 yards long and 75 yards wide. Soccer games last 90 minutes, with a possibility of 30 more minutes for overtime play.

In a soccer match, an athlete may cover from 2,000 to 10,000 yards or more. However, most runs are usually made for 5 to 30 yards and require an athlete to be able to accelerate and decelerate quickly with various movement patterns. Players will walk or jog in between runs, usually with a 1:3 work:rest ratio.

Given the length of play and the distances an athlete must cover, aerobic conditioning is required for soccer. This type of conditioning will be important to enable players to recover quickly from high intensity sprints and to maintain their energy levels and speed during the length of the game.

Development of the glycolytic energy system through sprinting is also going to be necessary for soccer performance. An overreliance on aerobic conditioning will develop an athlete's endurance, but leave him slow.

In addition to acceleration and aerobic endurance, soccer requires agility. An athlete needs to be able to be elusive, be evasive, twist, and change directions quickly. Ankle sprains and groin injuries are commonly seen in soccer players, so agility technique and conditioning will be important.

Other injuries commonly seen in soccer include hamstring and upper thigh strains, caused by a combination of sprinting, agility, and the amount of power that must be generated in order to kick the soccer ball. Due to the amount of running involved in the sport, attention should also be paid to preventing shin splints.

Dynamic flexibility exercises should be employed during the warm-up to reinforce technique and to help prevent injuries during practice and the game. As previously discussed, the advantages of a dynamic flexibility program are multi-faceted and most appropriate to the game of soccer.

A speed and agility program for soccer should target the following:

- Sprinting technique: helps with speed and helps prevent injuries.

- Acceleration: high intensity sprints and drills to improve an athlete's ability to accelerate for 5 to 30 yards.

- Aerobic conditioning: helps athletes recover from high intensity sprints and helps them perform for the entire game.

- Agility training and its subcomponents: teach how to change directions to help prevent injuries and develop agility to improve performance. Active recovery (i.e., light jogging) should be emphasized during rest periods.

- Work to rest ratio of 1:3 to mimic the demands of the game.

Beginning Program

The high school athlete's training will be organized around the following:

- 20-week general preparation phase

- 10-week special preparation phase

- 4-week precompetition phase

- 15-week competition phase

- 2-week transition phase following the season

The high school athlete's training should focus on the following:

- Building an aerobic endurance base in the general preparation phase
- Developing running technique
- Improving acceleration
- Improving speed
- Developing agility techniques

General Preparation Phase

During the general preparation phase, the high school athlete should focus on developing an aerobic endurance base, learning running technique, and learning agility technique. Athletes should train two to four times per week. Each session should focus on dynamic flexibility exercises, running technique drills, basic agility technique drills, and either acceleration drills or aerobic endurance training. Table 13-1 shows the types of drills that a high school athlete should focus on in the general preparation phase.

Physical Quality	Drills
Sprinting technique	• Arm swing drills • High knee drills • A drills • B drills
Speed	• 40-yard sprints
Acceleration	• Standing starts • Stick drills
Agility	• Shuffles • Backpedals
Conditioning	• Deceleration drills • Moderate intensity runs, 20-30 minutes duration

Table 13-1. Physical qualities to be developed and recommended drills for the high school soccer player during the general preparation phase

Table 13-2 outlines a sample workout for a high school athlete training four times per week during the general preparation phase. Because this athlete is a beginner, the focus is on fundamental agility and running skills. The workouts are divided into two days with a primary focus on aerobic endurance and two days with a primary focus on acceleration. Agility, sprinting technique, and dynamic flexibility are trained daily. Sprinting technique focuses on arm swing, the high knee movement, and pulling the heel to the hip. Agility technique focuses primarily on shuffling and backpedaling. Athletes should be allowed to fully recover for two to three minutes between sprinting technique, agility, and acceleration drills. The emphasis of drills should be on correct execution first and speed second.

Day	Primary Emphasis	Training Component	Drills
Mon.	Aerobic endurance	Warm-up	Dynamic flexibility exercises (10-15 minutes)
		Sprinting technique	Arm swing drills, 2x20 yards High knee walks, 2x20 yards Butt kicks, 2x20 yards A walks, 2x20 yards
		Agility	Shuffle (right, then left), 2x5 yards Backpedal, 2x20 yards
		Aerobic endurance	Moderate intensity run, 20-30 minutes
Tues.	Acceleration	Warm-up	Dynamic flexibility exercises for 10-15 minutes
		Sprinting technique	Arm swing drills, 1x20 yards High knee walks, 1x20 yards High knee skips, 3x20 yards Butt kicks, 1x20 yards A walks, 3x20 yards
		Agility	Carioca, 2x20 yards Shuffle right 10 yards, sprint 10 yards (2-3x) Shuffle left 10 yards, sprint 10 yards (2-3x) Backpedal 10 yards, turn and sprint 10 yards (2-3x)
		Acceleration	Standing starts, 3-5x20 yards
Thurs.	Aerobic endurance	Warm-up	Dynamic flexibility exercises for 10-15 minutes
		Sprinting technique	Arm swing drills, 2x20 yards High knee walks, 2x20 yards Butt kicks, 2x20 yards A walks, 2x20 yards
		Agility	Shuffle (right, then left), 2x5 yards Backpedal, 2x20 yards
		Aerobic endurance	Moderate intensity run, 20-30 minutes
Fri.	Acceleration	Warm-up	Dynamic flexibility exercises for 10-15 minutes
		Sprinting technique	Arm swing drills, 1x20 yards High knee walks, 1x20 yards High knee skips, 3x20 yards Butt kicks, 1x20 yards A walks, 3x20 yards
		Agility	Carioca, 2x20 yards Shuffle right 10 yards, sprint 10 yards (2-3x) Shuffle left 10 yards, sprint 10 yards (2-3x) Backpedal 10 yards, turn and sprint 10 yards (2-3x)
		Acceleration	Stick drill, 3-5x

Table 13-2. Sample general preparation phase workouts for high school soccer players

Special Preparation Phase

During the special preparation phase, the high school athlete should focus on applying the aerobic endurance base to the sport, emphasizing agility patterns and sprinting technique, and developing both acceleration and speed. As this phase progresses, drills should be performed with the ball or against another opponent. Examples may include the player shuffling for five yards with the ball, passing it, and then running for 10 yards. The same drill could be performed with two players executing it at the same time, i.e., each player attempts to complete the drill before the other player does.

Athletes should train two to four times per week. Each session should focus on dynamic flexibility exercises, running technique drills, specific agility technique drills, and either acceleration drills, speed training, or aerobic endurance training. Table 13-3 shows the types of drills that a high school athlete should focus on in the special preparation phase.

Physical Quality	Drills
Sprinting technique	• Arm swing drills • High knee drills • A drills • B drills
Speed	• Flying sprints • 40- to 100-yard sprints • Stride length drills
Acceleration	• Standing starts • Stick drills
Agility	• Shuffles—with and without the ball • Backpedals—with and without the ball • Deceleration drills—with and without the ball
Conditioning	• Pattern running • Interval training (1:3 work:rest)

Table 13-3. Physical qualities to be developed and recommended drills for the high school soccer player during the special preparation phase

Table 13-4 describes a sample week of workouts for the special preparation phase. Dynamic flexibility exercises are still performed at the beginning of each workout as a warm-up. Sprinting technique drills are performed at a faster pace and begin integrating more complicated A and B drills. While agility training still focuses on fundamentals, the fundamentals are now being incorporated into movement patterns that may be seen during the game. Pattern running, drills with the ball, and drills with

Day	Primary Emphasis	Training Component	Drills
Mon.	Speed	Warm-up	Dynamic flexibility exercises for 10-15 minutes
		Sprinting technique	High knee skips, 2x20 yards Butt kicks, 2x20 yards A skips, 2x20 yards B walks, 2x20 yards
		Agility	Shuffle (right, then left), 2x5 yards plus sprint 10 yards Backpedal, 2x20 yards, turn and sprint 10 yards
		Speed	3-5x40 yards, flying Stride length drills, 3x, 6-10 sticks set at 80% of stride length
Tues.	Conditioning	Warm-up	Dynamic flexibility exercises for 10-15 minutes
		Sprinting technique	Arm swing drills, 1x20 yards High knee walks, 1x20 yards High knee skips, 3x20 yards Butt kicks, 1x20 yards
		Agility	Carioca, 2x20 yards 20-yard bending run, right 20-yard bending run, left
		Conditioning	12-15x1' sprints followed by 3' jog
Thurs.	Acceleration	Warm-up	Dynamic flexibility exercises for 10-15 minutes
		Sprinting technique	High knee skips, 1x20 yards Butt kicks, 2x20 yards A skips, 3x20 yards B walks, 1x20 yards B skips, 3x20 yards
		Agility	Shuffle with the ball (right, then left), 2x5 yards, pass ball then sprint 10 yards Backpedal against an opponent, 2x20 yards, turn and sprint 10 yards
		Acceleration	Standing starts, 3-5x20 yards Stick drill, 3-5x
Fri.	Conditioning	Warm-up	Dynamic flexibility exercises for 10-15 minutes
		Sprinting technique	Arm swing drills, 1x20 yards High knee walks, 3x20 yards High knee skips, 3x20 yards Butt kicks, 1x20 yards A walks, 3x20 yards
		Agility	Carioca, 2x20 yards 20-yard bending run, right 20-yard bending run, left
		Conditioning	10-15x30" sprints followed by 90" jog

Table 13-4. Sample special preparation phase workouts for high school soccer players

other players should be integrated as the special preparation phase progresses. Speed work is now incorporated along with shorter distance acceleration training. Finally, the interval training allows the athlete to apply his aerobic endurance base to more sport-specific situations that incorporate active rest intervals.

Precompetition Phase

In the precompetition phase, training is scaled back so that the high school soccer player can focus more on game skills. Agility training should be performed with the ball and should require interaction with other players.

Physical Quality	Drills
Sprinting technique	• A drills • B drills
Speed	• Flying sprints • 40- to 100-yard sprints
Acceleration	• Standing starts • Stick drills
Agility	• Pattern running
Conditioning	• Shuttle runs • Interval training (1:3 work:rest)

Table 13-5. Physical qualities to be developed and recommended drills for the high school soccer player during the precompetition phase

In this phase of training, dynamic flexibility drills are still performed as a warm-up for each workout. Sprinting technique is trained daily; however, remedial exercises such as arm swings and high knee drills have been removed in favor of focusing on more complex movements such as A and B drills. Agility work focuses on movement patterns that are likely to occur in game situations, and should be performed both with the ball and with other players. Speed training is balanced between flying starts to simulate game situations and longer sprints done from a standing start. Finally, conditioning uses interval training to make it more soccer-specific.

Competition Phase

Training is scaled back in the competition phase for a number of reasons. First, athletes may be competing several times a week. They cannot be expected to compete at their best if they are exhausted from intense speed and agility training. Second, with the increased focus on sport practices and competition, athletes could become overtrained and injured if training is not cut back. As a result, during this phase, training will be scaled back to two days per week (three if the week allows) and will focus on maintaining conditioning and working on essential skills.

Day	Primary Emphasis	Training Component	Drills
Mon.	Speed	Warm-up	Dynamic flexibility exercises for 10-15 minutes
		Sprinting technique	A skips, 2x20 yards B walk, 2x20 yards
		Agility	10-yard shuffle with the ball (right/left), pass, then sprint 10 yards, 3x 10-yard backpedal, pivot, receive the ball, and sprint 10 yards with the ball, 3x
		Speed	3x40 yards, flying 2-3x60 yards, standing start
Wed.	Acceleration	Warm-up	Dynamic flexibility exercises for 10-15 minutes
		Sprinting technique	A walk, 2x20 yards B skips, 2x20 yards
		Agility	10-yard drop, dive right (left), 3x 20-yard bending run (right/left), 3x
		Acceleration	Standing starts, 3-5x Resisted starts, 3x
Fri.	Conditioning	Warm-up	Dynamic flexibility exercises for 10-15 minutes
		Sprinting technique	A skips, 2x20 yards B walks, 2x20 yards
		Agility	Agility pattern drill 4, 3x (40" to finish, 2' rest)
		Conditioning	12-15x1' sprints followed by 3' jog

Table 13-6. Sample precompetition phase workouts for high school soccer players

Physical Quality	Drills
Sprinting technique	• A drills • B drills
Speed	• Flying sprints
Acceleration	• Standing starts
Agility	• Pattern runs
Conditioning	• Interval training (1:3 work:rest)

Table 13-7. Physical qualities to be developed and recommended drills for the high school soccer player during the competition phase

In the competition phase, dynamic flexibility exercises are still performed at the beginning of each training session. Sprinting technique is still considered important; however, the drills are minimized with this phase. Acceleration and speed training is combined. For example, a coach might emphasize an explosive standing start as part of a 40-yard sprint. Agility training will focus exclusively on movement patterns that may be seen during the sport, with the emphasis being on correct execution and speed. Whenever possible, the ball (and other players) should be incorporated with agility training. Finally, conditioning will continue to be focused around interval training.

Day	Primary Emphasis	Training Component	Drills
Day One	Speed	Warm-up	Dynamic flexibility exercises for 10-15 minutes
		Sprinting technique	A skips, 2x20 yards
		Agility	10-yard shuffle with ball (right/left), pass, then sprint 10 yards, 3x 10-yard backpedal, pivot, receive ball, and sprint 10 yards, 3x
		Speed	3-5x40 yards, standing starts
Day Two	Conditioning	Warm-up	Dynamic flexibility exercises for 10-15 minutes
		Sprinting technique	B skips, 2x20 yards
		Agility	10-yard drop, dive right (left), 3x 20-yard bending run (right/left), 3x
		Conditioning	15-20x30" sprints followed by 90" jog

Table 13-8. Sample competition phase workouts for high school soccer players

The high school athlete needs to develop a fitness and movement skill base. As a result, many of the drills and exercises performed are fundamental in nature. While fundamentals are important at the college level, sports-specificity takes on even greater importance. The remainder of this chapter will focus on the college program.

Advanced Program

The collegiate athlete's training will be organized around the following:

- 20-week general preparation phase

- 12-week special preparation phase

- 4-week precompetition phase

- 12-week competition phase
- 2-week transition phase following the season

The collegiate athlete's training should focus on the following:

- Soccer-specific conditioning
- Perfecting running technique
- Improving acceleration
- Improving speed
- Improving soccer-specific agility

General Preparation Phase

For the collegiate soccer player, the general preparation phase focuses on developing a number of qualities. First, aerobic conditioning needs to be developed to allow the soccer player to maintain his intensity throughout the soccer game. Second, sprinting fundamentals should be emphasized, along with some speed work. Third, agility fundamentals should be developed and some time should be spent applying these techniques to soccer movement patterns. Fourth, acceleration should be trained. Training should take place three to four times per week. Table 13-9 lists the physical qualities to focus on in this phase and the drills for developing them.

Physical Quality	Drills
Sprinting technique	• Arm swing drills • High knee drills • A drills
Speed	• Flying sprints • Stride length drills
Acceleration	• Standing starts • Stick drills
Agility	• Shuffles • Backpedals • Pattern runs and drill #1
Conditioning	• Moderate intensity running for 20-30 minutes • Interval training (1:3 work:rest)

Table 13-9. Physical qualities to be developed and recommended drills for the collegiate soccer player during the general preparation phase

Day	Primary Emphasis	Training Component	Drills
Mon.	Speed	Warm-up	Dynamic flexibility exercises for 10-15 minutes
		Sprinting technique	Arm swing drills High knee skips, 3x20 yards Butt kicks, 3x20 yards A walks, 3x20 yards
		Agility	Shuffle right/left, sprint 10 yards, 3x Backpedal 10 yards, pivot and sprint 10 yards, 3x
		Speed	Flying 40's, 3-5x Stride length drills, 6-8 sticks 80% of stride length, 3-5x
Tues.	Conditioning	Warm-up	Dynamic flexibility exercises for 10-15 minutes
		Sprinting technique	High knee walks, 3x20 yards Butt kicks, 3x20 yards A walks, 3x20 yards
		Agility	Agility pattern drill 1, 3-5x
		Conditioning	8-12x30" sprints, 90" jog recovery
Thurs.	Acceleration	Warm-up	Dynamic flexibility exercises for 10-15 minutes
		Sprinting technique	Arm swing drills, 2x High knee walks, 3x20 yards Butt kicks, 3x20 yards A skips, 3x20 yards
		Agility	10-yard drop, dive right (left), 3x 20-yard bending run (right/left), 3x
		Acceleration	Standing starts, 3-5x Stick drills, 3-5x
Fri.	Conditioning	Warm-up	Dynamic flexibility exercises for 10-15 minutes
		Sprinting technique	High knee walks, 3x20 yards A walks, 3x20 yards
		Agility	Carioca, 3x20 yards Shuffle right/left, sprint 10 yards, 3x Backpedal 10 yards, pivot and sprint 10 yards, 3x
		Conditioning	Moderate intensity run, 20-30 minutes

Table 13-10. Sample general preparation phase workouts for collegiate soccer players

During this phase, fundamental movement skills are taught or refined. Sprinting technique is emphasized on all days with a greater volume than that seen on the high school level. Agility technique is also emphasized (i.e., shuffle, backpedal, etc.), and should be combined with sprinting to make it more soccer-specific. In addition, pattern runs and drills are included from the beginning to help reinforce quick starts, stops, and changes of direction. Conditioning is emphasized in this phase as its presence will determine whether the athlete can maintain his intensity during a long game. Table 13-10 provides a sample week of workouts during the general preparation phase for a collegiate soccer player.

Special Preparation Phase

The special preparation phase is designed to apply the physical qualities developed in the general preparation phase directly to the sport of soccer. This phase is meant to be a bridge between the general preparation phase and the precompetition phase. As a result, exercises and drills become even more soccer-specific. Moderate intensity runs and general agility training are de-emphasized in favor of more specific conditioning and agility patterns. In this phase, the collegiate athlete should train three to four times a week.

Physical Quality	Drills
Sprinting technique	• Arm swing drills • High knee drills • A drills • B drills
Speed	• Flying sprints • Stride length drills • Fast leg drills
Acceleration	• Standing starts • Stick drills
Agility	• Pattern runs and drills #1-3, 5
Conditioning	• Interval training (1:3 work:rest) • Shuttle runs

Table 13-11. Physical qualities to be developed and recommended drills for the collegiate soccer player during the special preparation phase

The training in this phase becomes faster and more complex. Sprinting technique drills predominantly focus on A and B drills. Agility drills only focus on fundamental skills when they are in combination with other movements to continue preparing the athlete for soccer. The ball and other players should be integrated into agility training as the phase progresses. Fast leg and stride length drills are added to the speed

Day	Primary Emphasis	Training Component	Drills
Mon.	Speed	Warm-up	Dynamic flexibility exercises for 10-15 minutes
		Sprinting technique	High knee walks, 2x20 yards A skips, 3x20 yards B walks, 3x20 yards
		Agility	Agility pattern drill 2, 3x Shuffle right/left with the ball, pass, then sprint 10 yards, 3x Backpedal 10 yards, pivot, receive the ball, and sprint 10 yards, 3x
		Speed	3-5x60 yards, flying Fast leg drills, 3-5x
Tues.	Conditioning	Warm-up	Dynamic flexibility exercises for 10-15 minutes
		Sprinting technique	High knee skips, 3x20 yards A walks, 3x20 yards B skips, 3x20 yards
		Agility	Agility pattern drill 3, 3x
		Conditioning	Agility pattern drill 4, 20 yards, 3-8x, 40" to finish and 120" recovery (jog)
Thurs.	Acceleration	Warm-up	Dynamic flexibility exercises for 10-15 minutes
		Sprinting technique	High knee walk, 3x20 yards A skips, 3x20 yards
		Agility	Agility pattern drill 1, 3x 30-yard bending run (right/left), 3x
		Acceleration	Standing starts, 3-5x Push-up starts, 3x Stick drill, 3x
Fri.	Speed/Conditioning	Warm-up	Dynamic flexibility exercises for 10-15 minutes
		Sprinting technique	A skips, 3x20 yards B skips, 3x20 yards
		Agility	Agility pattern drill 5, 3x Shuffle right/left with the ball, pass, sprint 15 yards, 3x Backpedal 10 yards, pivot, receive ball, and sprint 15 yards, 3x
		Speed	Stride length drills, 4-6 sticks put at 80% of stride length, 3-5x Fast leg drill, 3x
		Conditioning	Sprint 1', jog 3', 8-12x

Table 13-12. Sample special preparation phase workouts for collegiate soccer players

training. Conditioning centers around the shuttle runs and interval training to attempt to mimic the demands of soccer. Table 13-12 provides a sample week of the special preparation phase.

Precompetition Phase

In the precompetition phase, training is scaled back in favor of skilled practices. Therefore, the training must be prioritized to focus on the most important qualities, or training means should be combined to help develop multiple qualities. For example, a 50-yard sprint might be performed from a standing start so that starting, acceleration, and speed can all be emphasized in one drill. Table 13-13 shows the qualities to be developed and the drills to use during the precompetition phase.

Physical Quality	Drills
Sprinting technique	• A drills • B drills
Speed	• Flying sprints • 40- to 100-yard sprints from a start
Acceleration	• Standing starts • Resisted starts
Agility	• Pattern runs and drills #4, 6, 8, 9
Conditioning	• Pattern runs and drills

Table 13-13. Physical qualities to be developed and recommended drills for the collegiate soccer player during the precompetition phase

Due to time demands, very little work is spent on fundamentals in this phase. Sprinting technique drills emphasize A and B drills. Agility training deals exclusively with various patterns that simulate movement patterns that are seen in the game of soccer (i.e., working with the ball and with other players). Conditioning is becoming increasingly game-specific, with a combination of the pattern conditioning drill (which trains all components in addition to agility) and the shuttle run. Table 13-14 highlights a sample week from the precompetition phase.

Competition Phase

Due to the rigors and frequency of competition, speed and agility training will be scaled back during the competition phase. Wherever possible, training will use exercises that train multiple qualities (for example, agility/conditioning, acceleration/speed) to help save time. Table 13-15 shows the physical qualities to be developed during this phase and what means will be used to develop them.

Day	Primary Emphasis	Training Component	Drills
Mon.	Speed	Warm-up	Dynamic flexibility exercises for 10-15 minutes
		Sprinting technique	A skips, 3x20 yards B walks, 3x20 yards
		Agility	Agility pattern drill 6, 3-5x Agility pattern drill 8, 3-5x
		Speed	2x3-5x60-yard sprints, standing start
Wed.	Acceleration	Warm-up	Dynamic flexibility exercises for 10-15 minutes
		Sprinting technique	A walks, 3x20 yards B skips, 3x20 yards
		Agility	Agility pattern drill 9, 3-5x Shuffle right/left with the ball, pass, sprint 15 yards, 3x
		Acceleration	Standing starts, 2-3x Resisted standing starts, 3x
Fri.	Conditioning	Warm-up	Dynamic flexibility exercises for 10-15 minutes
		Sprinting technique	A walk, 2x20 yards B walk, 2x20 yards
		Agility/Conditioning	Pattern conditioning drill, 4-8x
		Conditioning	Agility pattern drill 4 (to 25 yards), 3-5x, 45" to finish, 135" recovery

Table 13-14. Sample precompetition phase workouts for collegiate soccer players

Physical Quality	Drills
Sprinting technique	• A drills • B drills
Speed	• 40- to 100-yard sprints from a start
Acceleration	• Standing starts
Agility	• Pattern runs and drills #4 & 7
Conditioning	• Pattern runs and drills

Table 13-15. Physical qualities to be developed and recommended drills for the collegiate soccer player during the competition phase

Sprinting and agility drills are minimized to focus on maintaining skills or to focus on combining qualities and enhancing sport-specific conditioning and skills. For example, the pattern running drill is included on the first day. This drill trains speed (40-yard runs), acceleration (many 10- to 30-yard sprints), agility (shuffles, bending runs, drop/dive runs, backpedals, etc.), and conditioning (it is repeated 8 to 12 times with a 1:3 work:rest ratio).

Day	Primary Emphasis	Training Component	Drills
Day One	All	Warm-up	Dynamic flexibility exercises for 10-15 minutes
		Sprinting technique	A skips, 2x20 yards
		Agility/ Acceleration/ Speed/ Conditioning	Agility pattern drill 7, 8-12x
Day Two	All	Warm-up	Dynamic flexibility exercises for 10-15 minutes
		Sprinting technique	B skips, 2x20 yards
		Acceleration/Speed	2x3x100 yards, standing start
		Agility/Conditioning	Agility pattern drill 4, 2x3-5x25 yards, 45" to finish, 135" recovery

Table 13-16. Sample competition phase workouts for collegiate soccer players

Agility Drills

Agility Pattern Drill #1

Purpose: Develop acceleration and stopping ability.

Objectives:

*   Incorporate decision-making.
*   Reduce unnecessary body movements.

Description:

*   Have the athlete sprint forward 10 yards, backpedals five yards, sprint forward 10, back five, then finish with a sprint forward to complete the drill.
*   The athlete should accelerate with 100% effort.
*   The athlete should maximize the forward lean when initially accelerating.
*   The athlete should use a forceful, high knee lift when initially accelerating.
*   The athlete should minimize braking distance by quickly dropping the center of gravity.
*   The athlete should use short, choppy steps to minimize stopping distance.

Increasing Complexity/Difficulty:

- Receive a ball kicked or tossed from the coach in the forward direction and pass it back.
- Add shuffles to the backwards runs.
- Perform the drill with the soccer ball.
- Use two identical patterns of cones and have athletes race each other through the drill.

Work Interval: Will vary on distance of cones and ability of athlete, but should be between 8 and 12 seconds.

Rest Interval: Once mastery of the drill has been reached, the rest intervals may be brought down to 3:1 rest to work interval.

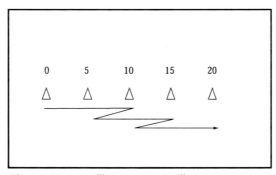

Figure 13-1. Agility Pattern: Drill #1

Agility Pattern: Drill #2

Purpose: Develop acceleration and stopping ability.

Objectives:

- Maintain body control.
- Develop specific rate of force production.
- Lower center of gravity when decelerating.

Description:

- The athlete starts at one end and runs forward to each cone in the series.
- The athlete should concentrate on running in straight lines.
- The athlete should make "tight" corners.
- The athlete should keep the elbows relatively close to the body.
- The athlete should drop the center of gravity while decelerating.
- The athlete should use short, choppy steps to decelerate quickly.
- The athlete should maintain a neutral spine at all times.

Increasing Complexity/Difficulty:

- Combine a forward run with side shuffling.
- Use shuffling only.
- Have the athlete run off the end of the drill to receive a ball.
- Perform the drill with a ball.
- Use two identical patterns of cones and have athletes race each other through the drill.

Work Interval: Will vary on distance of cones and ability of the athlete, but should be between 8 and 12 seconds.

Rest Interval: Once mastery of the drill has been reached, the rest intervals may be brought down to 3:1 rest to work interval.

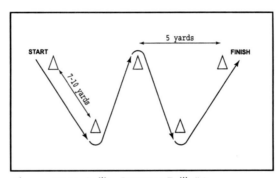

Figure 13-2. Agility Pattern: Drill #2

Agility Pattern: Drill #3

Purpose: Developing controlled running at maximal or near-maximal running speed.

Objectives:

- Incorporate decision-making.
- Control unnecessary body movements.

Description:

- Have the athlete use a "rolling" start for this drill.
- Once he reaches the first cone, he should be at a maximal controlled speed.
- The athlete should keep the corners "tight" when passing the cones.
- The athlete should keep the elbows close to the sides.

Increasing Complexity/Difficulty:

- Stagger the distance of the cones.
- Stagger the width of the cones.

- The coach can tell the athlete which direction to run (left or right) at the end of the drill.
- Perform the drill with a ball.
- Use two identical patterns of cones and have athletes race each other through the drill.

Work Interval: Will vary on distance of cones and ability of the athlete, but should be between 8 and 12 seconds.

Rest Interval: Once mastery of the drill has been reached, the rest intervals may be brought down to 3:1 rest to work interval.

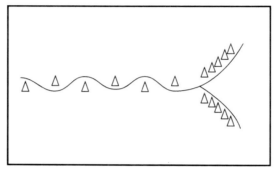

Figure 13-3. Agility Pattern: Drill #3

Agility Pattern: Drill #4

Purpose: Develop acceleration and stopping ability.

Objectives:

- Maintain body control.
- Develop specific rate of force production.
- Lower center of gravity when decelerating.

Description:

- Begin at the start line and run to the five-yard line, run back to the start, run to the 10-yard line, run back to the start, run to the 15-yard line, run back to the start, run to the 20-yard line, run back to the start.
- The athlete should accelerate with 100% effort.
- The athlete should maximize the forward lean when initially accelerating.
- The athlete should use a forceful, high knee lift when initially accelerating.
- The athlete should drop the center of gravity while decelerating.
- The athlete should use short, choppy steps to decelerate quickly.
- The athlete should maintain a neutral spine at all times.

Increasing Complexity/Difficulty:

- Stagger the distance of the cones.
- Increase the number of cones.
- Perform the drill with a ball.
- Use two identical patterns of cones and have athletes race each other through the drill.

Work Interval: Will vary on distance of cones and ability of the athlete, but should be between 20 and 40 seconds.

Rest Interval: Once mastery of the drill has been reached, the rest intervals may be brought down to 3:1 rest to work interval.

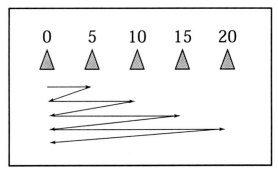

Figure 13-4. Agility Pattern: Drill #4

Agility Pattern: Drill #5

Purpose: Develop lateral acceleration, lateral stopping ability, and body control.

Objectives:

- Simulate movement patterns seen at all positions.
- Reduce unnecessary body movements.
- Train eye-hand-foot coordination.

Description:

- Place two cones two to three yards apart for shuffling.
- Place two cones 6 to 12 yards apart for running.
- The athlete should not cross over the feet during the drill if shuffling.
- The athlete should maintain a low center of gravity, keeping the knees and hips bent while shuffling.
- The athlete should move the feet as quickly as possible while shuffling.
- The athlete should lower the center of gravity while turning through the cones when running.

- The athlete should drop the inside shoulder and extend the arm toward the ground while turning when running.
- The athlete should emphasize a high knee lift while accelerating off the turn when running.

Increasing Complexity/Difficulty:

- The coach can pass a ball back and forth to the athlete during the shuffling portions of the drill.
- The coach can have the athlete run for a ball off the end of the drill.
- The cones can be spread further apart to emphasize stopping mechanics while running.
- The coach can time the drill for completed cycles through the pattern.

Work Interval: Will vary on distance of cones and ability of the athlete, but should be between 8 and 12 seconds.

Rest Interval: Once mastery of the drill has been reached, the rest intervals may be brought down to 3:1 rest to work interval.

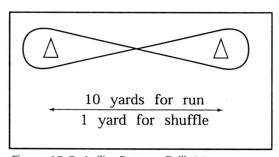

Figure 13-5. Agility Pattern: Drill #5

Agility Pattern: Drill #6

Purpose: Develop athletic stance, hand-eye-foot coordination, reactive ability, and lateral agility.

Objectives:

- Simulate movement patterns seen at all positions.
- Reduce unnecessary body movements.

Description:

- The emphasis of this drill is to have the athlete react to the random movements of the soccer ball.
- The athlete starts in an athletic stance.
- The coach lightly tosses the soccer ball to the ground in the direction of the athlete.

- The athlete reacts to the direction of the ball by shuffling.
- The ball is trapped and passed back to the coach.
- The coach redirects the ball in the desired direction.

Increasing Complexity/Difficulty:

- The coach can toss the ball a little harder to get the athlete to react more quickly.
- The coach can toss the ball further away from the athlete to increase the shuffling distance.
- A sprint after the pass back can be incorporated at the end of the drill.

Work Interval: The coach can use a determined number of tosses to complete the drill. Or, the coach can use an approximate time of the drill, ranging from 5 to 15 seconds.

Rest Interval: Once mastery of the drill has been reached, the rest intervals may be brought down to 3:1 rest to work interval.

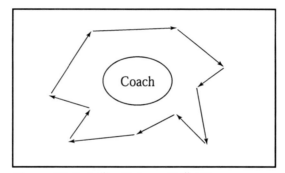

Figure 13-6. Agility Pattern: Drill #6

Agility Pattern: Drill #7

Purpose: Develop change-of-direction ability, acceleration, speed, and conditioning.

Objective: Require athletes to perform agility and speed tasks under fatigued conditions to simulate the requirements of the game.

Description:

- A number of agility, speed, and acceleration tasks may be incorporated into this drill and performed in a circuit manner. Some examples are (the number in parenthesis refers to the corresponding number on the illustration of the drill):
  - ❏ 40-yard sprint (#1)
  - ❏ 20-yard sprint (#2)
  - ❏ 20-yard backpedal

- ❏ 10-yard shuffle (right/left), sprint 10 yards (#3)
- ❏ 10-yard drop (right/left) (#4)
- ❏ 20-yard bending run (right/left) (#5)

- These tasks should be performed in a circuit fashion with a jogging active recovery (for example, the athlete may sprint 40 yards, jog back to start line, then perform a 20-yard backpedal, jog back, perform a 10-yard shuffle, etc.).
- Any number of tasks may be included and their order should be mixed up.

Increasing Complexity/Difficulty:

- Incorporate more tasks (i.e., make the drill longer).
- Perform more repetitions.

Work Interval: Will vary depending upon the tasks and the distances.

Rest Interval: Once mastery of the drill has been reached, the rest intervals may be brought down to 3:1 rest to work interval.

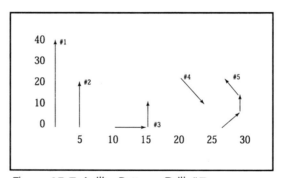

Figure 13-7. Agility Pattern: Drill #7

Agility Pattern: Drill #8

Purpose: Develop reactive and change-of-direction ability.

Objectives:

- Incorporate decision-making.
- Reduce unnecessary body movements.

Description:

- Start in an athletic stance.
- The athlete should accelerate with 100% effort.
- The athlete should cut sharply and sprint in the instructed direction.

- The athlete should maximize the forward lean when initially accelerating.
- The athlete should use a forceful, high knee lift when initially accelerating.
- The athlete should drop the center of gravity while decelerating.
- The athlete should use short, choppy steps to decelerate quickly.
- The athlete should maintain a neutral spine at all times.

Increasing Complexity/Difficulty:

- Instead of running, have the athlete shuffle.
- Vary the distances.
- Change the cutting angle.
- Perform the drill with a ball.
- Use two identical patterns of cones and have athletes race each other through the drill.

Work Interval: Will vary on distance of cones and ability of the athlete, but should be between 8 and 12 seconds.

Rest Interval: Once mastery of the drill has been reached, the rest intervals may be brought down to 3:1 rest to work interval.

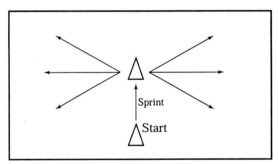

Figure 13-8. Agility Pattern: Drill #8

Agility Pattern: Drill #9

Purpose: Develop reactive and change-of-direction ability.

Objectives:

- Incorporate decision-making.
- Reduce unnecessary body movements.

Description:

- Start in an athletic stance.
- Backpedal on command, cut sharply, and sprint in the designated direction.
- The athlete should maintain a neutral spine at all times.

Increasing Complexity/Difficulty:

- Instead of running, have the athlete shuffle.
- Vary the distances.
- Change the cutting angle.
- Perform the drill with a ball.
- Use two identical patterns of cones and have athletes race each other through the drill.

Work Interval: Will vary on distance of cones and ability of the athlete, but should be between 8 and 12 seconds.

Rest Interval: Once mastery of the drill has been reached, the rest intervals may be brought down to 3:1 rest to work interval.

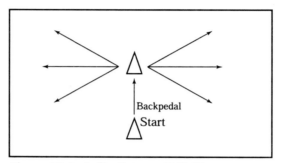

Figure 13-9. Agility Pattern: Drill #9

Suggested References

Abe, T., J.B. Brown, & W.F. Brechue. (1999). Architectural characteristics of skeletal muscle in black and white college football players. Medicine and Science in Sports and Exercise, 31, 1448-1452.

Asmussen, E., and F. Bonde-Peterson, and K. Jorgensen. Mechano-elastic properties of human muscles at different temperatures. Acta Physiologica Scandinavica 96: 86-93.

Barbaro, R. (2000). Elements of speed development. In Jarver, J. (Ed.) Sprints and Relays 5th Edition, pgs. 15-18. Mountain View, CA: TAFNEWS Press.

Bates, B. T. 1970, The relationships of performance on lateral change of direction agility tests. Health, Physical Education, and Recreation microfiche publication. Thesis. East Stroudsburg State College, PA.

Bergh, U., and B. Ekblom. Influence of muscle temperature on maximal muscle strength and power output in human muscle. Acta Physiologica Scandinavica 107: 332-337.

Blazevich, A.J. (2000). Optimizing hip musculature for greater sprint running speed. Strength and Conditioning Journal, 22(2), 22-27.

Bompa, T.O. (1999). Periodization: Theory and Methodology of Training 4th Edition. Champaign, IL: Human Kinetics.

Boyden, H. (1978). Power training for sprinters. In Jarver, J. (Ed.) Sprints and Relays 1st Edition, pgs. 65-68. Mountain View, CA: TAFNEWS Press.

Church, J.B., M.S. Wiggins, E.M. Moode, & R. Crist. Effect of warm-up and flexibility treatments on vertical jump performance. Journal of Strength and Conditioning Research, 15(3), 332-336. 2001.

Cissik, J.M. (2002). Techniques and speed development for running. NSCA Performance Training Journal, 1(8). www.nsca-lift.org/perform.

Conley, M. (2000). Bioenergetics of exercise and training. In Baechle, T.R. & R.W. Earle (Eds). Essentials of Strength Training and Conditioning 2nd Edition, pgs. 73-90. Champaign, IL: Human Kinetics.

Costill, D.L., J. Daniels, W. Evans, W. Fink, G. Krahenbuhl, & B. Saltin. (1976). Skeletal muscle enzymes and fiber composition in male and female track athletes. Journal of Applied Physiology, 40, 149-154.

Couture, C.J. & K.A. Karlson. (2002). Tibial stress injuries. The Physician and Sportsmedicine, 30(6).

Cunningham, M. (2000). Pure speed training. Coaches Review, 72(2), 26-28.

Elam, R. Warm-up and athletic performance: A physiological analysis. NSCA Journal, 8(2), 30-32. 1986.

Faccioni, A. (1995). Assisted and resisted methods for speed development. In Jarver, J. (Ed.) Sprints and Relays 4th Edition, 63-69. Mountain View, CA: TAFNEWS Press.

Fredrick, G.A. & D.J. Szymanski. Baseball (Part I): Dynamic flexibility. Strength and Conditioning Journal, 23(1), 21-30. 2001.

Gagua, E. (1995). Sprint reflections. In Jarver, J. (Ed.) Sprints and Relays 4th Edition, 20-22. Mountain View, CA: TAFNEWS Press.

Guyton, A.C. & J.E. Hall. (2000). Textbook of Medical Physiology 10th Edition. Philadelphia: W.B. Saunders Company.

Halberg, G.V. 2001. Relationships among power, acceleration, maximum speed, programmed agility, and reactive agility: The neural fundamentals of agility. Masters Thesis, Central Michigan University. Mount Pleasant, MI.

Harman, E. (2000). The biomechanics of resistance exercise. In Baechle, T.R. & R.W. Earle (Eds). Essentials of Strength Training and Conditioning 2nd Edition, pgs. 25-56. Champaign, IL: Human Kinetics.

Harman, E., J. Garhammer, & C. Pandorf. (2000). Administration, scoring, and interpretation of selected tests. In Baechle, T.R. & R.W. Earle (Eds). Essentials of Strength Training and Conditioning 2nd Edition, pgs. 287-317. Champaign, IL: Human Kinetics.

Harre, D. (1982). Principles of Sports Training. Berlin: Sportverlag.

Hedrick, A. Dynamic flexibility training. Strength and Conditioning Journal, 22(5), 33-38. 2000.

Hedrick, A. Flexibility and the conditioning program. NSCA Journal, 15(4), 62-66. 1993.

Hutchinson, M.R., S. Cahoon, & T. Atkins. (1998). Chronic leg pain: Putting the diagnostic pieces together. The Physician and Sportsmedicine, 26(7).

Jakalski, K. (2000). Parachutes, tubing and towing. In Jarver, J. (Ed.) Sprints and Relays 5th Edition, pgs. 95-100. Mountain View, CA: TAFNEWS Press.

Jarver, J. (1978). Sprinting in a nutshell. In Jarver, J. (Ed.) Sprints and Relays 1st Edition, pgs. 9-13. Mountain View, CA: TAFNEWS Press.

Knudson, D.V., P. Magnusson, & M. McHugh. Current issues in flexibility fitness. President's Council on Physical Fitness and Sports Research Digest 3(10), 1-13. 2000.

Kumagai, K., T. Abe, W.F. Brechue, T. Ryushi, S. Takano, & M. Mizuno. (2000). Sprint performance is related to muscle fascicle length in male 100-m sprinters. Journal of Applied Physiology, 88, 811-816.

Kurz, T. (1991). Science of Sports Training: How to Plan and Control Training for Peak Performance. Island Pond, VT: Stadion Publishing Company.

Kuznyetsov, V.V., V. Petrovskiy, & B.N. Schustin. (1983). The model for sprinters. In Jarver, J. (Ed.) Sprints and Relays 2nd Edition, pg. 30-31.

Letzelter, M., G. Sauerwein, R. Burger. (1995). Resistance runs in speed development. In Jarver, J. (Ed.) Sprints and Relays 4th Edition, pg. 82-86. Mountain View, CA: TAFNEWS Press.

Lieber, R.L. & S.C. Bodine-Fowler. Skeletal muscle mechanics: Implications for rehabilitation. Physical Therapy, 73(12), 844-856. 1993.

McArdle, W.D., F.I. Katch, & V.L. Katch. (1996). Exercise Physiology: Energy, Nutrition, and Human Performance 4th Edition. Baltimore: Williams & Wilkins.

McFarlane, B. (1987). A look inside the biomechanics of speed. NSCA Journal, 9(5), 35-42.

McFarlane, B. (1995). Speed…A basic and advanced technical mode. In Jarver, J. (Ed.) Sprints and Relays 4th Edition, 14-19. Mountain View, CA: TAFNEWS Press.

McFarlane, B. Warm-up pattern design. NSCA Journal, 9(4), 22-29. 1987.

Medvedev, A.S. (1986). A System of Multi-Year Training in Weightlifting. Translated by Charniga, Jr., A. Livonia, Michigan: Sportivny Press.

Negrete, R., and Brophy, J. (2000). The relationship between isokinetic open and closed chain lower extremity strength and functional performance. Journal of Sports Rehabilitation, 9, 46-61.